Intimate Animation

In recent years, there has been a surge in animated projects that have pushed boundaries, broken taboos, prompted discussions and wowed festival and online audiences alike through compelling storytelling and unmatched artistry.

Join Ben Mitchell and Laura-Beth Cowley of Skwigly Online Animation Magazine and the *Intimate Animation* podcast as they take you on a tour of the landscape of contemporary animated films that deal with themes of love, intimacy, relationships, anatomy and sexuality – and the incredible artists behind them. Through research and firsthand interviews with trailblazers such as Signe Baumane, Andreas Hykade, Ruth Lingford, Michaela Pavlátová, Bill Plympton and Joanna Quinn, as well as newer voices including Sawako Kabuki, Renata Gąsiorowska, Will Anderson, Sara Gunnarsdóttir, Michaela Mihalyi, David Stumpf, Levi Stoops, Lori Malépart-Traversy, Anna Ginsburg, Veljko Popović, Renee Zhan and more, *Intimate Animation* looks deeply at the role animation has played in presenting elaborate and complex concepts relating to love and sexuality.

Exploring the role animation has played in sex education, self-discovery, the body, lust and love, as well as how the medium can be used to visually represent emotions, feelings and concepts not easily described in words nor depicted through live-action filmmaking, *Intimate Animation* is the ideal book for professional animators, filmmakers, enthusiasts, researchers, academic and students of animation and film studies interested in the themes of love and sexuality.

Intimate Animation

Ben Mitchell and Laura-Beth Cowley

CRC Press is an imprint of the
Taylor & Francis Group, an **informa** business

Designed cover image: Still from SH_T HAPPENS (Dir. Michaela Mihalyi, David Stumpf) ©2019 BFILM s.r.o. / Bagan Films / BFILM.cz s.r.o. / FAMU. Image courtesy of Mihalyi/Stumpf

First edition published 2025
by CRC Press
2385 NW Executive Center Drive, Suite 320, Boca Raton FL 33431

and by CRC Press
4 Park Square, Milton Park, Abingdon, Oxon, OX14 4RN

CRC Press is an imprint of Taylor & Francis Group, LLC

ISBN: 978-1-032-54169-3 (hbk)
ISBN: 978-1-032-54150-1 (pbk)
ISBN: 978-1-003-41550-3 (ebk)

DOI: 10.1201/9781003415503

Typeset in Minion
by KnowledgeWorks Global Ltd.

Access the Instructor and Student Resources/Support Material: https://www.routledge.com/9781032541693

Contents

Preface

Before we start, it's probably best we get one thing out of the way: This is not a book about hentai.

Well, not completely. It'll get a mention here or there, but it's probably worth clearing up any potential confusion or disappointment at the outset given that, when it comes to the pairing of animation and sex, a big chunk of the population will probably think of hentai before anything else. We're not ignoring it out of any moral objection (save for some reports that suggest the folks who work on it are woefully underpaid[1]) and, given that the biggest complaint most animation advocates tend to have is that the general population thinks that "cartoons are just for kids," it'd be a bit rich to dismiss any form of adult animation outright. But just to clarify, while there are probably books out there about the history of hentai, this isn't one of them.

So what is this book about?

On reflection, *Intimate Animation* is about a sea change in the animation industry that we have observed since the early 2010s. Certainly, there has been no shortage of love stories since the dawn of animation, but where there was once an animated film landscape dotted with the odd sexually charged short or risqué indie feature, in recent years, there has been a noticeable surge in work that embraces sexuality and all that comes with it; intimacy, fantasy, masturbation, lust, passion, monogamy, polyamory, body positivity and social attitudes, not to mention the vast array of psychological positives and negatives that are rooted in love and sex itself.

This is a book about generations of filmmakers who have made it their mission to push boundaries, whether to prompt serious discussion of lofty issues, to educate the masses on subjects that are traditionally tricky to communicate in other forms of media, to self-therapize through artistic expression or simply to make audiences laugh and relax about a subject they might have previously been inhibited toward. It is also about the pioneers who blazed the trail in the world of intimate animation – the Michaela Pavlátovás, the Bill Plymptons, the Ruth Lingfords, the Signe Baumanes, the Joanna Quinns (we could go on, but it would look like we're just listing names to reach word count). More than anything, it is a celebration of the inherent power that a medium as rich and inspiring as animation can bring about, and its potential to surpass other forms of filmmaking and storytelling in the process.

The origins of this book begin with our earlier collaborations through the UK animation resource Skwigly. As partners in our daily life, one of our first points of familiarity was animation, particularly that which sits on the fringes of the mainstream with more of an adult focus. Through our respective work in events programming and curation, an early project that would help kick off *Intimate Animation* was a 2014 screening event in which we presented a selection of our favorite short films on the subject of intimacy, sex, relationships and love in the back of a brewery in Bristol. From this, we developed the *Intimate Animation* strand for Skwigly's animation podcast network, through which we conducted a series of interviews and episodic deep dives into the world of animated eroticism.

This book does not claim to be a complete dossier on all matters of adult animation, sex in the animated form, a full history of erotica in animation, nor an overtly unbiased account of the themes of sex, sexuality, sensuality, gender, equality, love, relationships, fetishism or any other aspect of what we discuss within these pages. Instead, we are offering a well-intentioned, *reasonably* comprehensive overview of noteworthy contemporary animation films and the artists behind them. From our perspectives through our work on Skwigly, as well as the assortment of international film and animation festivals we have been privileged to participate in (whether in a preselection capacity, as programmers, as jury members or as filmmakers ourselves), we hope for this book to shine a light on the work we feel most passionately about; animated films that can help us work toward a shared understanding of the intimate desires and experiences of ourselves and others. While it is a subject that far extends the confines of a single book, we hope what we have written here can be a springboard for further study, exploration, critical writing and, perhaps most importantly, more films from diverse voices that will continue to push animation that deals with themes of love, sex and relationships forward.

Note

1 Paulsen, I. (2019) *11 Shocking Facts About the Hentai Industry You Didn't Know*. Available at: https://vocal.media/filthy/11-shocking-facts-about-the-hentai-industry-you-didn

Acknowledgments

The authors would like to express their extreme gratitude to the following for their assistance in the creation of this book.

Floor Adams, Chloé Alliez, Will Anderson, Nádja Andrasev, Signe Baumane, Glen Biseker, Will Bateman, Efa Blosse-Mason, Robert Bradbrook, Ross Butter, Zuzana Černá, Annemie Degryse, Violette Delvoye, Nancy Denney-Phelps, Jeroen Derycke, Shamayita Dey, Pegah Farahmand, Tor Fruergaard, Renata Gąsiorowska, Anna Ginsburg, Sara Gunnarsdóttir, Shoko Hara, Steve Henderson, Delphine Hermans, Joel Hoffman, John Holderried, Panna Horváth-Molnár, Andreas Hykade, Draško Ivezić, Cathy Jefferies, Sawako Kabuki, Simran Kaur, Dimitri Kimplaire, Jean-François Le Corre, Manuela Leuenberger, Sara Jin Li, Ruth Lingford, Luigi Loy, Chintis Lundgren, Rebecca MacKillop, Lori Malépart-Traversy, Bastien Martin, Terri Matthews, Michaela Mihalyi, Les Mills, Veronica L. Montaño, Rob Mordue, Amy Morris, Jon Nunn, Diane Obomsawin, Matt Oxborrow, Michaela Pavlátová, Becky Perryman, Bill Plympton, Veljko Popović, Joanna Quinn, Nina Rebel-Faure, Pamela Ribon, Tobias Rud, Ramon Schoch, Jez Stewart, Levi Stoops, David Stumpf, Lukas Suter, Sissel Dalsgaard Thomsen, Nadine Viau, Joseph Wallace, Sturgis Warner, Shanice Williamson, Aaron Wood, Eleanor Wort, Julia Young, Renee Zhan and Virág Zomborácz.

Author Biographies

Ben Mitchell is a Bristol-based animator, filmmaker and writer. Alongside his work as an animation freelancer and independent director, he was written extensively on the animation industry, primarily as Editor in Chief of Skwigly Online Animation Magazine, for which he also hosts and produces several podcast strands including *Intimate Animation*, which began in 2016. As an educator Ben has lectured and tutored at several universities and is the author of the book *Independent Animation: Developing, Producing and Distributing Your Animated Films* (CRC Press, 2016). He has also worked with and alongside a number of international industry events (including Encounters, ITFS Stuttgart, Animafest Zagreb, the British Animation Awards, Fredrikstad Animation Festival, Manchester Animation Festival and Cardiff Animation Festival) in a variety of capacities spanning preselection, awards juries, programming, hosting and panel moderation.

Dr. Laura-Beth Cowley is an animator, filmmaker and educator based in Bristol, UK. She has a PhD from The University of the West of England, with a focus on the use of new technology within the animation industry, and has written academically, critically and journalistically for various online and print journals. She has spoken at multiple conferences, festivals and symposiums, taught at several universities and is the Second Year Stage Leader for MA Character Animation at Central Saint Martins, University of the Arts London. Alongside her academic work, Laura-Beth has worked in the animation industry for various studios and clients including Aardman Animations, Calling The Shots and BBC Arts and is a co-founding member of the Weird Eye Collective. She is the Features Writer and co-host of the *Intimate Animation* podcast strand for Skwigly Online Animation Magazine.

Introduction

A (Very) Potted History of Erotica in Animation

As it is largely to provide a general historical context for the rest of this book, whose contemporary case studies predominantly consist of works produced after 2010, this summary should not be taken as a fully comprehensive breakdown of every love- and sex-themed animation produced across the world.[1] As with the history of animation in general, the history of erotic animation is hard to appropriately put across in a single chapter, another shared difficulty being the determination of an exact starting point. If going by the definition of erotica as "works of art that show or describe sexual activity, and which are intended to arouse sexual feelings" and animation as "the process of making films in which [computer models], drawings or puppets appear to move" (https://www.collinsdictionary.com/), then we could potentially see examples of erotic animation in early examples of mutoscopes – hand-cranked devices similar to flip-books, first created in 1895 and largely found in arcade parlors.[2] As described by Rino Stefano Tagliafierro on his website for his 2016 short film *PEEP SHOW*,[3] mutoscopes were early forms of entertainment that displayed, among more innocuous fare, "pictures of indecent scenes."

Moving into the early 20th century, we can see more examples of what is traditionally recognized as drawn animation, the earliest example of salacious animation generally considered to be *Eveready Harton in Buried Treasure* (1928),[4] created by a group of anonymous animators, a pornographic romp in which the titular Harton wrangles an oversized appendage and attempts to have sex with women and animals (Figure 0.1). Although indisputably crude in nature, it dispels the notion that animation for adults is solely a modern endeavor.[5]

DOI: 10.1201/9781003415503-1

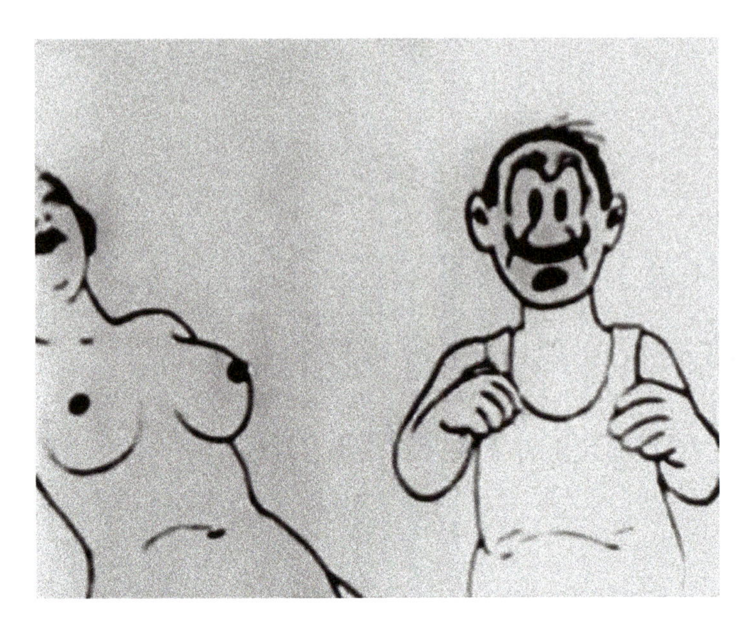

Figure 0.1

Still from *Eveready Harton in Buried Treasure* (Dir. Anon).

Considering the days and weeks that animators would have spent animating mere seconds of footage, it is not wholly surprising that some would have sought out ways to entertain themselves by slipping in innuendos and sexual references. More pronounced themes would follow in the late 1920s and 1930s, of which perhaps the most iconic is the Fleischer Studios' coquettish Betty Boop, whose early storylines featured nudity, groping and interspecies relations, as well as what have been seen as minor acts of immorality at the time. Betty's iconic look, characterized by a large head of curls sitting on top of a slender feminine body with a strapless black cocktail dress that revealed her garter, would be reworked as a result of the introduction of the Hays Office Production Code Administration (PCA) in 1934. The new classification of decency would see Betty's hemline lengthened and her chest and shoulders covered. The code would also affect other studios and cartoons of the time.[6] However, as is often the way, some elements persisted throughout the post-code cartoon landscape, largely involving the lascivious pursuit of females, often under duress, as well as the sexualization of women and female-coded animals and objects for comedic effect.

Come the 1940s, an undeniable horniness would pervade many animated shorts; looking to the work of *Looney Tunes* director Chuck Jones, Pepé Le Pew stands out as being perhaps the most infamous sex pest in animation (onscreen at least) in his relentless pursuit of an uninterested female cat believed to be a fellow skunk. Other films dotted throughout this era that swirl around the concept of male-coded characters seeking to conquer women include Tex Avery's iconic MGM cartoons *Red Hot Riding Hood* (1943), *The Shooting of Dan McGoo* (1945) and *Swing Shift Cinderella* (1945), that pit a perpetually inflamed Big Bad Wolf against the alluring nightclub dancer Red, the films' gags frequently oriented around her fending off his advances. While Jones and Avery were not the sole propagators of such mildly risqué cartoon antics, theirs are perhaps the films that have endured the most, thanks in no small part to the artistry behind them.

The troubled political climate of the 1940s would also see the production of wartime information films for soldiers, headed up by Jones alongside other prominent directors of the time and centered around the character of Private Snafu (1943–1945). Targeted at young men who might be swayed by the wiles of a flirtatious double agent, the films portray Snafu as a gullible army soldier prone to blabbing military secrets to enemy spies in the form of enticing females who make flagrant use of their sexuality to earn his trust.[7]

Following a postwar dearth of noteworthy animated films that took on themes of desire and amore, things would pick up again in the late 1960s, Sweden leading the charge with the live-action/animation hybrid feature film[8] *I huvet på en gammal gubbe* (*Out of an Old Man's Head*, 1968) that sees an elderly man reminisce on his life, including its occasional sexploits. In Japan, Eiichi Yamamoto would kick off what would become known as his "Animerama Trilogy" with *A Thousand and One Nights* (1969). The films, rounded out by *Cleopatra* (1970) and, perhaps the most well known, *Belladonna of Sadness* (1973) would be known for their adult themes and an avant-garde approach to combining traditional animation techniques with increasingly experimental and stylized methods of visual storytelling.

Bookending the 1970s, prolific UK animator Bob Godfrey (whose legacy spans prominent advertising campaigns, beloved television series and the Oscar-winning 1975 short *Great*) would cheerfully embrace sex-themed comedy in such work as *Henry 9 'til 5* (1970), in which an unassuming office worker extolls, in monotone, the virtues of harnessing sexual fantasy to make it through the work day (Figure 0.2), as well as *Kama Sutra Rides Again* (1971), a film chosen by Stanley Kubrick to play before UK theatrical screenings of *A Clockwork Orange* (1972)[9] that sees a middle-aged couple work their way through a variety of sexual positions, mostly with slapstick consequences. On the other side of his Oscar win, Godfrey would present a back-and-forth between a hapless would-be Casanova and a sex advice columnist in *Dear Margery Boobs* (1976) and collaborate with Croatian director Zlatko Grgić on *Dream Doll* (1979), which would get itself an

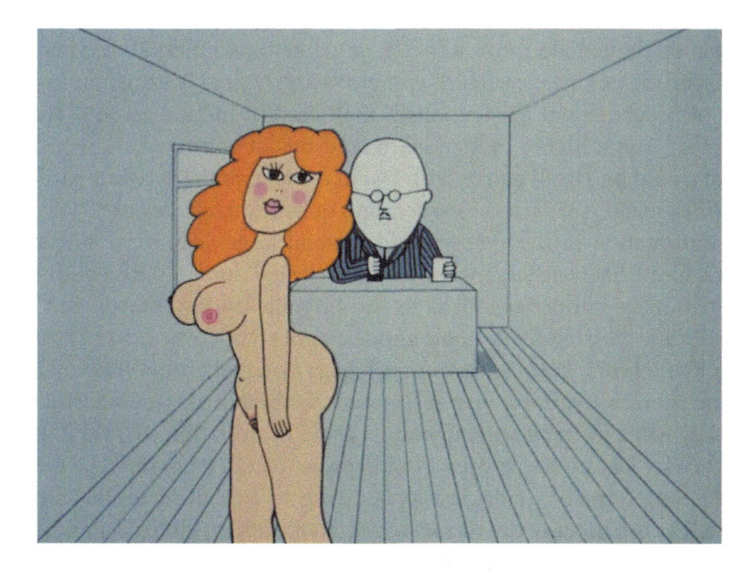

Figure 0.2

Still from *Henry 9 'til 5* (Dir. Bob Godfrey). ©1970 The Bob Godfrey Collection

Oscar nomination the following year. While Godfrey's previous films all share a mission statement in subverting misconceptions of the British public as conservative and prudish, *Dream Doll* edges more into general absurdism and *Le ballon rouge*-esque fantasy in its tale of a lonely man who finds solace in a blow-up companion, and the societal judgments this incurs.

In the States, independent animator Ralph Bakshi would establish a name for himself with the anti-authoritarian classic *Fritz the Cat* (1972), a translation of the Robert Crumb comic to cinema that, while not embraced by Crumb himself,[10] proved to be an extremely profitable success story for independent film.[11] Bakshi would not be involved in its less memorable sequel, *The Nine Lives of Fritz the Cat* (Dir. Robert Taylor, 1974), instead continuing to raise eyebrows with transgressive, sexually graphic, boundary-testing work the likes of *Heavy Traffic* (1973) and *Coonskin* (1975). Perhaps motivated by the original success of *Fritz the Cat*, in 1974, Charles Swenson would offer up his own low-budget take on the raunchy, animal sexploits premise with *Down and Dirty Duck*. Meanwhile in Europe, Belgian cartoonist Jean-Paul Walravens (AKA Picha) would pair up with Boris Szulzinger for the feature film *Tarzoon, la honte de la jungle* (*Tarzoon: Shame of the Jungle*, 1975), a sophomoric gag fest that would eventually see an English-dubbed US release in 1979. Back in the United States, Don Jurwich's anthology feature *Once Upon a Girl* (1976) would string together various adult reimaginings of fairy tales. Falling more into the category of pornography than the other works mentioned, the film is notably unique in its drawing upon the labor of animation for most of its content, preempting the rise of animated pornography in the early 1980s by some years.

Returning to that decade's short film offerings, projects that warrant mention include the captivating, sometimes suggestive imagery of Yoji Kuri's pixilation/2D animation hybrid piece *The Bathroom* (1970, Japan); Thalma Goldman's *Green Men, Yellow Woman* (1973, United Kingdom) wherein a woman who yearns for Clark Gable fends off the haranguing behavior of small green men who get up in her business; Zdenkó Gasparovich's *Satiemania* (1978, Yugoslavia), an animated tribute to the compositions of Erik Satie, pairing several with often-sensual depictions of the female form across a range of illustration styles; and Suzan Pitt's[12] experimental masterwork *Asparagus* (1979, United States),[13] an 18-minute odyssey of psychosexual existentialism that would function as both an installation piece[14] and a highly influential, mixed-media animated short in its own right that would find itself paired with David Lynch's similarly avant-garde debut feature *Eraserhead* (1977) in the earlier days of its theatrical release.[15]

Adult animation in the 1980s would, by and large, lean more toward sci-fi and genre films that were less inclined toward sexual themes.[16] Exceptions would include two more outings for Picha in the caveman buddy comedy *Le Chaînon manquant* (*The Missing Link*, 1980) and the apocalyptic war satire *Le Big-Bang* (*The Big Bang*, 1987), both abundant with gags oriented around sex, nudity and bodily functions in a similar vein to *Tarzoon*. Embracing the popularity of sci-fi and fantasy while lacing it with a good measure of titillation, Gerald Potterton's 1981 anthology feature *Heavy Metal* would prove a modest commercial hit[17] (later becoming something of a cult classic), boasting some legitimate stars among its cast as well as the noteworthy talents of segment directors John Halas, Jimmy T. Murakami[18] and John Bruno among others.

Stateside, Bakshi's 1982 release of *Hey Good Looking*, a reworked version of a troubled production that originally began in 1974, would weave appropriately calamitous sex scenes into the chaotic misadventures of a pair of Long Island gang members. Made in the United States and the United Kingdom, Robert Zemeckis's *Who Framed Roger Rabbit* (1988) can also be noted for slipping trace amounts of sexuality into what is essentially a family film, though in a way that can be considered charmingly innocuous and of its era; outside of vaguely euphemistic games of pattycake and the iconic, curvaceous design of its supposed *femme fatale* Jessica Rabbit (discussed further in Chapter 3), the only overtly explicit moment of the film can supposedly be found in early prints, wherein the most eagle-eyed of squinting, thirsty cineastes might spy a visible pudenda for a handful of frames in a scene that sees her flung, legs splayed, from a crashed car. Evidence of the moment is so low-resolution as to call its very existence into question, though at least one animator has reportedly taken credit for it.[19]

On the short form side, ribald political satire would be found in Marian Cholerek's phallic-soldier-infested *Z Górki* (1980, Poland) with more earnest introspection found in Michèle Cournoyer's experimental fantasy exploration *Old Orchard Beach P.Q.* (1981, Canada) and Krešimir Zimonić's visually poetic journey through womanhood *Album* (1983, Yugoslavia), while anarchic and bawdy comedy would alternately be represented by Piotr Dumała's fairytale subversion (a violent take on *Little Red Riding Hood* that ends with a debauched sex scene) *Czarny Kapturek* (1983, Poland) and Zlatko Pavlinić's *PLOP!* (1988, Yugoslavia) in which your basic lothario attempts to lure a sexual prospect into domestic servitude. Among the bigger names to make their initial mark in the 1980s would be Bill Plympton[20]; while an early short *Love in the Fast Lane* (1985) would demonstrate some traces of the skill and ability he would soon be celebrated for,[21] *How To Kiss* (1989) would serve as a far more cohesive example of his ability to pair unique animation concepts with romantic themes. This decade would also see the emergence of Joanna Quinn,[22] her debut short film *Girls Night Out* (1987) making huge waves upon winning multiple awards at that year's Annecy International Animation Film Festival.

While both Quinn and Plympton would continue to make a name for themselves (both discussed further in Chapter 3), other significant directors would make themselves known from the 1990s onward, such as Ruth Lingford (explored in Chapter 4) and Czech animator Michaela Pavlátová,[23] whose notable work throughout the decade would include the Oscar-nominated[24] *Řeči, řeči, řeči* (*Words, Words, Words*, 1991), which uses symbols and visual metaphors to represent various flirtatious interactions between patrons of a bustling cafe (Figure 0.3). Similarly, *Repete* (*Repeat*, 1995) uses the tone and textural quality of physical media to explore the desires of men and women to break free from the loops they find themselves in. Pavlátová, whose later work is discussed further in Chapter 4, would also collaborate with Pavel Koutecký on the documentary *Až navěky* (*Forever and Ever*, 1998), for which she provided animated segments.

Other important short film work to emerge during this era includes the BAFTA-nominated[25] *Achilles* (1995), an offering from respected stop-motion director Barry Purves[26] that, in a condensed retelling of Homer's *Iliad*, explores a homosexual relationship between Achilles and Patroclus that is doomed to tragedy. Preceded by two other films – *Screenplay* (1992) and *Rigoletto* (1993) whose stories touch upon love and sexual themes though primarily serving as tributes to theater and opera respectively – *Achilles* stands among the director's work as most demonstrative of raw sexuality, hidden love and the inevitable embroilment of emotional misery that can come with both. Compelling works that also

Figure 0.3

Still from *Řeči, řeči, řeči* (Dir. Michaela Pavlátová). ©1991 Krátký Film Praha

invite scrutiny include Andreas Hykade's[27] *We Lived in Grass* (1995), in which a young boy grapples with his cancer-stricken father's assertion that "All woman is whore and all man is soldier" (Figure 0.4); Raoul Servais's *Papillons de nuit* (1997) an Annecy Grand Prix and FIPRESCI award winner in which the inherent sensuality imbued in the art of Paul Delvaux is explored through animation; Lorelei Pepi's *Grace* (1998), a haunting, experimental reflection on "flesh, mortality, and sexuality"[28] that would pick up awards at the Ottawa International Animation Festival[29] and Fantoche International Animation Film Festival[30]; and Michèle Cournoyer's powerful, Jutra Award-winning return with *The Hat* (1999),

Figure 0.4

Still from *We Lived in Grass* (Dir. Andreas Hykade). ©1995 Filmakademie Baden-Württemberg / Hykade. Image courtesy of Andreas Hykade

in which an exotic dancer contemplates a pivotal instance of childhood sexual abuse and how it has lingered with her.

Stateside, the feature film landscape would not produce much by way of memorable original ideas[31]; Bakshi's *Cool World* (1992) is a chaotic tale in which cartoon vamp Holli Would (Kim Basinger) strives to have sex with a human (Gabriel Byrne) in order to become one herself. A victim of external tampering that resulted in a final product that barely resembles its original concept,[32] the film would be doomed to live in the shadow of *Who Framed Roger Rabbit* for its ropier execution of a similar mixed-media approach. Elsewhere, Japanese director Satoshi Kon would fare better with his directorial debut *Perfect Blue* (1997), a powerful psychological thriller in which a pop star takes on a difficult, sexually explicit acting role that appears to trigger a dissociative fugue state.

The 1990s would also bring with it an uptick in animated series ostensibly aimed at adults, yet rapaciously consumed by children and teenagers alike. In the United Kingdom, projects such as Bob Godfrey's 1990 adaptation of *Wicked Willie* (the hijinx of a jaunty, sentient penis created by cartoonist Gray Jolliffe) would find a place on the home video market, while Sarah Ann Kennedy's *Crapston Villas* (1995) and Candy Guard's *Pond Life* (1996) would prove well-received, gently cynical additions to the slice-of-life genre. In a similar vein, Alison Snowden and David Fine would develop the series *Bob & Margaret* (1998) from their Oscar-winning National Film Board of Canada short film *Bob's Birthday* (1993), both presenting an endearing look at the relatable lives of a middle-class British couple. Back across the pond, while not oriented around sex itself, the concept is an ever-present specter that simultaneously eludes and defines the protagonists of Mike Judge's *Beavis & Butt-Head* (1993). For all of the controversy it has relished in courting over the years, Trey Parker and Matt Stone's *South Park* (1997) would incorporate sexual politics (alongside a healthy barrage of barefaced smut) from its first season onward, the early episode *Big Gay Al's Big Gay Boat Ride* directly assuring its impressionable young audience that "It's okay to be gay," a uniquely progressive move considering the sitcom landscape at the time. Both shows would prove popular enough to receive feature film iterations, with *Beavis & Butt-Head* also spinning off into the tonally disparate *Daria* (1997), an altogether quieter and more thoughtful portrayal of 1990s teenagehood, its associated relationship dramas and, occasionally, sexual politics. Existing series would also get more adventurous; episodes of *The Simpsons* (1989), having previously relied on euphemistic asides in the dialogue, would become more direct in their depictions of its leading characters' sex lives in episodes such as *Grampa vs. Sexual Inadequacy* (Season 6, 1994) and *Natural Born Kissers* (Season 9, 1998). The decade would draw to a close with more adult series springing out of the woodwork, some short lived (*Stressed Eric*, *The PJs*, *Spicy City*), others persevering for decades (*Family Guy*), while at the same time the lawless landscape of online animation would begin to fully take shape, pushed forward by the likes of Mondo Media, Ice Box and Spümcø.

The rise of web cartoons did not bring with it much by way of exceptional work that explored sexuality or related themes; save for *Queer Duck*, an enjoyable 20-episode series embracing LGBTQ+ culture created by *The Simpsons* and *The Critic* alum Mike Reiss with animation by Xeth Feinberg, most shows would generally rely on absurd concepts, gross-out gags and cartoon violence. Ironically, it would be the broadcast television landscape taking risks, albeit fairly short-lived ones, in the form of such shows as *Playboy's Dark Justice* (2000), Stan Lee's

Stripperella (2003), *Drawn Together* (2004) and *Rick & Steve: The Happiest Gay Couple in All the World* (2007).

Feature films of the decade would prove to be fairly diverse, kicking off with the ill-received[33] sequel *Heavy Metal 2000* (Dir. Michael Coldewey and Michel Lemire, 2000). In Japan, Hiroyuki Imaishi would bewilder and amuse with *Dead Leaves* (2004) an abrasive assault on the senses, seemingly in imitation of Western animation sensibilities with uber-violent sexual motifs and character concepts. Ever prolific, Bill Plympton would continue to throw raunchy moments into his short and feature film work, including the sci-fi farce *Mutant Aliens* (2001) and retro high school romance (with zombies) *Hair High* (2004). Also on the independent end of the spectrum is the Brazilian offering *Wood & Stock: Sexo, Orégano e Rock'n'Roll* (2006) by Otto Guerra, with 2007 seeing the re-emergence of Picha with the British, Belgian and French co-production *Snow White: The Sequel*, a film as ribald as its predecessors, though perhaps to less effect at this point in history. Musician and director Rob Zombie would also throw his hat into the ring with *The Haunted World of El Superbeasto* (2009), a rescue odyssey rich in nudity and occasional sex that does perhaps the most successful job of embracing its own goofiness.

Established filmmakers producing new short form work on the subject during this time would include Michèle Cournoyer with *The Accordion* (2004), an examination of sex and love in the internet age, as well as Michaela Pavlátová, whose 2006 film *Karneval zvířat* (*Carnival of Animals*) would pair exaggerated, animalistic sexual behaviors of humans to stretches of Camille Saint-Saëns's famous musical suite. Meanwhile Signe Baumane, having animated since the 1990s, would start to get more visibility having moved to the United States, developing her own brand of comedic absurdism with such films as *Natasha* (2001) in which a neglected housewife begins an affair with her vacuum cleaner (Figure 0.5), and the surreal anthology *Five Fucking Fables* (2002), an assortment of visual gags that lay the groundwork for her later series *Teat Beat of Sex* (2007, discussed further in

Figure 0.5

Still from *Natasha* (Dir. Signe Baumane). ©2001 Dirty Ditties. Image courtesy of Signe Baumane

Chapter 2). The rise of digital tools to streamline the animation production process for independent studios and filmmakers would lead to the first stages of a new age for animated shorts, acclaimed films including Greg Lawson's pro-safe sex skit *Powerplay* (2003, Netherlands); Sylvia Kristel and Ruud Den Dryver's *Topor and Me* (2004), a memoir of the Parisian art scene as remembered by Kristel, famed for her leading role in the *Emmanuelle* movies; Édouard Salier's *Flesh* (2005, France), which uncomfortably combines 9/11 visuals with pornographic imagery; and Dennis Tupicoff's cuckold revenge tale *Chainsaw* (2007, Australia).

It is from roughly this point in history that the major case studies of this book pick up from, though to begin with, it is worth examining another historical aspect of the relationship between animation and sex; its educational value.

Notes

1. A more dedicated list can be found via Appendix B.
2. The Museum of Modern Art. (1967). [online] Available at: https://www.moma.org/momaorg/shared/pdfs/docs/press_archives/3932/releases/MOMA_1967_July-December_0014_82.pdf.
3. Tagliafierro, R. S. (no date) *History*. Available at: http://www.peepshowmovie.com/history.html.
4. It has been contested that an earlier example of erotic animation can be found as segments in a 1924 stag film titled *The Virgin with the Hot Pants*.
5. Cohen, Karl F. (2004) *Forbidden animation: Censored Cartoons and Blacklisted Animators in America*. Jefferson: McFarland & Co Inc., p. 12.
6. Cohen, Karl F. (2004) *Forbidden animation: Censored Cartoons and Blacklisted Animators in America*. Jefferson: McFarland & Co Inc., pp. 19–23.
7. Cohen, Karl F. (2004) *Forbidden animation: Censored Cartoons and Blacklisted Animators in America*. Jefferson: McFarland & Co Inc., pp. 40–42.
8. Each segment directed by Tage Danielsson and Per Åhlin respectively.
9. Stewart, J. (2013) *Bob Godfrey (1921-2013)*. Available at: https://www.bfi.org.uk/news/bob-godfrey-1921-2013.
10. Gibson, J. M. & McDonnell, C. (2008) *Unfiltered: The Complete Ralph Bakshi*. New York: Universe Publishing, pp. 80–81.
11. Gibson, J. M. & McDonnell, C. (2008) *Unfiltered: The Complete Ralph Bakshi*. New York: Universe Publishing, pp. 80–81.
12. https://www.suzanpitt.com.
13. https://www.suzanpitt.com/asparagus.
14. Buchan, S. (2018) 'Into the Doll's House: Libido and Desire in *Asparagus*' in Smith, V & Hamlyn, N. (ed.) *Experimental and Expanded Animation: New Perspectives and Practices*. US: Springer International Publishing AG, p. 206.
15. CRITERION (2018) *On the Channel: ASPARAGUS and ERASERHEAD*. 10 December. Available at: https://www.youtube.com/watch?v=LMqavuJzqLI.
16. Save for the rise of anime hentai with the Japanese original video animation series *Lolita Anime* and *Cream Lemon*, both kicking off in 1984.
17. The Numbers. (2024) *Heavy Metal (1981)*. Available at: https://www.the-numbers.com/movie/Heavy-Metal-(1981).
18. Murakami's own 1986 feature film *When The Wind Blows*, adapted from the Raymond Briggs graphic novel of the same name, also warrants mention through its depiction of an elderly couple held together by their love for one another in the face of the horrors of nuclear war.

19 As recounted by historian Karl Cohen in the Channel 4 documentary *Cartoons Kick Ass* (Dir. Stephen Lennhoff, 2000).
20 https://www.plymptoons.com/.
21 Plympton's 1987 short *Your Face* would be far better received, earning itself an Oscar nomination the following year.
22 https://www.berylproductions.co.uk/.
23 http://www.michaelapavlatova.com/.
24 Best Animated Short Film, 1991.
25 Short Animation, 1996.
26 https://www.barrypurves.com.
27 http://www.hykade.de/.
28 Pepe, L. (2024) *Grace*. Available at: https://www.loreleipepi.com/news/works/grace/.
29 https://www.animationfestival.ca/.
30 https://fantoche.ch/en.
31 An exception being Bill Plympton's *I Married A Strange Person* (1997), discussed further in Chapter 3.
32 Gibson, J. M. & McDonnell, C. (2008) *Unfiltered: The Complete Ralph Bakshi*. New York: Universe Publishing. pp. 219–227.
33 Rotten Tomatoes. (no date) *Heavy Metal 2000*. Available at: https://www.rottentomatoes.com/m/heavy_metal_2000.

1

Sex Education

As many an animation studio on-the-grow and thirsty for work will attest (often in large, attention-grabbing fonts on the "Why Work With Us?" section of their website), educational content is one of the more indefatigable and recession-proof branches of the animation industry. It is with us from an early age, in the form of preschool entertainment whose remit is to interweave didacticism into its stories and messaging for an audience learning the absolute basics of life, consistently rearing its head throughout formative education, accentuating – or even carrying – the documentaries we watch and the explainer videos we desperately punch up online when the mechanics of certain, seemingly basic adulting tasks elude us.

It stands to reason, surely, that sex education might benefit in the same way. The clinical specifics of sexual anatomy and activity are conveyed with far more palatability in a classroom setting through animated diagrammatic content than a potentially messy live-action alternative. Less tangible, more conceptual topics will invariably carry more weight through an animated, artistic interpretation than to-camera footage of a researcher drily breaking them down. More importantly, animation has a proven track record of being more fun and inviting repeat viewing (and now we're starting to sound like one of those studio websites).

In this chapter, we will be investigating the role animation has played in educational materials that cover a range of sex-related topics, from anatomy and reproduction through to intimate health and social discussions, from the early-to-mid-20th century up to now. Through the case studies that follow, we will see a wide variety of approaches to tone and presentation that different eras and areas of the world take, from stoic and clinical to relaxed and playful, and discern the pros and cons of both.

DOI: 10.1201/9781003415503-2

Keeping Up Appearances

To see one such juxtaposition, we can look, perhaps surprisingly, to Walt Disney Productions. Generally known for their unsurpassed legacy of translating children's books and fairytales into dozens of beloved, merchandisable hot properties, their earlier output would, against the backdrop (and in the wake) of the Second World War, lean toward educational filmmaking to be implemented by American companies and schools. One such project, produced as part of a series of hygiene-oriented health films between 1945 and 1951, is *The Story of Menstruation*. Originally released in 1946 during something of a postwar slouch for the studio (that would eventually be saved by the successful box office performance of *Cinderella* in 1950), the ten-minute piece aimed at schoolgirls on the verge of adolescence would reportedly[1] be shown at schools well into the 1960s.

The tone of the film as a whole is set up effectively by its opening credits, presenting the title against a classically arranged score in cursive lettering that denotes formal, mid-20th century conventions of femininity, followed by petals falling over the sponsorship declaration "A Walt Disney production through the courtesy of Kotex Products," who would benefit from the film being accompanied by a distributed pamphlet titled *Very Personally Yours* that advertised their product line. As narrator Gloria Blondell (a performer across theater, film, television and radio whose work with Disney would also include voicing Daisy Duck in a number of classic shorts) waxes poetic about the tireless efforts of "Mother Nature," we pan across a nursery to a bassinet containing the world's most made-up baby, a curious approach to its design and coloring suggesting the presence of mascara, eyeliner, lipstick and even microbladed eyebrows; whether this is intended to symbolically represent the dawning of feminine maturity thematic to the film is unclear, though we quickly cross-fade to a disquietingly featureless iteration of said baby whose pituitary gland is kicking into gear. Bolstered by growth hormones, we see her age up to 13 where, while at school, maturing hormones set their sights on her ovaries and, as Blondell forebodingly declares, "menstruation begins."

Created over three-quarters-of-a-century before periods would even warrant brief mention in an animated Disney feature (an honor eventually bestowed upon 2022's *Turning Red*), through a certain lens the film could be considered progressive for its time. Predictably, to modern viewers, it wears its age on its sleeve more glaringly; while the breakdown of the biological processes remains scientifically sound (the shedding of the uterine lining animated, true to Disney form, with a certain grace and elegance), the function of menses as regards reproduction rears its head in a way that politely abstains from acknowledging sexual intercourse. Ovaries, fallopian tubes, uteruses and vaginas are for making babies, yes, but getting the baby up there in the first place is a story for another day, evidently.

As a sex education film that essentially removes sex from the equation, what we're left with is a piece that is ultimately focused on intimate hygiene, and once the formalities of what exactly a period *is* gets out of the way, things take a bit of a turn. Interesting moments of narration include appealing to the viewer to "be very regular within yourself" as though they might have some ability to schedule their menstrual cycle with consistency, or willingly disrupt it by "getting overtired, emotionally upset or catching cold" in defiance of Mother Nature herself. By the seven-minute mark, things have noticeably shifted from a frank, though innocuous, educational video to a preemptive scolding of womankind for letting the side down. Illustrations of teenage girls, briefly brought to life through limited animation, are encouraged to shower because their periods make them sweaty – but remonstrated for having the water too hot or too cold. Exercise is encouraged, but exuberant horse-riding in white jodhpurs is off the menu ("Just use common sense!"). Feeling emotionally overwhelmed, lacking "pep," being constipated and – sin of all sins – *slouching* are all deficits of character that must be worked through for appearances' sake.

The overarching message to the young women of 1946 and beyond who might want to do more with their day than gentle housework is to stay in their lane. Interestingly, in their mildly slapstick approach to the characters' performances, these later scenes in the film seem intended to read more comedically than its first half, and in their earnestness of their "tradwife" depictions, they are probably most likely to get an amused/bemused response nowadays, for entirely inverse reasons. Yet it is these simultaneously well-intended and archaic qualities of the film that make it a particularly interesting time capsule. Its generation's expectations of comportment among society are seemingly as important as (or more than) learning of the biological process itself, preparations for womanhood presented as though rehearsing for a high-society debutante ball. The film concludes by perfectly summarizing this ethos with a montage of illustrations hammering home what the menstrual cycle is all in aid of – growing up to be a desirable woman, getting married at a traditional wedding and, ultimately, giving birth to a child of one's own.

Skipping ahead a few decades, we find several Disney short films that again lean into educational content, albeit more on the "playful" side of the spectrum. While the Walt Disney Educational Media Company would largely be responsible for films that educated its viewers on nonsexual matters such as table manners, cooperation, nutrition and the perils of smoking, often drawing upon the star power and appeal of its roster of characters across their feature films and shorts, 1972 saw the release of something of an outlier in *VD Attack Plan*, directed by the late Les Clark[2] with animation by Charlie Downs.[3] In stark contrast to *The Story of Menstruation*, the 16-minute film is an in-your-face, comedically aggressive jolt to the senses that sets out to warn a presumably young adult audience about the inherent dangers that might lie in wait should they engage in reckless, carefree intercourse; the Swinging Sixties are in the rear-view mirror, and now it's time to rubber up.

With a bold, daunting title card animated over an aggressive shade of red, *VD Attack Plan* initially plays out as a tongue-in-cheek military propaganda piece. We are presented with a stylized silhouette of a human figure, zooming in on their crotch to reveal an army of bacterium (the "Contagion Corps") divided into two factions, syphilis and gonorrhea, being compelled by their goofily designed Sergeant to spread venereal disease by any means necessary. Their success will be enabled by three crucial allies – fear, shame and, most importantly, ignorance, all manifested as scribbled blobs. As the Sergeant delivers his speech (the script performed with characterful relish by Keenan Wynn, reminiscent of his performance as Colonel "Bat" Guano in the Stanley Kubrick classic *Dr. Strangelove*), the spreading of VD is presented as an attack plan that does not discriminate against race, age or biological sex, the troops encouraged to target specific areas of entry for best effectiveness. He goes on to address the dangers of skin-on-skin contact, the ineffectiveness of birth control pills against sexually transmitted infections (STIs), leaving infection untreated or using apocryphal home remedies, albeit presented as strategic advice for the "troops" to follow. Putting this information across in such an indirect manner is an interesting concept, allowing it to acknowledge certain key details – such as the possibility of transmission between members of the same sex, the social responsibility of informing a partner they might have inadvertently infected and the notion of promiscuity increasing the odds of catching a disease – in a way that perhaps might have felt less confrontational or judgmental. At no point does *VD Attack Plan* chastise its audience for their lifestyle or lack of awareness, rather it invites them to know the "tactics" of their enemy, reinforcing the tenacity of the bacterium they are up against.

Though it refrains from pure scaremongering, even making a point of dispelling certain myths about the diseases in question such as being able to catch them from doorknobs and toilet seats, the cartoonish presentation starts to feel at odds with the more serious issues associated with untreated STIs. While the narration remains jocular (of Gonorrhea's effect on male genitals: "He'll probably notice some unusual fluid drippin' out. How 'bout that?"), the film makes the bold move of abruptly presenting the viewer with real photographs of extreme syphilitic chancres and the wide varieties of rashes that can plague those infected. The differences between how men and women can be affected venture into justifiable scare-tactics, frankly discussing gonorrhea's prospects for permanent damage and infertility as well as the potential for organ failure, insanity and damage to unborn fetuses that untreated syphilis can lead to. When considering the film's mollifying silliness at its outset, these scenes are comparatively brutal and in-your-face, casting the Sergeant's charm offensive in a more sinister light.

More optimistic is *VD Attack Plan*'s final section, presented as a "warning" to the assembled troops, which encourages viewers to use common sense and seek out reliably discrete, professional medical attention, as well as pointing them in the right direction as to where to seek it out and encouraging the use of condoms to help prevent transmission. In spite of a few dated instances of advice, such as the effectiveness of washing with soap and water and peeing after sex as preventative measures, what perhaps holds up the strongest is the film's main message to address the problem quickly and not be delayed by feelings of shame.

Baby Steps

No matter how well-meaning films tackling these subjects are in intent, as time passes, they will inevitably struggle to hold up to scrutiny. While very few historical examples of educational films, sexual or otherwise, are completely evergreen in how they choose to present their information, as we move closer to the present day, we start to see some examples that hold together a little better.

Those who grew up in the 1970s or later may very well have been introduced to the birds and the bees via the disarmingly relaxed and lighthearted books of the late Peter Mayle, *"Where Did I Come From?" The Facts of Life Without Any Nonsense and With Illustrations* (Lyle Stuart Inc., 1974) and *"What's Happening to Me?" An Illustrated Guide to Puberty* (Lyle Stuart Inc., 1975). Mayle, who would later become known as a writer of memoirs such as the best-selling *A Year in Provence* (Hamish Hamilton, 1989), kicked off his writing career with several educational books for children and young adults, often teaming up with illustrators and generally aiming to demystify some of life's grander topics, including divorce, theology and pregnancy. These first two books are especially notable for their playful approach to a subject that parents might very well struggle to comfortably convey, helped in no small measure by the characterful illustration work of Arthur Robins. Ultimately going on to sell in the millions, each book also saw an animated adaptation in 1985 and 1986, respectively.

Perhaps the most widely known and best-remembered, *"Where Did I Come From?"* stands out for presenting the (somewhat shrouded) facts of life to a particularly young audience of children who have just reached the age of wanting to know how babies are made. The film's animation, taken on by Burbank Films Australia and directed by Ian MacKenzie, stays true to the tone of Robins's original illustrations and, while certainly boasting design sensibilities more specific to the decade it was produced, would likely retain the attention of its young viewers then and now.

Gently taking the burden of responsibility away from parents, the film kicks off by dismissing the variety of placeholder explanations they make to avoid the subject of where babies come from – left by a stork, a present from fairies, found in cabbage patches, randomly appearing in a glass of beer, and so forth. At two-and-a-half minutes long, the point is a little overstated, but it does help further establish the cartoony, kid-friendly tone as an excuse to come up with some innocuous visual skits similar to what children of the 1980s would be used to in the shows they watched.

The sequence also creates a buffer before one of the film's more frank scenes in which the fundamental differences between male and female anatomy are broken down, potentially revelatory information to some children who might not have seen their parents or siblings naked. A cartoon man and woman stand in as placeholders for the viewers' parents ("The important parts are the same") sharing a bubble bath together, a baffled rubber duck blowing off suds to reveal more of each of them, focusing on the outward differences rather than getting into the weeds of internal anatomy. True to Mayle's general approach toward softening the facts while not misrepresenting them, breasts are explained as a "a mobile milk bar" and, to instill hope in the young male viewers, the film declares "It will grow bigger as *you* grow bigger" as regards penis size, prompting a slightly odd cutaway of a baby morphing into a toddler, marveling at the growth of his genitals.

We cut to the man and woman in bed as the narrator discusses intimacy, kissing and arousal of the penis, which "gets bigger because it has a lot of work to do." Penetration is described but not depicted, though the bouncy animation of missionary position sex is surprisingly frank, if not especially adventurous. Intercourse as a whole is slightly dressed up with the qualifier "It's called 'making love' because it starts with the man and the woman loving each other" as we go into another perhaps unnecessary cutaway to the baby, tickled by a floating heart as the narrator attempts to explain the specific qualities of sexual pleasure. Overall, the film is fascinating for how it, in some instances, glosses over certain areas while overexplaining others. On the subject of orgasm, we see a cascading tidal wave representing ejaculation, overselling it slightly. The visual metaphors continue to take artistic license as cartoonified, synchronized-swimming sperms race toward the edge of a pool, cheered on by a similarly anthropomorphized egg (brushing past a morbid moment in which one of the "unlucky" sperm appears to drown), the pool metaphor abandoned with fertilization depicted as the sperm and egg tango-ing before combining to create a fully formed baby.

The last stretch of the film goes into fetal development leading up to childbirth, sticking with your common or garden variety visual presentation of gestation and replacing the metaphoric approach with a framing device that sees multiple children – and a dog – gather in a big playroom to watch the "sciencey" part. Presumably because this is the film's driest segment that feels at odds with its pacing thus far (clocking in at nearly five minutes), to make it more interesting for viewers, we repeatedly return to the playroom in a series of slightly distracting cutaways as the gathered kids increasingly fidget and misbehave; whatever the intention, ultimately this draws attention to it being the least interesting stretch of the video rather than pepping it up. Although they deserve points for keeping the line "that's all part of womb service."

The birthing process itself is, again, packaged with extraneous descriptive elements, this time regarding labor pains and contractions, making it clear just how uncomfortable and drawn-out the whole ordeal is likely to be, considering "how small the opening is." Wrapping up with a brief note on the function of the umbilical cord and how it results in a belly button, the film ends on a bit of a visual non sequitur as multiple babies of varying ethnicities appear in front of a spinning globe; while this is doubtless to highlight the universality of the topics being discussed transcending race and background,[4] when considering the median age of its main audience, it is one area that might have benefited from more explicit narration.

Although fun and worthy of some praise for its free-spiritedness and relaxed attitude about the subject, the cultural impact of the film adaptation certainly does not appear to match that of Mayle's original book, which would get itself a warmly received 50th anniversary edition in 2022. While it's harder to gauge the overall response to the animation, customer reviews for a 2005 Stateside DVD release[5] of essentially the same film with an alternate narration provided by Canadian television personality (and sometimes Mogwai) Howie Mandel are a little more divided (more conservative viewers left "Horrified"[6] or likening it to something from Cartoon Network's Adult Swim[7]), though still largely positive.

Its successor, 1986's *"What's Happening to Me?"* would also see its animation handled by Burbank Films Australia, this time with animation direction by Greg Ingram. Retaining the same overall "cartoon" vibe that would have very much felt at home in much of that era's children's television programming, the tone is firmly set as we see various young teenagers of various ethnicities blighted by the hallmarks of puberty – erections, breasts, pubic hair and, bizarrely, oil rig compliant towers (tangentially representing acne) springing up out of nowhere, and at inopportune moments. With the narrator establishing the reason for the film's existence is to address "The world's most embarrassing questions" young teenagers won't want to ask their parents (and their friends likely won't know the answers to), the film's jumping-off point is the slightly reductive argument that all matters of sexual maturity stem from an inherent instinct to reproduce as seen throughout nature; to its credit, later in the film, the script brings up having children "*If* you decide to." The journey of pubescence is visualized through two young teens careening chaotically through a metaphorical pinball machine. It is among several aesthetic qualities of the film that, while consistent with its predecessor, come across as slightly at odds with its intended audience. Given the subject matter of this film is clearly targeted toward preteens rather than the younger children who would be watching *"Where Do I Come From?"* the cutesy, almost preschool quality of certain segments (such as goofily anthropomorphized estrogen, testosterone and sperm cells) would possibly prompt some weary eye-rolling from viewers. On a similar note, the oversimplification of certain diagrammatical segments could potentially cause confusion, such as a cross-sectional illustration of a scrotum brimming with spermatozoa but no visibly separate testicles.

Nevertheless, the brass tacks are presented clearly and with levity, rattling off various physiological changes ("Breasts are lovely and useful") and emotional developments, though it makes no effort to address the subject of attraction other than the limited, heteronormative take that girls will become attracted to boys, and vice versa. Periods and the menstrual cycle are explained informally and in stark contrast to Disney's *The Story of Menstruation*, the narrator conceding "It often makes ya feel grouchy." After acknowledging the cosmetic concerns of pimples and voice changes, the film moves on to masturbation as an inevitability in both young males and females; while the relaxed verbiage of the script and the brevity of the scene glosses over some of the finer points, the film scores points for acknowledging the role – and existence – of the clitoris, and for its sex positivity insofar as it encourages potential feelings of shame the viewer might grapple with be dismissed; all of these sticky new developments are a completely normal part of growing up.

Northern Exposure

A significant factor in just how formal or informal the broaching of a potentially difficult subject through animation might be is the area of the world in which it is produced. Mayle's adaptations, being largely produced in and for Western, English-speaking territories, have less to worry about as far as how well they translate across Australia, the United Kingdom and the United States. It is interesting to note how, as relaxed as *"Where Did I Come From?"* is about its depictions and descriptions of sexual activity, other territories are even more laid back. Liller Møller's[8] 1990 Danish Film Institute piece *Sådan får man altså børn* (*That's How You Have Children*), a comparable production, considering the appealing, cartoonish way it portrays procreation, is far more direct in its depiction of sex. With no bed sheets covering them up, the couple who are aiming to conceive take up multiple positions from missionary to riding cowgirl, penetration and ejaculation explicitly shown; at a later point in the film where the child is born, it is dragged out of the birthing canal accompanied by jets of blood that continue to spurt out of the new mother's vagina as the baby is handed to her for the first time, a slice of realism many such videos would be more inclined to omit. In spite of such imagery, the film is able to retain an "A" classification (equivalent to a British Board of Film Classification "U" or American Motion Picture Association "G") for its educational value, one would assume.

Glaringly different cultural attitudes to certain subjects, whether due to societal conventions, religious attitudes or the realities of their public health conditions, are also evidenced in the education materials of different parts of the world. To cite one example, *Menstrual Hygiene* – an animated film commissioned by India's Water, Sanitation and Hygiene (WASH) Institute – pushes through its economic production values to convey essential information on intimate health maintenance and hygiene product usage and disposal that, judging by its YouTube view count (upward on 10 million as of 2024) and appreciative comment section, is in high demand. The disparity between approaches is especially apparent when looking at modern-day equivalents of *The Story of Menstruation* produced in the United States, such as the videos of amaze.org (discussed further on in this chapter) or, to hone in on one specific example, *You & Your Period*, produced by medical technology company Hologic as part of the informational series *Lady Parts with Sarah Hyland* for popular US talk show *The Ellen Show*'s

YouTube channel.[9] Animated by Vannick Douglas, the short piece comes in at under two minutes and is awash with high-energy positivity and verbiage clearly aimed at younger audiences, seeing a 2D animated presenter and her disembodied (in a cute way) uterus rattling through all of the usual brass tacks of the changes a biologically female body endures during puberty – throwing in a few lesser-mentioned ones to boot ("Yes, nipple hair is a thing"). The overall effect is more a ripping-off-the-bandage approach than the softly-softly angle many other such videos take. While this quickfire method puts a positive spin on the topic, brief asides in the narration poke fun at itself and make it clear that the filmmakers are keenly aware that puberty and periods aren't always a walk in the park.

Heading away from the United States and North of the International Boundary, anyone familiar with the National Film Board of Canada's (NFB) output in general will be aware that it has never been an organization to shy away from any form of progressive filmmaking, least of all that laced with sexual themes and messaging. While some particularly notable examples of fictional storytelling and personal memoirs that populate its enormous roster of animated short films will be explored further on in this book, the Film Board's work in using animation for the purposes of sexual education warrants consideration. Certain films in its catalog stand out for marrying an auteur filmmaking approach to factual content, an early standout example being 1972's *About Conception and Contraception*.[10] Animated and designed by Ishu Patel, whose film work with the NFB has garnered many prestigious awards and distinctions – including the Annecy Grand Prix for *Afterlife* (1979) and an Oscar nomination/BAFTA win[11] for *Bead Game* (1977) – the entirely silent film "designed to be used by professional personnel" (as per the NFB's description) consists entirely of rudimentary, analogue paper cutout animation communicating the main areas of sexual activity and various contraceptive methods that can be implemented.

The film begins on two silhouettes, anatomically male and female, approaching one another. Following the superfluous detail of a large red heart appearing to indicate they're in love, we move on to a stylized, cross-sectional image of penetrative sexual intercourse and male orgasm, sperm leaving the testicles and combining with seminal fluid produced by the seminal vesicles. Post-coitus, we see the female reproductive system produce an egg as the sperm races through her cervix to meet it, forming an embryo and a sudden time-shift as the fully developed baby is delivered. Variations on this same basic sequence play out throughout the film, demonstrating how condoms, diaphragms, the contraceptive pill and intrauterine devices obstruct the meeting of sperm and egg. The basics of vasectomy and tubal ligation (described, with chilling formality, as "male sterilization" and "female sterilization" respectively) are similarly visualized.

The overall effect of the piece, when viewed through a modern lens, makes for something of a curiosity. Without any narration or soundtrack whatsoever (one assumes it would be presented in a classroom setting, with a teacher elaborating on the visuals while projecting the film), there are moments in *About Conception and Contraception* that now seem almost comedic in their simplification of the elaborate biological processes; the frantic wriggling of sperm "trapped" inside a removed condom, or as they appear to earnestly charge the diaphragm as though in hope of breaking through. The often-shakey stop-motion movement of the cutouts feel reminiscent of children's programming at the time, such as *Sesame Street* (a show to whose French-Canadian iteration *Bonjour Sesame* Patel also contributed segments), and also evocative of the early days of *South Park*.[12] Of course, at the time, these quirks would have stood out far less, and what the film can certainly be credited for is successfully communicating what it sets out to – perhaps barring the sequence related to the contraceptive pill, whose functionality proves trickier to visualize and, as such, seems a touch vague relative to the rest of the film.

Flashing forward through the NFB back catalog to 1989, we find *Growing Up*, a trifecta of mixed-media films directed by Moira Simpson and written by John Carroll. This short series mostly takes place within a Canadian elementary school classroom in which visiting performers Barbara Duncan and Blu Mankuma field seemingly nonscripted questions from its preadolescent students. While predominantly live-action, the information relayed by the duo to the class is often accompanied by animated sequences helmed by Jill Haras. Taking an altogether different approach to these visuals than Patel (though sometimes essentially illustrating the same concepts), Haras's design sensibilities are looser, brighter and more playful.

The first two films of the series (the third's focus being more on the general topic of peer pressure) do a fairly commendable job of laying out information for its young audience on sex and related topics, in particular *Head Full of Questions*, wherein the attending children are given *carte blanche* to fire off any enquiries they might have. The animated segments introduce us to Fred and Anna – a miscellaneous young couple rendered as felt-tip 2D drawings, fitting for the schoolyard theme of the series – who initially dislike each other, but soon develop a mutual attraction "for no scientifically explainable reason." Beginning with general conversations about the nature of love, the session moves on to discussions of arousal, sexual intercourse and orgasm with a fairly surprising degree of frankness when considering the era in which the film was made, as well as the median age of the children in the classroom, who fire off such blunt questions as "Is 'cum' semen?" to the unfazed adults. Another notable strength of a film made in the late 1980s is the encouragingly progressive impulse to present homosexual relationships in a positive light when the subject arises. When the conversation later moves to the subject of AIDS it is similarly constructive, putting the scaremongering of the times aside in favor of encouraging safety over abstinence. As such, it does a good job of destigmatizing the disease at a point in history where misinformation was both rampant and politicized.

Truth be told, the strength of the live-action portions of the film almost render the animated sequences redundant; as they take more of a poetic license with the subjects being discussed, their illustrative value occasionally gets confused by unusually timed moments of cartoonish slapstick, as well as an inclination toward absurdism; among the unusual portrayals of smitten playfulness between the couple is a scene where Fred vacuums Anna's sock off her foot while she arbitrarily holds a sofa above her head. Another visually contrived scene that takes place later in the film sees Anna orchestrate a pregnancy reveal wherein she hides their cat under her sweater to form a faux baby bump, as she delivers the news to an indoor-roller skating Fred's delight. The diagrammatical elements, however, are relatively straightforward and carry with them enough informational value as to make sense to a younger audience, and certainly, the animated sequence depicting sexual intercourse is presented in a more fluid, playful way than the clinical, static cutouts of *About Conception and Contraception*.

The second film in the series, *Changes*, begins with to-camera clips of older teenagers reflecting on their own pre adolescence and the range of attitudes they had toward the prospect of growing up. We return to the same classroom of students discussing their own uncertainties, grilling Duncan and Mankuma about what puberty has in store. This film pairs the animation and discussion points a little more clearly, conveying biological processes such as the administering of hormones by the hypothalamus and showing the different effects said hormones have on young males and females respectively (via a vaguely unsettling visual of children wrenching pull-down diagrams from their abdomens). Certain moments feel reminiscent of Peter Mayle's films, such as intuiting the internal importance of penis and breast size to children who may already be anxious or insecure about the subject. Importantly, the film's candor as to certain subjects – including masturbation ("If you do, that's okay. If you don't, that's okay too"), unwanted erections, nocturnal emissions and affirming that all experiences can occur at drastically different ages – helps it hold up, irrespective of some of its more dated production aspects.

Other NFB productions that warrant mention include Derek Lamb's 1990 short *Karate Kids* (an educational film presented as a risk-reduction cautionary tale, set in an unspecified developing country's market town wherein a pair of mischievous, unhoused children – Mario and Pedro – are warned about the dangers of sexual predators and AIDS by their older friend Karate) and Liz Scully's 1992 short *Good Things Can Still Happen* (in which Lucy, a young girl who has experienced sexual abuse, confides in her friend Kirby about the situation). Both films present cruel realities of the world in a way that combine both emotional and pedagogical storytelling, and in more brutal moments where some films might hold back (such as the inevitable consequences when Mario ignores Karate's warning and steps into the car of a stranger offering money), elect not to.

Outside of the NFB's documentary strands are a wealth of animated shorts, both fictional and either quasi or directly autobiographical, that deal with sexual themes from experimental and narrative perspectives as well as educational.[13] Indeed, the Film Board's sex positivity has extended to other ventures beyond narrative shorts and documentaries, to multimedia projects including the animated mobile interactive game *Clit-me*, developed in collaboration with the Université du Québec à Montréal (UQAM) and released in the lead-up to International Women's Day in 2019. The five-minute, animation-heavy online experience was created with the intention to educate users on bridging the "orgasm gap," a disparity that sees 62% of heterosexual women and 75% of lesbian women able to reach orgasm from their first sexual encounter with a new partner, as opposed to 85% of men.[14] The project was developed at the NFB's Digital Studio by participants in UQAM's Jeunes pousses interactive school, which brought together eight participants from programs spanning journalism, interactive media and graphic design working under executive producer Hugues Sweeney and editorial manager Valérie Darveau. Rather than a po-faced remonstration on gender inequality, *Clit-me* instead takes a cheerful, brightly colored approach to the subject of female sexual satisfaction, using a mixed-media combination of stop-motion and 2D animation for users to interact with a customizable clitoris avatar, exploring a variety of motion "techniques" to see what yields the best results.

Looking Under the Hood

The city of Montreal as a locale for heightened clitoral awareness via the medium of animation (a claim to fame disappointingly absent from its tourist literature) had in fact been established a few years previously with the success of Lori Malépart-Traversy's breakout student film *Le clitoris* (*The Clitoris*) (Figure 1.1), completed in

Figure 1.1

Le clitoris poster (Dir. Lori Malépart-Traversy). ©2016 Lori Malépart-Traversy

2016 at the Mel Hoppenheim School of Cinema, Concordia University. The project would pave the way for a filmmaking career that would eventually see her joining forces with the NFB for the episodic series *Caresses magiques* (*Magical Caresses*) in 2022, both presenting a potted history of societal attitudes to – and subjugations of – taboo discussion points around sex and anatomy.

Having initially taught herself animation while studying Fine Art at Concordia, Malépart-Traversy became so enamored with the process that she sought out a dedicated Animation program at the university, staying on for three more years to do a second degree. In developing *Le clitoris* as her final year film, she drew upon previously established interests that she was keen to explore further.

> Before doing *Le Clitoris* I already had an interest in sexology. I took a sexology class after high school and I was a bit disappointed with what we learned; we didn't learn about pleasure or orgasms, for example, we focused on specific stuff like fetishism. It was more scientific than social. I think it was something personal, a curiosity that was not fulfilled completely. I had questions and I was interested in that subject and it's something I liked – and I still like – to discuss with my friends, to know what their questions and concerns are.

Channeling this curiosity into a concept for a film came with some parameters, chiefly a limitation of three minutes in length due to being required to work alone (other than the music, the main aspects of production such as writing, animation and even voice narration would fall on Malépart-Traversy's shoulders). On the flip side, it also came with a welcome free reign as regards subject and technique, which emboldened the director to put forward her idea for a film that took on a then-relatively obscure – and potentially taboo – topic.

> I wanted to do something about female sexuality, but I wasn't sure exactly what – I just knew I wanted to talk about it. So I started to do some research and I found that the clitoris had so much funny and weird information about it. I thought that maybe I could make a short film just on the stuff I didn't know about the clitoris that I wanted to make people aware of.

Taking inspiration from Jean-Claude Piquard's 2012 book *La fabuleuse histoire du clitoris* (H&O) and with a color palette that evokes the stark pink tones of the organ under scrutiny (heightened by the black and white line-art of the character animation that plays out in the foreground), *Le clitoris* begins by breaking down the external and internal anatomical structure of the clitoris (that, chillingly, was not to become common public knowledge until the mid-2000s, largely thanks to the research efforts of urology Professor Helen E. O'Connell AO). Adopting a charming, faux-naive design style that sees the clitoris anthropomorphized as a playful entity who yearns to be loved and exists solely for its owner's pleasure, the film documents the extent to which male academics have "discovered" the organ (Figure 1.2), notably Realdo Colombo in 1559, and how its very existence has been queried and minimized by patriarchies of various cultures in the years since.

> I was really surprised – but not that much – when I learned all that in my research. I wanted to 'take back' the clitoris, to have a woman's perspective on it and stop these men having their opinion on it. It's kind of funny and ridiculous at the same time, the way they're treating the female body in the history of medicine. We often see the penis is more represented as some kind of character, in a way, but I wanted

Figure 1.2

Still from *Le clitoris* (Dir. Lori Malépart-Traversy). ©2016 Lori Malépart-Traversy

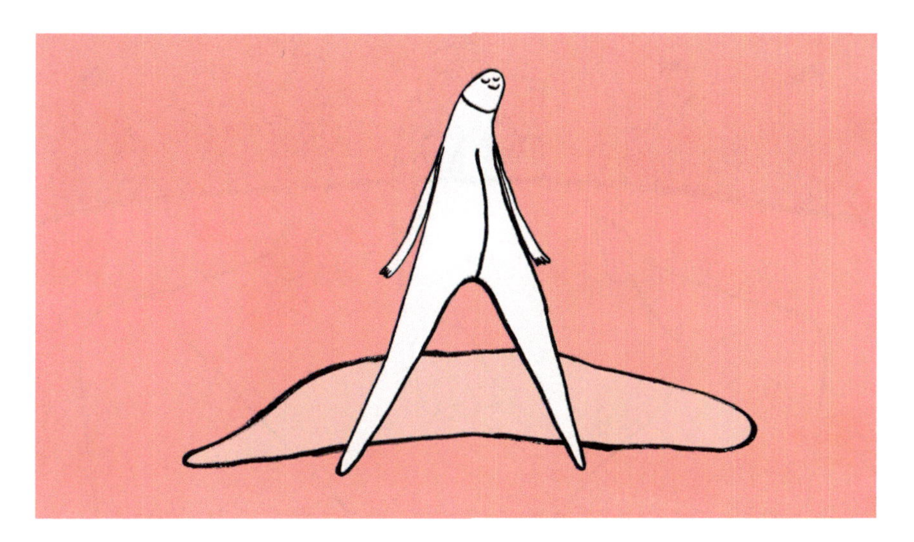

Figure 1.3

Still from *Le clitoris* (Dir. Lori Malépart-Traversy). ©2016 Lori Malépart-Traversy

> to present the female sexual organ as something that is alive as well, something that can have a personality, something that you can treat as a little person that actually exists, not just something you point at but don't know exactly what it is.

Certainly, a major component of the film's success is its sense of levity and visual humor, helped in no small measure by the characterization of the clitoris itself as a lovable, mischievous "creature" with a cute and appealing design (Figure 1.3). On the heels of the film's positive reception, Malépart-Traversy would even find herself able to "merchandise" the film through the creation of bespoke plushies of the character to sell online. As she recalls, the design of the film's titular lead would prove one of the more effortless aspects of production.

> I saw an image on the internet, when I was looking for clitoris images, with a penis and a clitoris side-by-side; their little roots really looked like feet to me. It started from that, I could see a little funny face on the end, and some arms. As I was doodling the clitoris I started to make it more simple; it's already a simple shape, the real anatomy of it, so it came easily and I was having a lot of fun just drawing the clitoris in different ways and doing different things.

From a structural perspective, the film also serves as a strong example of the power of animation as a medium through which to carry potentially heavy-handed social and cultural discussion points across. A standard, live-action documentary on the subject – and there have been a fair few – would struggle to maintain the same level of universal accessibility or communicate its concepts with such brevity; more pointedly, a live-action anthropomorphized clitoris wandering about without a body would be the stuff of nightmares, Freudian or otherwise.

> The way I did my little character is kind of impossible to do in live-action; you have to add some animation in it. This way it can be presented to younger people because it's a bit more metaphorical. I think that's why animation is perfect for my subject. [Audiences] think it's really funny, but at the same time some people are a bit shy about it, because it's all new information to them.

Figure 1.4

Still from *Le clitoris* (Dir. Lori Malépart-Traversy). ©2016 Lori Malépart-Traversy

The film goes on to address how this subjugation of female pleasure serves as a significant societal step backward when considering the degree to which it is documented to have been encouraged in the Middle Ages and Ancient Greece, up to the 19th century. Of its detractors, Sigmund Freud, "the Number One enemy of the clitoris," is pilloried for his unevolved stance on vaginal orgasm and fundamental misunderstanding of female anatomy (Figure 1.4). In spite of the 21st century's more enlightened attitudes toward female pleasure and anatomy, the film concludes with a lament that the clitoris is still considered a relatively obscure organ in the grand scheme of things.

> I think it's both men and women who don't know exactly what the clitoris is, where it is, how big it is, what it's used for. Hopefully both could learn more about the clitoris, because I feel that men and women know much more about the male organ than the female organ. So I think there's information that needs to get out more.
>
> First I wanted to inform myself, as it was all new information for me, and secondly I wanted to inform my classmates and my friends and my family – but I see that it's much bigger than that. I would like to inform everybody who encounters my film, and I think that it's a nice way to do a short film that is funny and fun to watch where, at the same time, you can throw some real information in it.

A hit on both the festival circuit (15 awards and special mentions across 150+ official selections) and online,[15] a lot of what succeeds about the film is rooted in the sweetness of its presentation; while not infantilizing the subject, it presents the information in a good-natured and easily comprehensible way, with a clear intention to spread awareness and invite further learning rather than lecture or lambast. Gauging audience reactions from YouTube comments in the years since its release, it is clear that there remains a staunch appreciation for the film that far outweighs its dissenters ("Some people are super enthusiastic about it – and others are shocked, or they don't like my accent!"). Even in its criticisms of specific males who alternately claimed ownership of the clitoris's existence or felt compelled to deny it, there is nothing about it that screams "anti-men"; rather, pro-body/sex positivity. The clitoris is not anyone's enemy, but rather something interesting to learn about – and fun to play with.

Brain Power

The clitoris is, if you'll pardon the analogy, just the tip of the iceberg when it comes to the sheer breadth of sexual discussion points whose dissemination everyone can benefit from. Educating the masses about these interwoven topics has taken on a huge variety of forms in more recent times, with a number of new considerations and necessary approaches, especially considering the evolved social conversations around LGBTQ+ issues and appropriate methods of communication that won't be considered outmoded, antiquated, offensive – or just plain cringey. However earnest in intent, getting these conversations started inevitably becomes a better sell when packaged alongside something more in the realm of light entertainment. The Channel 4 series *Naked Attraction*, produced by Studio Lambert and which premiered on UK screens in July 2016 to a mix of amusement and furore,[16] takes an altogether lighthearted approach in the presentation of its informational, animated illustrations. The sequences, juxtaposed against the show's main premise of a clothed contestant whittling down six naked romance prospects – housed in boxes behind screens that reveal more of their bodies with each round – to one, generally depict the results of research studies into people's romantic, cosmetic and sexual preferences, sprinkled in among banter between the choosing contestant and the show's host. The segments take an almost corporate approach in their design and execution, a style less-often paired with such subjects as intimate grooming, polyamory, penis size and cunnilingus (to name a few).

Brooklyn-based Latvian director Signe Baumane takes a not entirely dissimilar approach in her interweaving of simultaneously entertaining and educational scientific data, albeit as part of a quasi-biographical independent animated feature. In *My Love Affair With Marriage* (2022),[17] intricately researched vignettes that explore and elucidate how our brains and bodies react to physical and emotional attraction make regular appearances, in service to the film's narrative in which Zelma (Dagmara Dominczyk), a likable and relatably idiosyncratic Latvian woman, searches for love against the turbulent political backdrop of the Soviet Union. The film generally presents more as comedy drama than a dedicated educational tool, though the information is incorporated in such a way and with such endearing visual flair as to prove legitimately informative; its audience is likely to come away from it knowing more about our internal chemistry and behavioral prompts than they went in with.

"Actually learning about neuroscience was one thing that really expanded the way that I look at relationships," says Baumane, "Or even short communications between people – the knowledge that a lot of our interactions are biochemical processes."

With Biology manifested as an anthropomorphized neuron (voiced by Tony Award-winner Michele Pawk) (Figure 1.5) who narrates these segments, the film begins with the introduction of its protagonist at her youngest conceivable (pun inevitable) age, breaking down the fertilization process of spermatozoa meeting egg, accompanying Zelma throughout her troubled childhood (attributing her impulse to conform to her school's standards of femininity to her "still-developing limbic system"), adolescence (crediting estrogen with her increased physical

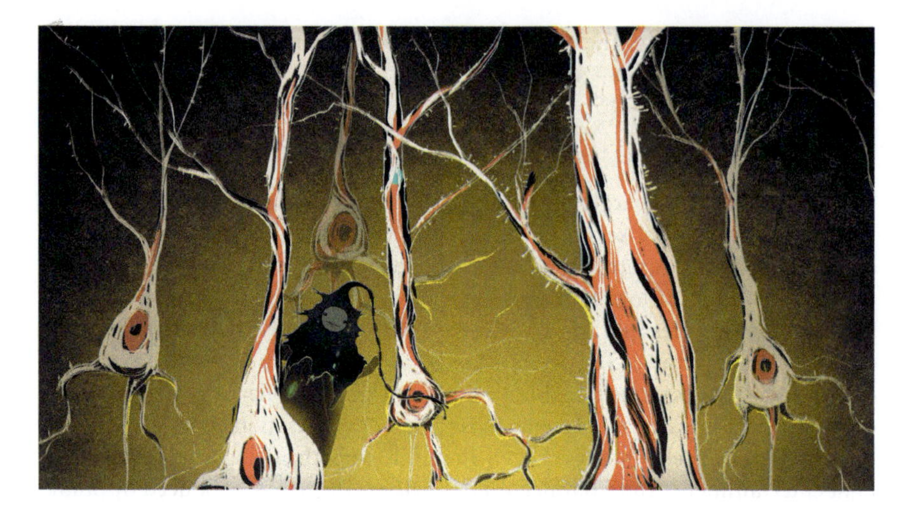

Figure 1.5

Still from *My Love Affair With Marriage* (Dir. Signe Baumane). ©2022 The Marriage Project LLC / Studio Locomotive / Antevita Films. Image courtesy of Signe Baumane

appeal to others and a fundamental restructuring of her brain prompting her to seek out thrills) and young adulthood.

At this point in the narrative, the Biology interludes become even more compelling as they step away from the perhaps-familiar territory of school-age biology classes and more into the realm of popular science and psychology. As Zelma makes faltering steps throughout several doomed relationships toward the destination of self-assurance and fully realizing what she wants from life and her prospective relationships, we are guided through what motivates her more dubious decision-making; often it is reactive, in the face of both passive and direct abuse at the hands of her partners.

Importantly, we are also given insights into the root causes of her spouses' ingrained issues through glimpses at crucial, defining incidents in their respective childhoods. In the case of her first husband Sergei, having stumbled upon alcohol at age 8, we see him beguiled by how much it lifts the drabness of his world, in turn making him feel safe against his mother's bipolar behavior and wavering affection. For Bo, her second husband, it is sneaking into his parents' bedroom, also at age 8, and the feelings of comfort that accompany secretly trying on an extravagant dress that belongs to his mother.

The development and deepening of Zelma's love for these men, one an insecure and volatile abuser, the other struggling with gender dysphoria that inevitably bleeds into her expectations of their marriage, is fascinatingly laid out through the Biology segments as a chemical dance of norepinephrine, serotonin, dopamine (a neurotransmitter cocktail that instigates her initial feelings of attraction) and – a recurring culprit – oxytocin, surges of which keeping her from leaving when common sense would otherwise dictate that she should. Says Baumane,

> The biggest surprise for me when I was researching neuroscience was learning about oxytocin. That was really eye-opening, because oxytocin has the reputation as the 'hormone of love', the solution to all our problems, right? But then when you look at oxytocin you ask *What is this neurotransmitter actually? What is the purpose? What is it really doing?* It is a primary neurotransmitter that is actually a

hormone for contracting the uterus at childbirth. Then, when the baby is born, it is also opening the nipples for the milk to flow out, and as a side effect, this neurotransmitter, this hormone, creates the feeling of bond between mother and the baby. And the baby, because it's fed with the milk that is full of this hormone, also feels the bond to the mother. But the side effect of that is that everybody outside the bond is the 'enemy'. It's like when a dog gives birth to a litter of puppies, and the owner of the dog wants to pet it, and it growls, it is because of oxytocin. That was what my discovery was, that this oxytocin creates the love and the bond, but it also creates the hatred.

The phenomenon is one we are all likely familiar with, not just as far as our romantic or sexual relationships are concerned but also when considering our allegiances to sports teams, political parties – essentially any scenario in which we find ourselves associated with one group over another. It is a human condition that makes the populace especially susceptible to manipulation and division, and in the context of a particularly intense relationship it can wreak havoc.

So the message of the film is 'use your prefrontal cortex'. Every time that you feel this strong bond, if you're able to analyze what is happening to you, you're kicking in the prefrontal cortex: *This is a hormone working, and I should really make a more rational decision about my actions.* (Figure 1.6)

This speaks to what is especially valuable about these sequences, that they elaborate on how beholden we are to biological impulses we have no rational control over, how manipulatable we can be and, crucially, that it is not our fault if we find ourselves manipulated. Certainly there are plenty who might not just relate to Zelma's odyssey, but gain some comfort in having a greater understanding of why certain troubled relationships in their own lives may have been the way they were.

That is kind of my hope, for people who watch the film to understand that they shouldn't be puppets in the hands of this hormone, they should be really aware. I think that knowing that gives you so much power over your actions.

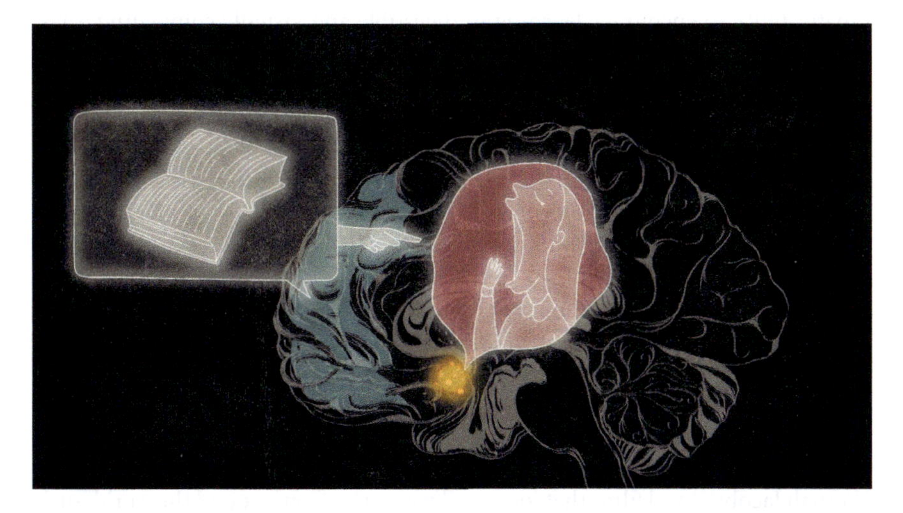

Figure 1.6

Still from *My Love Affair With Marriage* (Dir. Signe Baumane). ©2022 The Marriage Project LLC / Studio Locomotive / Antevita Films. Image courtesy of Signe Baumane

Other areas covered by Biology throughout the film span self-control, stress, the menstrual cycle, the effects of lysergic acid diethylamide (LSD) on the brain, fetal development, microbial clouds and the role they play when kissing, along with the physical structure of the hymen and the social importance that only humans ascribe to both its preservation and eventual loss. Another factor that makes them stand out is their visual execution; while the main narrative of *My Love Affair With Marriage* is presented through 2D character animation inhabiting constructed, live-action/stop-motion sets (a motif established in Baumane's previous feature film *Rocks in My Pockets*),[18] the Biology scenes take on a unique 2D approach somewhere between illustration and motion graphics visualized fully by animator Yajun Shi, who was sought out specifically by Baumane on the strength and aesthetic of her award-winning Pratt Institute's student film *Parasite* (2018).[19] Much like Baumane's own work (the feature built on a foundation of celebrated, independently produced short films and the episodic, "explicitly educational" series *Teat Beat of Sex*, discussed in the following chapter), Shi's ability to take on all of the primary aspects of an independent production – design, color, animation, compositing – made her a valuable asset to the production, her sequences effectively punctuating the main narrative of the film while retaining enough of the same independent spirit to not distract from it.

Resourcefulness

Outside of standalone films and animated segments of longer-form projects, dedicated educational resources have also tapped into the value of animation as a communication tool. A contemporary example of sexual education aimed at a range of ages is TED-Ed,[20] an initiative of the world-famous TED Talks, a nonprofit that specializes in creating content and distributing thoughts and ideas through physical conferences, online videos and partnerships. With the organization providing free content to support educators, students and the general public on various topics, TED-Ed Animation is their collection of original short-form content, some of which are award-winning, that uses animation's innate ability to encourage learning in digestible and visually compelling ways. As with much of TED's content, the animation produced for TED-Ed covers a multitude of subjects and themes.[21] Within the remit of sex and relationships, their YouTube channel has two playlists that fit these subjects: *Love, Actually* and *Understanding the Adolescent Brain*; there are, however, many other films that discuss love, relationships, sex and sexual health in a broader sense across TED-Ed's wider range of animation content.

The films generally fit within three categories that often intersect – first, those that deal with the science of sex and sexuality as found in the natural world, including the effects of hormones and other chemicals in the cycle of the body. Films such as *How Does This All-Female Species Reproduce?* (2023) directed by Petya Zlateva, looks at parthenogenesis, a form of reproduction that allows animals to develop an embryo without fertilization.[22] Second, many films look at various cultures, their histories and art, often with a focus on love, such as films in their *There's a Poem for That* series like *First Kiss by Tim Seibles* (2019, Dir. Hannah Jacobs)[23] and films that focus on love stories from around the world, such as *The Irish Myth of Diarmuid's Betrayal* (2022)[24] directed by Efa Blosse-Mason (more of whose work is discussed further in Chapter 6) that follows the princess of Tara in a story full of magic, revenge, heartbreak, love and loss. Third, films that approach the subject from a psychological or sociological position, focusing on the role relationships play both in our own lives and within society at large, as seen in films such as Rod Phillips's *When Did Humans Start Getting Divorced?* (2021)[25] directed by Chintis Lundgren (also discussed further in Chapter 6) and Gerta Xhelo. On the TED-Ed website, each film is accompanied by "Think," "Dig Deeper" and "Discuss" tabs that offer tests and additional resources to help explore the subject of the video further. The range of films, collectively viewed by millions of people, offer bite-sized information and stories to explain, inform, entertain and enlighten a global audience.

Similarly, The School of Life[26] is an organization that offers support on various aspects of life and insight "from psychology, psychotherapy, philosophy, art and culture," with an aim to "teach people how life can be lived and what can make it truly worthwhile, effective and fulfilling."[27] Through their YouTube channel, audiences can educate themselves on various subjects to do with the self and the betterment of life. Their many videos span subjects relating to relationships, sex and our connection to one another, the latter being one of the key areas, as it is one of the key aspects of life. There are dozens of films, many – if not most – making use of animation created by various talented individuals to bring this knowledge to life. By using visual metaphor to aid in the transfer of information, these frank but calmly narrated videos are enjoyable while being useful in unpicking what makes us tick by uncovering aspects of ourselves and our relationships that might be improved upon.

Some examples include *Our Secret Wish to Never Find Love* (2024)[28] delicately created by Deanca Rensyta, which discusses how we may unconsciously not want to find a partner despite our external attempts to find one, for various complicated and often emotionally fraught reasons. *The 17 Secrets to a Successful Relationship* (2023),[29] animated by Hannah O'Brien, is a step-by-step listicle-styled video that focuses on ways one can maintain a healthy relationship; the characters within the film are diverse, affording prospective viewers more of an opportunity to see themselves and their relationships reflected within the film. Animated by James Carbutt, *On Still Being a Virgin* (2017)[30] looks at the social changes to our relationship with sexual shame and how it has changed over time, using a blocky, minimalistic style to create a film that can talk about the individual among the many who, for whatever reason, remain virgins into their twenties. These are just a few of the hundreds of short digestible films on offer, for free, that give insight into our psyches and the psyches of those around us, opening up subjects for further conversation with friends, family, lovers or indeed professionals (a service that the organization also provides, along with articles, an app, corporate training, various books, games and other products aimed at helping couples and individuals open up, have conversations and better inform them about how to make healthier relationships).

Another free online resources in a not-dissimilar vein is AMAZE[31] whose primary aim is to "take the awkward out of sex ed" via a comprehensive library of animated videos alongside other helpful teaching tools. With a mission statement that "envisions a world that recognizes child and adolescent sexual development as natural and healthy," the videos cover a wide range of topics, with major category groupings spanning healthy relationships, sexual orientation, gender identity, STIs, puberty, body positivity, pregnancy and personal safety.

In the years since its inception, the organization has forged relationships with a variety of global partners[32] in an ongoing effort to cast as wide a geographical net as possible, its videos providing subtitles in multiple languages with associated YouTube channels featuring videos targeted at viewers from East and Southern Africa, China, Finland, Germany, Japan, Laos, Maharashtra, Russia, Spain, Thailand, Vietnam and Arabic-speaking countries.

As well as the above-listed themes and discussion topics, there are several videos that expand on sexual autonomy and consent. An especially important topic when contemplating the societal effect of #MeToo, a movement that shed alarming light on just how flimsily grasped the subject is by a worrying percentage of the global population, to see it incorporated into educational materials of this variety is encouraging. Among the videos put out by AMAZE that make use of animation in communicating the topic are *Consent Explained: What Is It?* (animated by Nadav Arbel), which analogizes the concept to a range of sporting activities in which one party is clearly unhappy with being involved, *Consent and Communication* (scripted and animated by Ron Levin), in which a grizzly bear infiltrates human society and reflects on what he has learned about impropriety and respect as far as the physical space of others, and Allie Mehner's *Saying Yes or No: What Is Consent?* – a longer piece in which two sisters discuss the warning signs of being pressured to move faster in a relationship than all parties are comfortable with.

Outside of AMAZE's output, another standout example of just how impactful an animated explainer can be when dealing with this topic is demonstrated in *Consent: It's Simple as Tea*, one of a series of licensable teaching aids created by Providence, Rhode Island–based Blue Seat Studios. Originally uploaded in May 2015, the video carries its message through rudimentary, stick-figure animation by Rachel Brian, the founder and CEO of Blue Seat Studios, the simplicity of the visuals being a parallel to what *should* be a simple concept (sexual consent is presented as analogous to a guest consenting to an offered mug of tea; any form of refusal in either scenario is not to be disputed or dismissed) that seemingly need not warrant explanation. The enormity of the film's public reception is a strong indicator that, in fact, its message was sorely needed.

Fueling its viral visibility as a YouTube upload, in the years to follow the piece would be reuploaded across a bevy of video platforms and social media channels by regional police departments and news outlets such at *The Washington Post*, *Metro* and *The Independent*. Ultimately the video would spread like wildfire, accruing over 150 million views across the world, as per the studio's website. Preceding the #MeToo movement by over two years, *Consent: It's Simple as Tea* would spark a wealth of gratitude from viewers praising its ability to bring such a frequently debated topic to its fundamental brass tacks in a way that anyone can appreciate and learn from, even finding organic ways to interject memorable humor. A significant portion of the original upload's comments section is people perhaps drawing on their own observations and lived experiences to expand on the analogy.

Another organization whose efforts to increase public awareness and understanding of the topic of consent through animation was the volunteer-based, nonprofit initiative Project Consent.[33] Taking an entirely different approach that brings sexual anatomy itself to the front and center, the main campaign consists of three short, CG animated videos carrying the message "Consent is Simple," starring a cast of simultaneously disembodied and anthropomorphized body parts enacting scenarios in which consent is assumed but not explicitly granted. *Whistling* sees a set of male genitals nonchalantly approach a set of buttocks, who deny him access when he gets too close; in *Laughing*, a hand and a breast share a friendly moment, the hand misreading the situation and grabbing the breast, who sets him straight; *Dancing* features a vagina dancing next to a penis, who similarly makes an advance and is rebuffed. The project was run by Sara Jin Li, having conceived of it at 17 years old.[34]

> We wanted the campaign to be cheeky (no pun intended) because we wanted to break the ice. Sex education, especially in the United States, where I'm based, is quite lacking and there's a huge discomfort in just talking about sex. Consent, anatomy, all of it have this very harmful taboo when it shouldn't. The idea for Consent is Simple is in the name itself: we want folks to feel entitled to talk about their bodies without shame or discomfort. We aimed to have a body-neutral conversation about consent by just being like, "Yes. These are body parts. We have them. Don't be weird about them!"

For their brevity, playfulness in execution and innocuousness of message – that basic consent should be indicated beforehand or, at the very least, boundaries should be respected once firmly drawn – every video is nonetheless blighted by comments, often facetious and largely from men,[35] that appear to have either missed the point or feel targeted by it. Certainly this is a reaction that many of the other videos discussed are not immune from, though it seems curiously concentrated in these instances. The fact that, for so many viewers, their first impulse is to shirk responsibility or dismiss the basic aim of a campaign with inarguably noble intentions outright is indicative of just how necessary such endeavors are in this day and age.

"When it went viral, I think it held a mirror up to our culture's faces because it forced people to examine why they're uncomfortable talking about sex and consent," reflects Li. "It's a silly concept, but not an unserious topic. The reactions we got from the campaign are just as telling as the videos themselves."

While the project itself would draw to a close in September 2019, the three main campaign videos have proved an enormous hit online, the YouTube uploads alone accruing over 15 million[36] views between them.

A similar project that favors simplicity of visuals in service to its message not being distracted from is *Consent*, also a three-part series produced to raise awareness about the subject for Somerset and Avon Rape and Sexual Abuse Support (SARSAS).[37] The animations, produced by Bristol, UK studio Rumpus Animation[38] and funded by the Armed Forces Covenant Fund Trust (although available online, they were initially commissioned for use in the armed forces), take a decidedly different approach by presenting their characters in a distinctly sexless way. Designed by Rumpus animator and director Marta Dias,[39] the studio would initially put forward animals of no specific gender (Figure 1.7), before settling on an altogether more abstract style. As Rumpus creative director Joe Wood recalls:

> We love minimal design, making characters out of lots of minimal shapes, and trying to get as much animation out of the simple shapes as possible. In the original proposal we'd shown the client how little, minimal blobs could work, and then we sent a few examples of animal characters, but I think everybody just agreed that the blobs were kind of 'human', in a way that felt right.

Wood and team would choose an approach that paired the factual, informative scripts with visuals that had scope for personality and humor. While the first video in the series, *Sexual Harassment in the Workplace* (Figure 1.8), plays darker

Figure 1.7

Early character designs by Marta Dias for *SARSAS: Consent* (Dir. Joe Wood). ©Rumpus Animation

in its presentation of a problematic, antagonistic office worker souring their environment with threats, intimidation and lecherous behavior (ultimately leading to their arrest), the series gets progressively lighter as it goes. In the follow-up video *Alcohol and Consent*, playful humor and even slapstick are comfortably set against a narration that presses forward the importance of alcohol consumption inhibiting a prospective partner's ability to make decisions that they won't regret later. The third entry, *Consent: More Than No Means No*, shows the variety of ways in which a person can communicate nonconsent through their body

Figure 1.8

Still from *SARSAS: Consent* (Dir. Joe Wood). ©Rumpus Animation language, general behavior, state of consciousness, visible uncertainty and other tells. The film also communicates the importance of how consent can be established or reinforced by nonverbal behaviors, an aspect of the discussion that is valuable to those who find the concept something of a minefield. From Wood's perspective, this entry proved the most gratifying to work on.

> I like the consent film best, because you can see the little character is actually having some thoughts about what is the right thing to do. *Consent: More Than No Means No* was the sweetest of a lot, because it's almost like a little love story. One of the little characters learns what is wrong, what things you shouldn't do, and then it all ends very happily. I'm glad that there were three of them; it goes from dark to happy.

By dispelling myths and encouraging open conversation, these and other films have helped aid in the understanding of the biological, emotional and social aspects that matters of sexuality bring to both individuals and society as a whole. In the following chapter, we will look to work that explores how we come to understand our sexuality and, ultimately, embrace it.

Notes

1 Griffin, Sean (2000). *Tinker Belles and Evil Queens: The Walt Disney Company from the Inside Out*. NYU Press. pp. 35–37. ISBN 0-8147-3123-6.
2 One of Disney's famed "Nine Old Men," whose work with the studio went back to animating on the 1929 *Silly Symphonies* film *The Skeleton Dance*.
3 Whose career would also include animating on Gerald Potterton's *Heavy Metal*, discussed in Chapter 3.
4 It is worth noting that it would not be until 2000 that an adapted, "African American Edition" of Peter Mayle's original book would be published.
5 amazon.com. (nodate) Where Did I Come From? [DVD]. Available at: www.amazon.com/Where-Did-Come-Howie-Mandel/dp/B000BITVGU.
6 Niki Marie Schering (2005) *Horrified*. Available at: www.amazon.com/gp/customer-reviews/R7PY6RSVRA4FB.
7 Cara Kara Bo Bara (2010) *Not for young children*. Available at: www.amazon.com/gp/customer-reviews/R1YC0YULLGFDNS.
8 A director whose work with the DFI would also include the 1987 sex education film *Sex—en brugsanvisning for unge* (*Sex—A Guide for Young People*).
9 https://www.youtube.com/@TheEllenShow.
10 NFB (no date) *About Conception and Contraception*. Available at:
11 Best Short Fictional Film, 1978.
12 Retroactively, considering the show would not exist for three decades to come.
13 NFB (no date) *Sexuality and Reproduction (21)*. Available at: https://www.nfb.ca/subjects/sexuality-and-reproduction/.
14 Statistics from—Garcia, J. R. Lloyd, E. A. Wallen, K. Fisher, H. E. (2014) Variation in Orgasm Occurrence by Sexual Orientation in a Sample of U.S. Singles. *The Journal of Sexual Medicine* [online]. 11(11), pp. 2645-2652. Available at: https://onlinelibrary.wiley.com/doi/abs/10.1111/jsm.12669.
15 The film has received more than 14 million views across YouTube and Vimeo alone, as of January 2025.

16 In spite of receiving nearly 250 complaints in regard to its focus on naked bodies in the first months of the show's airing, UK's communications regulator OFCOM ultimately determined said nudity was "justified by the context of the programme"—Wightman, C. (2016) *So nearly 250 people complained about nudity in Naked Attraction—but Ofcom won't be investigating.* Available at: https://www.digitalspy.com/tv/reality-tv/a807624/people-complained-nudity-naked-attraction-ofcom-wont-investigate/
17 www.myloveaffairwithmarriagemovie.com.
18 www.rocksinmypocketsmovie.com.
19 www.yajunshiportfolio.com/parasite.
20 https://ed.ted.com.
21 TED-Ed (2024) *About TED-Ed.* Available at: https://ed.ted.com/about.
22 TED-Ed (2023) *How Does this all-female species reproduce?—Susana Freitas and Darren Parker.* 6 April. Available at: https://www.youtube.com/watch?v=hdkcXqQPMdM.
23 TED-Ed (2019) *"First Kiss" by Tim Seibles.* 1 April. Available at: https://www.youtube.com/watch?v=dv9sgFHS2Do.
24 TED-Ed (2022) *The Irish myth of Diarmuid's betrayal—Iseult Gillespie.* 5 May. Available at: https://www.youtube.com/watch?v=fZNUcyAhOGI&t=2s.
25 TED-Ed (2021) *When did humans start getting divorced?—Rod Phillips.* 28 January. Available at: https://www.youtube.com/watch?v=Zj089JLYdMA.
26 https://www.theschooloflife.com/.
27 The School Of Life (2024) *About Us.* Available at: https://www.theschooloflife.com/about-us.
28 The School Of Life (2024) *Our Secret Wish Never to Find Love.* 10 january. Available at: https://www.youtube.com/watch?v=oDjlHY5Z2xI.
29 The School Of Life (2023) *The 17 Secrets to a Successful Relationship.* 2 August. Available at: https://www.youtube.com/watch?v=ak4j5pVHDGg.
30 The School Of Life (2017) *On Still Being a Virgin.* 26 September. Available at: https://www.youtube.com/watch?v=e-WCz951EBc.
31 www.amaze.org.
32 amaze.org (no date) *Partners.* Available at: www.amaze.org/partners/#international-partners.
33 https://www.youtube.com/@ProjectConsentVlog.
34 Escandon, G (2016) *Sara Li.* Available at: https://22under22.hercampus.com/2016/sara-li.
35 One could go out on a limb and assume there are probably a few bots in the mix as well.
36 As of September 2024.
37 www.sarsas.org.uk.
38 www.rumpusanimation.com.
39 www.marta-dias.art.

2

Self-Discovery

As demonstrated in the previous chapter, a fully developed sexual awakening is rarely an instantaneous thing, although it often has significant milestones and catalysts along the way. The road to a grounded and full appreciation of our sexual proclivities, boundaries and limits is not always a smooth one, the journey often involving baggage from our earliest relationships and even childhood. For some, it can be a miasma of shame, guilt and contradictory emotions about our bodies and interpersonal relationships; for others, a beautiful, organic and intuitive phase of life with plentiful rewards. Of course, there's the far greater percentage of the population that fall somewhere in the middle, who experience universally relatable but ultimately mild embarrassments and victories alike as they "come online," so to speak.

Animation's capacity for visual abstraction and accessible symbolism has made it a valuable medium for stories of sexual development and awakening, particularly through filmmakers' ability to depict our formative sexual urges, fantasies and the complex social and psychological considerations that impact upon our earliest sexual development. These include – but aren't limited to – religion, recreation, food, family, body image and personal identity.

One film that expertly presents the interweaving of burgeoning romantic desire with religious leanings is *Altötting*, a 2020 Studio Film Bilder, National Film Board of Canada and Ciclope Filmes production written, directed and narrated by Andreas Hykade, known previously for such libidinously charged films as *Ring of Fire* (2000, explored further in Chapter 6). Having incorporated autobiographical elements into his previous work (such as the later-discussed "Country Trilogy" that groups *Ring of Fire* and *The Runt* together with his 1995

DOI: 10.1201/9781003415503-3

Filmakademie Baden-Württemberg student short *We Lived in Grass*), *Altötting* draws upon Hykade's childhood remembrances of a devotion to the Virgin Mary and the emotional, artistic, architectural and geographical associations that came with it. Indeed, the film's themes and setting take their cues from what the director considers to be one of his most crucial formative influences.

> I was brought up in the Bavarian countryside in the '70s. This was before the internet, and the cultural program was very limited in this area. 20 kilometers from where I was brought up is Marktl am Inn, the birthplace of Pope Benedict XVI. If you go 20 miles to the other side, it's Braunau am Inn – the birthplace of a guy known as Adolf Hitler; that's the cultural setup there. So I was desperately looking for something to connect with, and I would find it at this little chapel, the Shrine of Our Lady of Altötting. The outside of the chapel is plastered with hundreds and hundreds of paintings, all centered around the Holy Mary. And there are autobiographical paintings; whenever you survive a tragedy that happens to you, you praise the Holy Mary and thank her for still being alive. So if, for example, you're a farmer that fell under a tractor, you'd paint yourself and the tractor, with your limited abilities, and put it on the wall for everybody to see. I was very much inspired by that, because, even from a very young age, I could see this connection between the personal myth and the collective myth. By putting yourself on the same painting as your goddess, you become part of this collective story. As this was the earliest reference point, I would say that it's probably the strongest. It's a natural thing, it's almost as if it's pressed in your genes.

While aspects of this experience and inherent connection doubtless bubble away in the background of much of Hykade's work, it is most explicitly referenced in the film *Altötting*, which straddles the line between personal memoir and philosophical musings on the crucial roles played by religion, time and place during our formative years. Hearkening back to his first experience of visiting the chapel and being entranced by the wall of votive offerings, many of which depicting the horrors of war, the young Hykade conjures a fantasy image of the Virgin Mary as a comforting protector who cradles him, lovingly. As he grows older, his idealization of her as a maternal figure develops into her as a figure of desire (Figure 2.1). The monochrome drabness of his world is brightened by golden hues as his attachment develops, conjuring scenarios in which she appears naked before him, inviting him to embrace her and share a somewhat intangible form of physical love (the symbolism of which will be familiar to viewers of *Ring of Fire*, whose Water Woman bears a near-identical design and otherworldly physiology to the Virgin Mary as depicted). The intensity of Hykade's reads as comparable to the idealized infatuations many of us find ourselves stricken by in youth and, as with all infatuations, a time eventually comes when the fog lifts and we move on, however begrudgingly. For the director, this crucial "first love" came tied, unsurprisingly, to his relationship with religion as a whole.

> I grew up as a devoted disciple of the Virgin Mary. It was a personal choice, nothing that was forced upon me. Then I slowly progressed toward being a secular person. This meant losing the Catholic Church, the Pope, the Bible, God, Jesus and, finally, the Virgin Mary. It was a process that would take me thirty years. Then it took me another five years to craft the film.

A revelatory development for the Hykade of the film comes when he asks Mary why she does not age. In response, the film's color theory shifts to a richer,

Figure 2.1

Still from *Altötting* (Dir. Andreas Hykade). ©2020 Film Bilder / NFB Canada / Ciclope Films / Hykade. Image courtesy of Andreas Hykade

darker, more foreboding palette as she pulls him further into her world. There he witnesses her take on multiple forms across time, embracing a parade of admirers, some enduring great suffering and seeking solace, all of whom wither and perish in her arms to be discarded. Testament to the power of the film's artistry and animation, it is a sequence that carries with it tremendous weight, albeit one that is inarticulable.

> You see, when you talk about the subject of religion you come to a kind of mystic component—something that cannot be explained with words. [This scene] is the part where the visuals take over. Hopefully the mind of the audience takes over as well.

An especially significant component of the power *Altötting* holds in its visuals is the distinct talent of fellow director Regina Pessoa, known for such films as *Kali, the Little Vampire* (2012) and *Uncle Thomas, Accounting for the Days* (2019) and an instantly identifiable approach to elaborate linework and shading, not entirely dissimilar to that employed by Hykade in his preceding films.

> Regina's work had a huge influence on my work, in a weird way. I saw her debut, *The Night*, in 2000, the same year that my film *Ring of Fire* came out. Both films had these "scratchy" elements, only her scratches were full of life, while mine were just stiff. So I thought: *I'll leave the whole scratching thing up to her, because she is obviously the queen of scratch.* So I turned to simple stick-figure-with-flat-colors kind of stuff, but fifteen years or so later I needed that scratchy element.

In joining forces, *Altötting* boasts some of the richest and most engaging visual sequences of the director's filmography, in part owed to a style progression seen throughout the film as young Hykade's relationship with the Virgin Mary and religion shifts as he grows older.

> The whole thing had to make some overall sense. This entailed starting very simply, perhaps primitively, in the "real" world. Then, to show the power and the beauty of religion, we had to become more elaborate in the "Virgin Mary" parts.

Then, when religion sets our hero on fire, we had to dive into this beauty, become overwhelming. [Finally] we had to turn this beauty into darkness. In the end we go back to a certain kind of simplicity, but with a touch of light. A touch of Virgin Mary-spook. The sound and the music[1] do the rest and turn it into a kind of ghost story in the end.

This final phase of the film's look comes after the intensity of the death parade, which ends with the narrator seeing himself taken into Mary's arms, jarred by its implication. Suddenly in darkness, the pair embrace one final time before she withers in his arms and floats away. It is a haunting moment that evokes the intangible love stories of classic literature; as with the doomed romance between prince and rose in Antoine de Saint-Exupéry's *The Little Prince*, there is a mournful component to letting go of a love that is unsustainable. A superficial reading of the film might be that Hykade's relationship with religion is analogous to a young man's infatuation that he has moved on from, although the variety and depth of images it conjures suggests something more substantial. While this artistic enrichment of the film owed to Pessoa's presence, their collaboration would prove beneficial to all aspects of the film. On top of her involvement leading to additional funding and production assistance from Portugal, Pessoa's intuition would directly improve aspects of the story itself.

There were some crucial moments when it was about defining the specifics of the narrative. The specifics of the narrator. I always included Regina, discussed these issues with her and followed her direction. I trusted her. She kept reminding me that the film is a love story. And because I trusted her, I wanted to satisfy her. I didn't want an artist like her to devote so much time and in the end not be satisfied with the result. So I wanted her to like the film. I hope she does.

In the film's final moments, we return to the monochrome "real world," Hykade's onscreen counterpart emerging from the church, older, wiser and – perhaps – freer, though "haunted by the memory of her beauty." As he walks away, the sky changes from gray to the golden hue previously only seen in the Virgin Mary's presence, possibly suggesting that comparable beauty might be found elsewhere. Though a deeply personal reflection, there is a certain lightness to the film, particularly in its opening moments depicting the chapel's worshippers that shows off Hykade's flair for getting appealing performances out of minimally designed characters. While the film draws a line under certain relationships that were of enormous importance in his younger days, the role of the real life Shrine of Our Lady of Altötting played will always be significant.

This chapel in Altötting, with its thousand drawings created by devotees over hundreds of years, was my doorway to the spiritual world and to the past when I was a boy (this was the '70s). It had huge relevance for me when I was a boy. Now I visit the place like someone who's visiting the grave of a long-lost lover.

I hope the film speaks for itself. I also hope it leaves enough space for the audience to bring their own experiences to it. So I don't want my interpretation of the film to overshadow it; I want to leave it to the audience. One thing I can say: I don't believe in God and the afterlife anymore. But I see religion as part of the history of humankind. We are what we are partly because of religion. Now I think we should bring the power of religion into the secular world.

Obstacles and Triumphs

Another such tale of formative sexual growth is *Ivan's Need* (Figure 2.2), a warmly received project produced at the Lucerne University of Applied Sciences and Arts in 2015. Made by filmmaking trio Veronica L. Montaño,[2] Manuela Leuenberger[3] and Lukas Suter,[4] the six-minute short combines stark, lustful imagery with a playful, at-times surreal sense of dream logic and an endearingly innocent protagonist, resulting in a faintly absurd but strangely relatable coming-of-age fairytale. Its positive reception on the festival circuit would see it snatch up major awards at the Fantoche International Animation Film Festival and Neuchâtel International Fantastic Film Festival in its home country of Switzerland, Montreal's Les Sommets du cinéma d'animation and the Stuttgart International Festival of Animated Film in Germany on top of official selections at the Annecy International Animation Film Festival, Ottawa International Animation Festival and the Encounters Film Festival in the United Kingdom.

Gravitating toward one another during their studies, the trio of Montaño, Leuenberger and Suter would exchange ideas, quickly determining that they would create a better film working collectively than on their own. Taking inspiration from the likes of Yoriko Mizushiri (whose work, such as 2012's *Futon*, would use animation and sound to convey sensuality in a manner that draws upon tactile sensation) and the absurd, whimsical style of Michaela Pavlátová, the group would ultimately develop the premise of *Ivan's Need* from a basic concept of Montaño's:

> I didn't have an ending, but I had the basic idea – I knew I wanted it to be sensual and I had the idea of a baker kneading dough and likening it to a woman's breasts, but that was it, the rest we developed together.

These ingredients are present from the opening moments of the film, which opens on a wall of yellow dough. Turquoise hands (establishing the film's uniquely vibrant color palette) enter the frame, prodding, manipulating and fingering the

Figure 2.2

Stills from *Ivan's Need* (Dir. Veronica L. Montaño, Manuela Leuenberger, Lukas Suter). ©2015 Veronica L. Montaño / Manuela Leuenberger / Lukas Suter. Images courtesy of Veronica L. Montaño

malleable backdrop, at first tentatively before graduating to fully kneading the substance with both hands as their owner, young Ivan, makes excited noises. The animation, primarily taken on by Leuenberger and Suter to Montaño's design work, depicts Ivan's bliss as he throws his whole body into the process with perfect fluidity, until his crotchety employer Horst snaps him out of his reverie. Clearly less interested in the hard bread the dough is destined to become, Ivan begrudgingly accompanies his boss to deliver loaves to their sultry neighbor Alva. His attitude improves enormously at the sight of her impossibly long breasts, draped around her body like scarves before unraveling, Rapunzel-like, from her apartment window. Ivan is inflamed with ardor at the sight while his boss, all business, ties the bread to her breasts for her to retrieve. The visual is one of many that leans into an inherent silliness of the film and the logic of its world.

"It's a combination of two things, I guess," recalls Montaño. "I love wearing scarves and I always thought it would be nice if they were made of body parts, because it's a nice feeling, and the nearest thing I could imagine were the breasts." This, combined with the inherently sensual visual of classical snake dancers, would inform Alva's design (Figure 2.3), one with which Ivan is instantly infatuated.

Back at the bakery, Ivan's sensual dough-kneading takes on a new dimension as he imagines himself grabbing up handfuls of breasts, frolicking and cuddling them while in the nude (special credit for the film's ability to tow the line between sensual and unsettling is the masterful sound design by Etienne Kompis and Thomas Gassmann, which gives the film an almost ASMR quality at certain moments). It's a fantasy scenario perhaps relatable to those whose first inklings of sexual desire may have come before a full awareness of the mechanics of sex itself; in Ivan's case, an extra dimension is added to his daydreaming insofar as the world he occupies is a relatively fantastical one in and of itself. Scolded again by Horst, who slips on a slab of dough and burns his hands on the masonry oven, Ivan gleefully takes the opportunity to visit Alva again under the pretense

Figure 2.3

Alva designs by Veronica L. Montaño for *Ivan's Need.* ©Images courtesy of Veronica L. Montaño

of delivering more bread. She welcomes his enthusiasm for her breasts and uses them to carry him up to her room, where his fantasy becomes reality.

Although it is never explicitly stated what age Ivan is meant to be, Alva certainly reads as the older, more experienced party. Something the film achieves well is sidestepping the potentially problematic concerns of an age difference by giving the characters almost inhuman characteristics; they don't read so much as literal people than manifestations of desire and self-discovery; in Alva's case, it is assured and solicitous, while in Ivan's, it is wide-eyed and driven by exploratory wonder. Says Montaño,

> We had reactions from people who felt weird that it was 'sexy', yet they liked it. Maybe that's it, because Ivan is cute and sensual and wrapped up in this weird concept of ours. It's difficult because, for us, it was always natural and made sense. In the beginning [Ivan] was more of a creeper, but as the story was developing the character did too, and at some point he became pretty young and cute. We knew this innocence and curiosity was really important to us.

"We wanted to present sex as a natural thing," adds Leuenberger. "So we needed an honest, innocent character. It's just how it came together. He has no other intentions except he's just going for what he sees and wants to touch what he sees, like a child."

Without any dialogue to speak of, a major player in the characterization of Ivan came from the voice performance of the directors' coursemate Frederic Siegel, a noteworthy filmmaker in his own right who would go on to create films including the multi-award-winning *The Lonely Orbit* (2019). Rebuffing the suggestion of using a "proper" actor, the team found themselves far more enamored of Siegel's youthful tone and ability to produce exactly the right kind of "weird sensual noises." Similarly, the inviting, seductive moans of Alva were "nailed" by Michiko Hanawa, one half of the duo Tim & Puma Mimi, who took on the film's music.

Leuenberger:

> We wanted the sounds not to be typical porn sounds. We wanted them to be funny and a bit weird, so we would ask her to do some high pitch and some low pitch, to go up and down with her voice.

The pair luxuriate in Alva's bare, unraveled flesh until Ivan is overwhelmed by sensation, resulting in her breasts transforming into hard, baked loaves.[5] Doleful at the apparent loss of what had so entranced him initially, Ivan is comforted by Alva, who coaxes him toward her crotch. Finding a new area of her body to be captivated by, he willingly slides inside her, finding refuge in her pulsating vaginal walls that prove to be an impossibly expansive terrain he is curious to explore. Crawling further into her body, Ivan eventually alights upon a heart, whose texture he finds most appealing of all. We end on Ivan, having achieved perfect euphoria, submerging completely into Alva's heart. The route to this bizarrely sweet final destination of Ivan's odyssey came, as Montaño remembers, after some degree of trial and error before deciding to take the plunge (so to speak) into full-on, sleep-deprived absurdity.

> It was funny because we had a lot of endings, but they always involved Ivan running away when Alva's breasts turned into bread. We had one night where we got into a bit of a crazy state and needed sleep, and at some point we thought *What if we go* inside *the vagina? Yeah, totally, that would be perfect!* We always thought that he needed to find

the "internal" dough, the internal feeling, and we didn't want him to find that in sex. We thought it would be nice if he found it in something more deep, more important.

Adds Leuenberger,

We always had that structure where, pretty much from the beginning, we knew that there'd be that climax followed by some disappointment; he thought he'd found what he was looking for, but then gets disappointed – but then what he finds next is even better.

In some respects, *Ivan's Need* speaks of a young man's discovery of a previously dormant side to himself, one inflamed by arousal and in dire need of taming so that he might find true peace and satisfaction. Another piece that metaphorically lays out the concept of wrestling with new, hard-to-control urges is *Growing Pains* (2014) (Figure 2.4). Directed by Tor Fruergaard and written by Sissel Dalsgaard Thomsen, the film explores the unusual affliction of Fabian, a young man amid the throes of puberty who discovers, to his horror, that when he becomes aroused he turns into a werewolf. Thomsen and Fruergaard had previously collaborated on multiple films, including *Venus* (2010), which is discussed further in Chapter 6. Although the film would receive full funding and complete artistic freedom from The Danish Film Institute, an undoubtedly ideal situation

Figure 2.4

Stills from *Growing Pains* (Dir. Tor Fruergaard). ©2014 First Lady Film. Images courtesy of Tor Fruergaard

for any filmmaker, the duo originally applied to the organization with an entirely different project, according to Fruergaard:

> Just before we went into the first meeting, we were like, should we have a backup? We talked really briefly about maybe making something with a werewolf. Then when we got into the meeting, the commissioner was really not into the idea we had, so we looked at each other and said we also had an idea for a werewolf film. The commissioner said "Wow, that sounds exciting." Then we started to work on it, so that's how it got into the world.

Thomsen, whose works prominently features themes of sex and sexuality, explains:

> Tor and I really have a common love for all sorts of creature films and horror films. So I was just like, "Yay, werewolves!" But Tor was the one who brought it up as an idea and I added the sex. A lot of the time, sex can be a lot like therapy. It reaches into a lot of other aspects of life. And some of those may be psychological issues, emotional or other kinds of issues in life that can be channeled through the sexuality of a person. You can use [sex] to embody something that's maybe emotional or psychological.

The film's protagonist Fabian lives with his prudish and overprotective mother. One day when assisting her at her veterinary clinic, he meets and instantly falls for Felicia, a pretty new girl in town. Later, while fantasizing about his new crush, his body begins to change – growing fur and claws – as he becomes aroused. Only when he climaxes does he revert to his human form, his confusion diverted when his mother enters the room. He later invites Felica to walk with him in the woods; the two grow closer and develop more of an affection for one another. Hormones raging, they return to Fabian's house and begin to make out, prompting another werewolf transformation, a clear metaphor for pubescence and burgeoning sexuality, as Thomsen explains: "This whole idea of the wolf being this very aggressive, classically masculine monster – a strong but also possibly destructive force – just made sense to use."

Continues Fruergaard,

> When we kind of settled on the werewolf as a one-to-one image for puberty, sexuality and going from childhood to manhood, that was where we really had the DNA of the film. I remember that I said to everybody on the team that we don't want any full moons, we don't want any silver bullets, all that. It needs to be about how it is to go into puberty, to feel something for another human being in a very different way, and suddenly realize that you are turning into a grown-up, with everything that follows.

This same werewolf imagery also has a darker side that can be seen to represent male urges, as Thomsen expands upon.

> The idea of actually being afraid that your sexuality might hurt another person, and the shame that can come along with that is, I think, a very male issue, or a very male worry. As a teenage boy coming into your own sexuality, it just fits perfectly with the werewolf.

This concept plays out when, as Fabian's animalistic side takes over, he unintentionally scratches Felicia's back deeply. He retreats to the bathroom after she recoils in horror and, riddled with fear, shame and self-loathing, mutilates his wolf-like appendages. Concerned, Felicia enters the bathroom, shocked to see

Fabian in his werewolf form, fleeing as his mother returns home while he escapes through the bathroom window. Once returned to his normal state, Fabian attempts to apologize, but a fearful Felicia rejects him. Returning home, he is confronted by his mother who suggests a cure – castration. As they prepare for the procedure at the clinic, Felicia interrupts and attempts to stop the procedure. Moved by Felcia's words of protest and her obvious care for him, Fabian changes his mind and harnesses his werewolf abilities to escape his bindings, fleeing with Felicia as his mother cowers in fear. Safe in the woods, the couple successfully have sex; with compassion and understanding, Fabian's animalistic sexuality remains a present but controllable part of his sexual identity.

For Fruergaard, the themes raised by the film, specifically those regarding male urges and the potential for violence, were important to unpack:

> It's a very personal film for me, because, as a man, you get that story a lot, that men are violent, and men hurt other people, and they hurt each other and women. I think a lot of men (and I know this is kind of a slippery slope) want to be one of the good guys but still have to live with that image, that men are violent because that's the story that we tell. Obviously, there's a good reason why we tell that story. But it's not like that with everybody.
>
> Sometimes I get people saying "Oh, yeah, #NotAllMen," but you also get these very black-and-white preconceptions, asking "why tell a story about a man that's innocent?" Because no man is innocent, and that's fine, but I think it's still interesting to tell a story about men who struggle with having that image glued to them, even though they want to be different.

Thomsen adds to this, by evidencing how this idea is resolved within the film itself.

> I think the whole point of the ending, in particular, is that you can be authentic in your male sexuality and control it at the same time. You don't have to remain a little boy and stay completely outside of this zone, you can step into it and embrace the beast, so to speak – but you can control the beast at the same time. That, to me, is a very important message with the ending [...] I can imagine that if you put on a certain kind of filter, it can seem like a very controversial film, but in my opinion it really isn't. I mean, the whole point of the ending is that it's not controversial, that this is who he really is, it's the natural part of him – and it doesn't have to be violent.

The film answers these questions elegantly by addressing the old adage of "boys will boys" and the outdated idea that men – hormonal young men in particular – cannot control themselves, by showing that in fact, they can, while also embracing their natural virility.

Another key element of the film is Fabian's relationship with his overbearing mother, a single parent who conceived Fabian through the use of a sperm donor and whom Fabian says "doesn't really like men." Her lack of boundaries and militant attitude toward sex later leads her to attempt the unthinkable in castrating and mutilating her own son in a bid to "resolve" the issues raised by his budding sexuality, an act that potentially shows her to be not only against sex but fearful of male sexuality. Although the mother character is not explored at great length in the film, partially due to its time restraints and primary focus on Fabian's own journey to sexual understanding, her actions and reactions leave us wondering what may have made her this way. Was the sperm donation a lie? Did she know Fabian's father? Was he potentially a violent man, who didn't learn to control his own "monster"?

Ultimately, these are questions that are left unexplored in the film, though her function in the story is important and serves a clear purpose, as Thomsen explains:

> The mother is kind of a caricature, and she is kind of an archetype. But I also don't find it to be that much of a problem, because it is a fairy tale in a way – and when you tell fairy tales, the characters are sometimes symbols of something [...] and she's an embodiment of this feeling of shame, in a way.

The film makes use of physically constructed paper backgrounds, with paper texture-overlaid 2D animation composited into the scenes. Director Fruergaard states that this paper world, in which even the sounds have an appropriately textural quality to them, affords a level of fragility: "This boy is, of course, a monster, but he is also a little boy made out of paper, and you can rip him if you want to." He continues by explaining how the look of the film is not supposed to be challenging but instead a means to open the film up as a coming-of-age tale for young adult audiences.

> If you're 15 years old, you should want to see this film. And if you are 15 years old, and you see something that looks like it was made for children, then maybe you don't want to see it.

This consideration opens up *Growing Pains* to potentially being viewed not just as entertainment but also something with education value. As evidenced previously with the Danish Film Institute's sex ed film *Sådan får man altså børn* (Dir. Liller Møller, 1990) in Chapter 1, Denmark has a particularly open and liberal attitude toward sex, an idea attested to by Thomsen:

> It's a bit difficult when you don't know how to compare it, because I don't know what it's like in Britain, for instance, but my perception is that it is pretty liberal still. Children and young adults get sex education in schools. I'm really happy that [my son's] school is talking about these issues, or these subjects in a very age-appropriate, but very liberal, open-minded way. And it's not a taboo subject in Denmark with children or young people.

This mentality is clearly a very important factor in both *Growing Pains* and in their previous film *Venus*, as Thomson explains:

> I think a message that they have in common, which I also try to implement in a lot of my other work and is not necessarily sexually themed, is being open to the idea that other people are different from you; opening the audience's mind to something that they might not be used to in their own life. Other people can live lives that are very different from yours, and that doesn't make them any less than you. Both of these films deal with something that is, in a sexual way, somewhat shameful, or something that some people at least think should be hidden. We tried to bring it out into the light and have an open conversation about it, saying "It's not dangerous, nor something you should feel shame for in any way."

This sentiment is shared by Fruergaard:

> It's not just about sexuality, it's about being human in a way, keeping an open mind to everything and telling stories about people who are struggling with not being normal. I can totally relate to that.

In contrast to the character of Fabian, whose canine transformation is initially unwanted, Terri Matthews's 2016 film *The Wrong End of the Stick* tells the somewhat inverted tale of Malcolm Fetcher, a married, middle-aged teacher who finds himself increasingly unable to hide a secret longing to live his life as a dog. Created at the world-renowned National Film and Television School (NFTS) in the United Kingdom, the film is distinct from the other voyages of self-discovery discussed in that Fetcher's crisis is one of full-on species dysphoria.

Matthews, who would go on to work as a Story Artist for various children's shows, cites her passion for adult animation as her inspiration

> to tell a grippingly awkward, darkly comic and crazy story for a mature audience. I was inspired by old British series such as *Monkey Dust* (and the character Clive in particular), so I ultimately wanted to make a film that would pay tribute to long absent, mainstream British adult animated series.

In the film, we initially join Malcolm at home watching unseen, potentially insalubrious videos on his computer before his wife Beverly interrupts, asking him to join her in bed. When he eventually crawls into bed with her, their intimacy abruptly stops when he begins humping her leg, our first hint of the story to come. The next morning, a concerned Bev tries to question Malcolm, but he quickly deflects and leaves for work. At school, Malcolm and his students are distracted by two dogs mating in front of the window. On returning home, Malcolm finds the house empty save for the family dog, Francis. Drawn in by Francis's carefree life, Malcolm seeks to mimic him, dropping onto all fours and drinking from his water bowl (Figure 2.5). As he continues to live out his best dog life, he follows Francis under the table, where a flexible Francis begins to lick himself. An inquisitive Malcolm attempts to copy him. When an out-of-context utterance and unfortunate angle leads Bev to find Malcolm in a compromising position under the table, next to Francis, she jumps to the reasonable conclusion that something unseemly is at play. Distraught and sickened, she kicks Malcolm out of their home.

Malcolm attempts to find solace and, while searching online, finds an event that seems to cater to people like himself. Arriving at an apartment building in a makeshift dog costume, he is transported into a fantasy world. In a scene that

Figure 2.5

Still from *The Wrong End of the Stick* (Dir. Terri Matthews). ©2016 National Film and Television School

Figure 2.6

Still from *The Wrong End of the Stick* (Dir. Terri Matthews). ©2016 National Film and Television School

showcases the medium of animation to full effect, we see him transform into his dog persona, welcomed by a bunny before an elegant deer leads him through a door to a beautiful space, with other animals. Here, Malcolm "believes he is being taken somewhere where he can truly be himself. Venturing into a beautiful glade is Malcolm's 'this is it' moment: he thinks he's found his people," Matthews explains (Figure 2.6). This idyllic scene is quickly shattered as the animals begin to engage in interspecies sex, the fantasy crumbles and we witness fur-clad people engaged in sex play. Continues Matthews,

> He realizes he's totally misread the situation. He takes off his mask and everything comes crashing back to the dank reality the partygoers are trying to escape from. These guys are just there for the sex (apart from the rabbit, Harlequin T. Fluffball, who is there for the crisps) and this is not what Malcolm wants at all.

Bewildered at the debauchery, Malcolm states he only wishes to be a "good boy" and flees. Meanwhile, back at home, Bev has steeled herself to look at her husband's computer history. Fearful of what she may find, she is relieved to uncover innocuous dog behavioral videos through which Malcolm can better hone his canine instincts. Relieved that his inclination is not a deviant perversion, she looks at their wedding photo and, in a moment of acknowledgment, sees that his doggy ideations have been there from the start. On returning home, Malcolm pleads with Bev, willing to forgo his true self should she be willing to take him back. Bev silently reveals her feelings on the matter by presenting Malcolm with a reconciliatory cup of tea in a dog bowl, showing her willingness to accept him as he is. The end of the film finds the two engaging in bedroom play that satisfies both of their needs. Despite the sometimes explicit imagery in the film, for Matthews, there is a clear line between Malcolm and the perceived proclivities the audience may infer from the scenarios.

> I could argue that none of it is sexual to him. We discover that the video he was watching in the opening scene was actually a playful documentary about Border Collies.

He's then playful in bed with Bev but gets lost in his own world. When he sees the dogs shagging in the school field, he's not longing to shag like a dog; he's actually taken by their freedom to express themselves and do what comes naturally to them.

Since Malcolm wants to be a dog in all ways, his sexuality might be tangled up in there somewhere. I leave that up to the audience to decide whether or not that's important, since it's not really the true intention of the film.

As well as Malcolm's journey, Bev is seen to change throughout the film. We see her acknowledge what, on some level, she may have always secretly known about her husband; that she is able to accept his true nature is a heartwarming step in their relationship, as Matthews notes – "She is the person Malcolm wants to be with and be his true self with, he didn't want anything else."

Initially driven by Matthews's desire to make the "darkest, grossest, most appalling thing the NFTS had ever produced," she was promptly encouraged to change paths as it was felt that audiences would reject a film that had no "redeeming moments." The film itself came from other short films that Matthews, producer Sam Bank and writer Chris Cornwell pitched to their course leaders. Unsatisfied with any one idea, the trio looked for common themes – "hiding an identity; a sex scene featuring awkward eye contact; and making the audience squirm" were, according to Matthews, all elements they were keen to explore.

We also had a fourth, more surreal idea where a character turned into a horse to escape their lonely, monotonous life. It had a flavor of the furry community to it, something that I've been fascinated with for yonks. So *The Wrong End of the Stick* came from a mix of all of these things.

While aspects of the furry fandom are featured within the film itself, the director maintains that Malcolm's story is not intended as a statement about "a whole community," rather one man's specific journey, the hope that he may not be entirely alone and discovering what is truly important to him (Figure 2.7).

It was always intended to be an identity crisis, something innocent. Malcolm has always been the way he is. We even designed him intentionally to have some dog-like features! And we meet him when he is already at breaking point, and finally ready to explore who he really is and discover what he really wants. It's not really about kinks and sex stuff, because Malcolm turns down the invitation to join the furry sex party. The film is more about the freedom of expression and identity amongst the boredom and the mundanity of life, exploring who we are and how we connect with others.

The film takes advantage of the NFTS's well-established live-action facilities by combining real sets and live-action shooting with 2D animated character animation. Driven by a desire to take the opportunity to work closely with a production designer and cinematographer (and a general disdain for drawing backgrounds), the bold, mixed-media approach taken by Matthews creates a synergy between the mundanity of Malcolm's real life and the fantasies of his dream life.

"I've always loved this kind of aesthetic, from productions like *Who Framed Roger Rabbit* and *The Amazing World of Gumball,* where each has created their own completely believable and engaging mixed-media worlds," says Matthews. This combination was also created to enable audiences to "more easily connect with and embrace the 2D animated characters" and, importantly, when combined with the more adult themes in the film, "keep audiences engaged and

Figure 2.7

The Wrong End of the Stick dog costume designs by Ockeroid. ©Image courtesy of Terri Matthews / Ockeroid

rooting for Malcolm until the very end, so they were not completely thrown off by surprise testicles and Francis the dog's red lipstick."

The process required actors to perform shots where characters interacted with real-life objects that were later rotoscoped.

> Our willing participant Hedley Roach took on Malcolm's role in the living room scenes, but we didn't have the budget to have a stand-in actor every day and ended

> up doing a lot of the acting ourselves. The challenge when filming the naughty bits was really just surviving the burning-hot embarrassment of being filmed pretending to take one for the team! I had to do those ones.

Matthews's willingness to throw her all into the film is commendable, and the overall look and quality of the animated performance lends the subject further credibility, allowing the audience to remain engaged, even when pushing the subject and the use of innuendo in the film.

> We wanted to play with the audience's expectations – it definitely became a fine line of leading and misleading the audience, but we found that by allowing brief moments of relief where the audience could laugh and breathe out before being subjected to another bizarre event meant they stayed connected to Malcolm, not to mention watch the rest of the film. If you look at it completely objectively, it is really the audience jumping to conclusions while watching a well-meaning man trying to copy his dog and lick his own balls.
>
> We had crafted the story in a way to not completely alienate the audience. We didn't just chuck as much gross stuff at the audience as we could. Everything was there for a reason, most of all to bring things back to cold reality, make the audience laugh and diffuse the tension so they didn't die cringing. Looking back, the trust that our course leaders placed in us was pretty amazing!

Although Matthews remained pragmatic about the film's prospects, stating that she didn't think any film with "swinging ball sacks (was) ever going to be in contention for a BAFTA," having a film that would most likely be destined for more niche, late-night, out-of-competition screenings was still somewhat difficult.

"It was a shame, because curators and judging panels seemed to only focus on the content and didn't appreciate the high level of skill it took to create such a seamless world," says Matthews.

In spite of this, *The Wrong End of the Stick* went on to have a strong festival run, picking up multiple awards including Best Animator Award at Underwire Festival 2016 as well as a Best Student Film nomination at the 44th Annie Awards in 2017. Its online reception is perhaps best exemplified by the film's top comment on YouTube, which reads "Excellent production of the worst story I could possibly tolerate"[6] demonstrating that, like Malcolm himself, the film has found its own place in the world.

The perception of what is "normal" is a problematic and generally antithetical concept when it comes to sexuality and the pursuit of an intimate relationship, particularly when there are additional external factors that hinder this process further, whether that is due to something physical, social or neurological. As tricky as it can be to navigate our sexuality under any circumstances, the journey can sometimes become especially compounded if neurodivergence is a factor. One film that does a commendable job of portraying this struggle is 2019's *Mind My Mind*, written and directed by Dutch filmmaker Floor Adams of Curious Wolf.[7]

After a near decade of development and production, during which the length and scope of the project would shift (from an initial proposed runtime of 11 minutes, it would expand to 30), *Mind My Mind* premiered at Anima Brussels in March 2019, kicking off a run of screenings that would bring Adams, already a respected animator in the Netherlands, a significant degree of international acclaim and respect for the way in which the film addressed the struggles of its protagonist Chris, a young, autistic model plane enthusiast embarking on his first significant romantic relationship.

The unique sensitivity of the film is likely owed to Adams's atypical background; prior to becoming a filmmaker, her work had spanned art therapy and psychiatry with a focus on disabled persons, as well as running animation programs for young artists with autism spectrum disorder. As Floor recalls:

> During my days as a teacher, when I was teaching animation to autistic students, I thought *Well, this is my subject. This is something I can relate to and I think I'm the person to make a film about this.* And that's what I did, for ten years of my life! It was a big project for me.

Taking inspiration from her own personal relationships, notably a romantic partner diagnosed with what was then-known as Asperger's syndrome (now considered part of ASD) and the sometimes-revelatory interactions with her students' thought processes and fixations, the premise of *Mind My Mind* would take shape, fleshing out its lead as an ostensibly well-rounded, if socially anxious, young man whose brain function is manifested as Hans, a nondescript[8] creature constantly busying itself with making sense of the array of stimuli Chris is barraged with (Figure 2.8).

> Once you're in someone's environment, you see there are a lot of things that are difficult for them. So I wanted to make a film about that, about people who, when you meet them, there seems to be nothing wrong, but in their heads there's a lot going on, a lot of things you don't see and don't know.

Adams would further draw upon the experiences of her former students by canvassing willing participants via questionnaire, an exercise not taken lightly and with as much consideration toward boundaries as possible. The group were encouragingly receptive and open in their responses, something that proved invaluable to the development of the film's script.

> I don't want to generalize anything, because everyone is different, but people were very open about it. A misconception about people with autism is that they can't lie, which is not true, but there is an openness to their conversations. They gave me the most beautiful answers, but you have to be really careful what you ask for, so

Figure 2.8

Still from *Mind My Mind* (Dir. Floor Adams). ©2019 CinéTé Filmproduktie / Fabrique Fantastique / Curious Wolf. Image courtesy of Floor Adams

> as to not open up any traumas or any feelings of anxiety or shame. It's like being a journalist, maybe, or a researcher. It's not only talking about sexuality or love but also what your special interests and preoccupations are. Some people may like to keep those things secret.

In a story device vaguely (and unintentionally) reminiscent of Disney/Pixar's *Inside Out*, *Mind My Mind* takes us back and forth between Chris's external life and the inner processes handled by Hans, from which we discern that certain "banal" topics and scenarios create anxiety for him, whereas thoughts of military aircraft, specifically warplanes, keep him grounded. His routine is disrupted when his brother calls, gently pressuring him to come to a party and potentially spend some time getting to know Gwen, an attractive herpetologist he is interested in. In preparation, Hans works overtime to get Chris into an appropriate headspace for the party; once there, he struggles to think of appropriate things to say, to his naturally sociable brother's chagrin. When Gwen joins them, she and Chris make small talk over the nature of pheromones in the animal kingdom. In spite of her personable nature putting him at ease, Chris begins to feel overwhelmed and leaves shortly afterward, Gwen following him outside to invite him to visit her at the zoo where she works. Back at home, he calms himself with his model kits, though is unable to sleep as Hans scrambles to put his thoughts about Gwen in order. It is important to note that the character of Hans is not, according to Adams, intended to represent Chris's autism specifically; rather, he is an "information processor" that anyone might have, albeit with an at-times more pressing workload.

> I watched the film with students who are studying to be teachers, so I was looking at the film through their perspective in the cinema, on a large screen, and thought *The audience needs to work really hard to understand everything*, because there was so much information in it that, to me, was so logical at the time of writing it and creating the storyboards, and now I'm thinking *Wow, there's so much, you can watch it over and over again to see different things.* I think that's the way all brains are – they're complicated, but when you carefully look at what Chris is doing, it's very logical, because it's just a more slow-motion type of information processing. You see all the steps and you see how it is without any filters; we have filters, because we're able to organize all the information more quickly, but it is the same, in a way.

Over the coming days, Chris pragmatically approaches the concept of relationships and flirting through observation and studying books, eventually building up the confidence to visit Gwen and make an effort to focus on her interests. Though the visit goes well and he finds himself in good spirits, introducing Gwen into his thoughts and routine becomes noticeably disruptive to Hans, who struggles to keep up with the new onslaught of emotions and information to digest. Their relationship continues to progress in a positive direction (Figure 2.9), though, to some extent, he finds himself masking, compelled to keep his own specific interest in planes hidden.

One night Gwen, sad that a chameleon at her work has died, shows up unannounced; they kiss and, in one of the film's more pointedly comedic beats, Chris asks if she'd like to have sex, the bluntness of which amuses her. Once inside, he makes a similarly pragmatic leap and abruptly appears naked before her.

> When I came up with the idea that he just wanted to pop that question, many people on the crew felt that it was too huge a leap for him. But I thought it wasn't, because I

Figure 2.9

Stills from *Mind My Mind* (Dir. Floor Adams). ©2019 CinéTé Filmproduktie / Fabrique Fantastique / Curious Wolf. Images courtesy of Floor Adams

> wanted to make it very logical; it's funny, but you can understand why he's doing it. So to me it made sense, and then when he undresses it's the same thing. In my experience, and what I've read in books also, it's that some people without boundaries tend to be less concerned with appearances; if you're going to have sex it has to be practical, so you just undress. It's nothing to do with foreplay, or being sexy or leaving things covered or uncovered, it's just "this is me" (I'm not trying to say that everyone is the same, of course it's more nuanced than that). Also walking around without putting on trousers afterwards, there's no inhibition or worry about what people may think.

Chris and Gwen start being intimate, while Hans goes into an organizational overdrive as he sifts and catalogs a deluge of sexual information at warp speed. This sequence in particular drew upon Adams's research and discussions with former students, so as to present Chris's struggle with as much authenticity as possible.

> I just thought *If you have so much struggle with organization and emotional stuff and you have to have everything explained, how would it work in these kinds of situations?* I also talked to people with autism of course, there was one girl for example who said "When I'm thinking about kissing or something then I have these movie scenes in my head, like *This is the way it works.*" I think those conversations made me realize that everything's going to be step-by-step and in some sort of order. How a neurotypical brain works when it comes to sex and relationships is almost the same, but it's less overwhelming, I think.

In spite of Hans's best efforts, during intercourse, Chris becomes overwhelmed and has to stop (Figure 2.10); when Gwen attempts to comfort him, he angrily grabs her arm and pulls it away in annoyance. While the moment is charged with aggression, for Adams, it is less about Gwen feeling threatened by his physical outburst than hurt by his rejection. While we have already gleaned

Figure 2.10

Still from *Mind My Mind* (Dir. Floor Adams). ©2019 CinéTé Filmproduktie / Fabrique Fantastique / Curious Wolf. Image courtesy of Floor Adams

from her dialogue earlier in the film that she is personable and empathetic, this a scene that speaks volumes about her character's ability to intuit that she is not in any danger, and the degree to which she accommodates his behavior suggests that she, on some level, is aware that there is something more complex that Chris is struggling with, beyond a bruised ego.

> I thought *He's frustrated, it didn't work out, he's had a sensual overload, and now she's trying to touch him* – I figured that would be too much for him, and it would be totally understandable that he rejects her when she touches him. The only thing that bothered me and was hard for me, during the writing, was *Why does she stay? Why doesn't she leave?* Or *Why doesn't she go after him?* She stays in his bed. She's vulnerable at that moment, because of course she's naked as well and she just gave herself to him. Nobody told me that it wasn't clear enough, but maybe I would leave if someone had just rejected me in this way – so she really has to understand him to stay, right?

While we know far less about Gwen than Chris, these brief insights into her behavior and how she responds to his difficulties throughout the film are enlightening. Her sense of empathy is seeded in the first scene that we meet her in, when she intuits that he is struggling to hold a conversation amid the loudness of the house party. She courteously keeps it going, contributing discussion points that she correctly gauges will keep his interest; when he feels compelled to leave shortly afterward, she respects his decision while letting him know she would like to see him again, a small but significant kindness when contrasted with the frustrations of others who unthinkingly chastise "Don't be so autistic" when frustrated by his limitations. These casual cruelties appear to have instilled in Chris a masking instinct, unnecessarily hiding his interests in model aircraft from Gwen. Her empathetic nature suggests that she is perhaps aware of Chris being on the spectrum, though another read, when considering her own niche, focused interests in her work, could be that she is neurodivergent herself.

> Many people ask me the same sort of question, "Is she also autistic?" or "How much has Gwen got to do with you personally?" I think that maybe she has something to do with me, because of the way that she relates to Chris. I thought that this is the way that people can connect to each other – you have to listen to each other, try to understand each other and then you really "meet" each other, in a way. I've heard from other people that it's quite atypical that she's so accepting so quickly, but to

me that's something I would do because I want to see through people's awkwardness or quirkiness, so I think that's more biographical.

The final scenes of the film see Chris retreat to his model studio, leaving Gwen alone in his bedroom while he works through his frustrations. The morning brings something of a breakthrough when he shows her his collection of models. It is a powerful moment in the film, sidestepping the usual tropes of an elaborate apology or grand, redemptive gesture; in being let in to his world, one ordinarily so closed off to outsiders, Gwen offers her immediate understanding and, to his relief, interest in that which he is so passionate about. In many respects, it is a more significant and intimate step in their relationship than the sex scene that precedes it. Some time later, we see a more socially relaxed Chris leave his apartment to meet up with Gwen, suggesting they are still together.

While Chris's inner struggles are a notable part of the story, *Mind My Mind* does a commendable job of avoiding certain pitfalls that other stories about neurodivergence find themselves falling into. When considering the harsh backlash ignited by Alex Oates's 2019 stage play *All in a Row* or Sia Furler's 2021 feature film *Music*, both heavily pilloried by critics and the autism community for their respective handlings of their subject matter, approaching the topic with an appropriate sensitivity that won't prove divisive is no easy task. In the case of *Mind My Mind*, its success could be reasonably attributed to it focusing not on what makes Chris perceivably different, but the relatable aspects of his struggles.

> It's a very universal theme, I think. It's not just about autism, but it's about everyone who thinks differently, and a lot of people who are wired differently, and so I hope it opens up conversations. Up until now it has, because people are talking about it, they relate to the film or know someone who does act "strange." I love the outcome, people respond to the film in the way that I'd hoped for all this time. And I didn't want to generalize, I just wanted to open up the conversation in a subtle, not in-your-face way.

Women in Love

Diane Obomsawin (also known by her pen-name Obom) has been a staple of the Montreal underground comics scene since the mid-1980s. Cutting her teeth in the world of animation while studying at Concordia University, since the late 1990s, she has enjoyed a harmonious relationship with the National Film Board of Canada, producing several commissioned films dealing with civil law and personal rights before her first original animated short *Here and There*, an autobiographical film based on her tumultuous childhood, which went on the win Best Narrative Short Animated at the Ottawa International Animation Festival in 2006.

Subsequent films have been based on Obomsawin's acclaimed work as a comic book writer and artist, with her 2008 award-winning graphic novel *Kaspar* (Drawn & Quarterly) (inspired by the life of Kaspar Hauser) adapted into a similarly accoladed NFB film in 2012. As Obomsawin herself acknowledges, being heavily involved in both comics and animated filmmaking, sometimes adapting one to the other, has served to highlight just how different the two mediums are when it comes to the demands on her time and attention:

> It's strange – doing a comic book I find more difficult, because I have to make a lot of decisions more often; for each panel I have to choose how to do it well, the best

way to do the framing, I have to think with each panel. So the drawing is quite fast but afterwards there are other problems to solve for the next panel. Animation is the opposite, I just do what I've decided to do and don't think so much. With comics, I'll want to make coffee and muffins all the time, do other things, but when I have a film I have to run after it. I run and run and don't stop.

Later comic projects would include *J'aime les filles*, a collection of ten reflections by women on their first same-sex attractions, exploring topics such as coming out, early attempts at sexual expression, affection both reciprocated and not, all presented with honest humor and pathos. The "ordinariness" and relatability of each memoir makes them all the more compelling, with Diane's distinct illustration style – in which people are depicted with animal heads that vary from story to story – imbuing them with an apropos sense of naivety.

At times explicitly sexual, there's no sense of an impetus to provoke, shock or titillate; these sequences instead serve to round out the authenticity of each recollection, appearing alongside endearing anecdotal details that broaden each story's relatability. Although the stories are bound by the theme of women's affection for one another, there's a universal accessibility inherent in its themes of yearning, rejection, adolescent confusion and, in its cheerier moments, the unbridled joy of romantic dreams coming true. The genesis of the project, as with many of the case studies in this book, came from Obomsawin's real-life experiences, and the realization that she had spent multiple years cycling through a series of romantic infatuations.

I was always in love with someone. It was a pattern that came from childhood. I tell that anecdote in the film, that I went to about fourteen different schools and I would unconsciously find a girl who I would fall in love with intuitively, from the age of four. That was my *raison de vivre*, I'd want to go to school to see her and focus on that. Looking back, I realized the first thing I did when I was in a new school was choose someone who would be important to me and with whom I didn't speak, just to know she's there. I kept doing this all my life. Then I was interested in knowing about other girls. At the same time I was reading from a book by Michel Tremblay, a well-known gay Quebecois author who explained that, when he was 16, he noticed that each time he saw a man and a woman kissing on the cover of a book, he always identified with the woman receiving the kiss, and realized that maybe he was more attracted to men. So my question for my friends was not about their very first love, it was the very first attraction, even semi-unconsciously, toward a woman.

Having been translated to English as *On Loving Women* by renowned Canadian publisher Drawn & Quarterly (who also released an English translation of *Kaspar*), in 2016, four of the ten stories were adapted into the above-mentioned animated NFB short film *J'aime les filles* (*I Like Girls*), an eight-minute anthology that would win the Grand Prize for Independent Short Animation at the 2016 Ottawa International Animation Film Festival and Best LGBT Short at the 2017 New York City Short Film Festival, alongside a plethora of Official Selections at major events including Sundance and Annecy. Though based heavily on the original book, the film presents a smaller range of case studies to more appropriately fit the format.

In the film I had to do a very concentrated version. In the book it's ten different stories separated into chapters that have the name of each woman. The first woman

I interviewed spoke for two hours and was completely depressed after that because it came with some pain for her. So afterwards I told my friends not to speak for more than twenty minutes.

Accompanying Obomsawin's personal segment *Diane* (which parallels Tremblay's awakening with one of her own when watching a charged kissing scene between two women in the progressive German movie *Girls in Uniform*) are remembrances from three other women who trace their earliest sapphic stirrings back to a particular individual in their life. Horse-obsessed Mathilde finds herself beguiled by a classmate with equine features, a trait shared by the woman she eventually dates later in life, while Marie's first crush is on a neighbor who resembles singer Françoise Hardy, the intensity of the moment their arms first touched burned into her memory. The film's opening segment tells perhaps the most straightforward journey of self-discovery, in which Charlotte is guided through her first experience of woman-on-woman intimacy by a classmate on the last night of boarding school. Their closeness develops organically, initially holding hands, then kissing and finally making love when Charlotte is invited to stay overnight at her new companion's family home. The following morning they emerge for breakfast, the mother either unaware or unfazed by their coupling. While doubtless a monumental event for Charlotte, the domestic scene is a heartening normalization of their love for one another in that the world carries on as it would any other day. Other points in the film, or curious incidental details, carry a similar weight, such as the frugal living circumstances of one of Marie's later girlfriends that sees her family enjoying a makeshift treat of ice cream cones (sans ice cream) dipped in cola. While Marie's story has a less happy ending, being wrenched away from the quaintness of that scenario by her mother and sent to work on a farm, the oddly specific nature of such details communicates a certain importance and value in how it contributed to her journey.

The thing that touched me the most was the fact that the people I interviewed said that they totally recognised themselves yet, at the same time, there was enough of a distance that they could laugh about themselves. I was really pleased with that, there was a sense that I didn't betray what they said at all. Maybe because of the animal heads, it helped them to de-dramatise or distance themselves, but at the same time they totally recognised themselves.

Another visual approach when looking at the animation itself is the occasional incorporation of rotoscopic elements, such as when Mathilde and a later girlfriend dance atop a pride float for the hearing impaired alongside a deaf lesbian couple who they have befriended. Although live-action reference footage has a tendency to be jarring when it rears its head among sequences that do not make use of it, Obomsawin's character design and line style allows the two approaches to coexist harmoniously.

We often say that animators are actors, but usually the traditional animators have a mirror beside them to do the action and then reproduce it. But as a not-quite-as-good animator I prefer the technique of rotoscoping. It comes from my lack of knowledge, but I don't think it's a bad thing that, if you have a lack of knowledge, you're able to go another way. For *I Like Girls* it was important because I really wanted to make a sensual film. My style of drawing is not naturally sensual, so I

> wanted to really be sure that the gestures were. Also it's difficult to animate two bodies together that are kissing or caressing, so we hired two dancers, because they understand the movement more than actors.

The end result works well in that, for the most part, it avoids the immediate tells of rotoscoping done in haste that often results in an uncanny, quasi-naturalistic quality of movement that sticks out like a sore thumb. By going hand-in-hand with the characters' animalized design sensibilities, Obomsawin's approach is a lot more subtle and understated, such as when Marie nervously walks alongside her neighbor, sweetly imitating specifics about the way that she carries herself.

As the film offers the briefest of glimpses into its respective contributors' blossoming desires and personal journeys, it is afforded some degree of wholesomeness by focusing on their romantic successes and, as previously mentioned, limiting the length of each testimonial so as to limit the potential for painful memories overshadowing the positive ones. While there are nods to the fact that there is needless hostility that nonheterosexual people still find themselves having to contend with, such as the aggressiveness of Marie's mother's "solution" for a daughter who is gay, or the aggrieved side-eye Mathilde and her partner endure from a woman they are sharing an elevator with while being physically affectionate, these events do not determine each woman's narrative. While perhaps not deliberate, this curatorial approach to each story might convey an underlying message for those on a similar journey themselves to take such criticisms and hostilities for what they are and, as best one is able, not be fazed by them.

A similar project in its being rooted in proclamations of love for women, albeit with a more tongue-in-cheek approach, is French-born director Chloé Alliez's La Cambre graduation short *Toutes nuancées* (*All Their Shades*, 2015) (Figure 2.11). Making effective use of found objects (in particular, light switches that serve as the heads of her puppets), the film is a celebration of – and tribute to – womankind in all its idiosyncratic glory.

Figure 2.11

Still from *Toutes nuancées* (Dir. Chloé Alliez). ©2015 ENSAV La Cambre. Image courtesy of Chloé Alliez

"I wanted to show the absurdity of some clichés and make fun of them," says Alliez of the project, which features a seemingly male narrator extolling perceived virtues of women, juxtaposed against scenarios involving women that are alternately comical, flawed, grounded and mundane.

> Many sentences in the film seem really too stereotypical (some people even thought it was a misogynistic movie because they didn't get the sarcasm). But it's a fact: when I asked men around me they gave me these kinds of answers. In our society, women are always associated with this picture of a beautiful creature and perfect mother, so when you are a woman, it's hard to disconnect from this and to just be considered as a person.

The depiction of the female form as a combination of found objects gives the film an inherently charming vibe off the bat, playing off the sentimentality of the narration by showing woman in a variety of nonglamorous scenarios such as shaving body hair, exhibiting road rage, doing home repair, menstruating in the shower and (against the declaration "they smell so good") farting a photo collage of pot-pourri. As the film goes on, it leans away from strictly subverting the voiceover and, at times, reinforces it. Positive presentations of womanhood, such as the ability to be nurturing and considerate, protective and maternal, glamorous and seductive, sexually inquisitive and politically engaged are shown, giving the film an extra layer of legitimate appreciation for the subject wrapped around its wry, self-aware core.

> In the beginning I had a few ideas of funny discrepancies between the voice and the pictures. Of course it wasn't enough! I tried to find clear reasons to love women, whether stereotypical, serious or even very personal. First it was difficult to get ideas but, as time went on, I found I couldn't stop. The story would build even after the shooting had begun. When I found a funny accessory I immediately thought *I have to find a sketch with that!* So the narration and the visuals fed each other.

As the film concludes, the narrator is revealed to be a woman herself, her monologue delivered in contemplation of her partner, whom she joins in bed. While a slight subversion of expectation given the script's performance by a male actor, the moment essentially hammers home just how universal the desirable traits of women are to people who sincerely love them without any interest in subjugation, oppression or exploitation.

> All the ideas were based on this ending revelation. The audience is supposed to imagine they are the words of a man. Then, at the end, the spectator understands it's a woman speaking about her reasons to love women, the same that a man could have had.

While Alliez originally hoped to achieve this with a female actor, it ultimately failed to translate, "We recognized the femininity in the voice (even in a very deep one) when I asked them for more punch. Luckily someone gave me the contact of the actor Pierre-Paul Constant and he was just perfect."

After the success of *Toutes nuancées*,[9] Alliez would team up with cowriter and director Violette Delvoye to work on her next film *Les liaisons foireuses* (*Inglorious Liaisons*, 2022). The film, set at a teenage house party, follows Lucie

Figure 2.12

Still from *Les liaisons foireuses* (Dir. Chloé Alliez, Violette Delvoye). LES LIAISONS FOIREUSES ©2022 Vivement Lundi ! / Zorobabel / ARTE France

and her best friend Maya, who has caught the eye of their peer group's "it" boy Jimmy. It becomes quickly apparent, however, that Maya secretly harbors feelings for Lucie, and when a discreet kiss outside on the patio reveals her true desires, it is Lucie who is left unexpectedly derailed. Progressing the unique character design motif of recycled light switches to include plugs for each character's body type, the style comes into its own in its characterization of the clumsiness of teenagers. The partygoers are a diverse group of relatable characters full of bravado, showing off and trying to figure out who they are while attempting to maintain a sense of right and wrong (Figure 2.12). According to Alliez, at the start of the project, there was no intended main character.

> Maya and Lucie's story was more mixed in with the other small stories. But it was a bit too messy, we needed someone to follow, and choosing Lucie was quite obvious. She was the most interesting, because her mood changes a lot during the film, and she is pretty dynamic, so we can see the development of her feelings.

After Maya kisses Lucie, they are interrupted by the oblivious Jimmy, as a confused but unwittingly jealous Lucie slips back inside, hurt by Maya's lack of action.

> Lucie probably had feelings for Maya before the kiss but didn't dare to let them exist, even for herself. When Maya opens this door, it's mind blowing for Lucie. Because of her dynamic and more impulsive temper, she would be a bit more ready than Maya to keep on exploring this new feeling. But Maya is too insecure, too preoccupied by everyone else's opinion. Lucie respects her choice but it also makes her angry, so she is sad and frustrated at the end of the film.

After studying together and helping each other on their film at La Cambre in Brussels, Alliez and partner Delvoye traveled across Europe in a van for a year, to create a participative animated series with recycled objects called *World in (Stop) Motion*,[10] through which they discovered a fondness for working together. Having started to write the original script for *Inglorious Liaisons*, by herself on a residency at l'Enclume studio and Zorobabel studio in Belgium (who would also become the first producers for the film), Alliez turned to Delvoye to help with storyboards, at which stage she was brought on as a codirector.

> She offered a new point of view on the story, more sensitive and complex. My first version was more oriented on jokes and graphic ideas. We mixed those two different approaches to work together on the script and storyboard. But I kept the lead of the visual part, as my ideas always tend to come through images.

They would later join forces with French production studio Vivement Lundi and, over the next three years, would make revisions to the script while securing funding for the film. Eventually, they were able to start production with a small team, animation taken on by Alliez and Delvoye themselves.

"[Violette] took mainly the smooth and precise scenes – very sensitive, and I preferred the dynamic ones," explains Alliez. "For the other tasks, like the editing or the sound, we always worked together."

The film itself is inspired by Alliez's past, in which she had a similar relationship with a best friend that they were unable to speak about, either with each other or their peer group.

> It was a forbidden love. During my teenagehood it was impossible to publicly accept this kind of feeling and we didn't have so many representations of homosexual people, famous or not. Because of that, it was hard to understand this kind of feeling and to allow yourself to live it.

This lived experience incentivizes Alliez to, through her work as a director, bridge this gap and show more representation of queer stories on the screen by queer authors.

> I think the queer representation is better today, but we clearly have to continue to progress. There are a lot of movies and series showing queer people and this amount of visibility helps, for sure, to demystify them and make it "normal." Sadly, very often the stories don't come from queer people themselves. So there are still too many clichés.

Alliez furthers this sentiment by expressing how this is possibly worsened in animation, where "directors tend to push the caricature. And in films and TV series for children, there are still a lot of stupid things that are considered harmless, but that I find dangerous."

Les liaisons foireuses took inspiration from many sources, including the dark humor and writing of animation director Niki Lindroth von Bahr, the theatrical and graphic approach to filmmaking of Wes Anderson, the life given to found objects by PES, as well as the feature film *Les Beaux Gosses* by Riad Sattouf.

> It's our favorite teenage movie, because it's more realistic than usual. He shows, with great humor, the ridiculous but touching attitude of teenagers, in all their integrity. It's closer to reality than those movies or series showing perfect and sexy teenagers (whose actors are actually 20 years old).

This drive to show real teenagers led Alliez and Delvoye to base the characters on their own experience, setting the story during the time period of their own teenage years rather than present day and avoid the pitfalls of misrepresenting the struggles that today's youth are up against.

> A lot of things changed in our society, specifically with the use of the smartphone. We would have had to include it in the narration, and we weren't comfortable with this. I also wanted to stay closer to my memories and my feelings.

Another inspirational figure was director and screenwriter Céline Sciamma who, along with her representation of women and queer people in such celebrated works as *Portrait of a Lady on Fire* (2019), also wrote the screenplay for Claude Barras's stop-motion feature *Ma vie de Courgette* (*My Life as a Courgette*, 2016) which, as well as providing a reference for the group dynamic of *Les liaisons foireuses*, also influenced the voices in the film.

> We knew they recorded the voices in real acting conditions, and we were really convinced by this method. Our objective was to make the voices as natural, alive and spontaneous as possible. So we cast non-professional teenagers, directly in their school, and we did our best to record them together.

Through these recordings, Alliez and Delvoye also allowed the teens to express the dialogue in their own way, keeping the recording going throughout takes to capture moments of hesitation and laughing to allow for a sense of naturalism. This approach would pay off and give the film a level of meaningful and empathetic authenticity that allows for conversations about a particularly difficult time of our lives. On showing the film to young audiences, Alliez notes they often have a lot to say.

> I was surprised to discover that it's still not so easy to claim homosexual feelings today. But what made us happy was to discover that the film was received not only through this perspective. In fact, this film talks about the difficulty of pulling out of the group and being yourself [in the face of] pressure. Homosexuality is presented as a context, but the real topic is more about those fragile, out of control feelings that you don't understand yourself. It's new and you need time to separate facts and fiction. Some teenagers shared with us how problematic it is to become someone real, far from the group life.

This particular frustration is beautifully put across in the film's final scene, in which Maya and Lucie meet on the dance floor for a slow dance (Figure 2.13). Seemingly on the precipice of voicing their true feelings, or acting further on them, both are swept away by their male suitors. We leave them staring across the room at one another, like two ships drifting apart. Alliez says:

> From the beginning we wanted an open ending. This kiss between them and those intense looks suggest a desire, but they still have to understand it. We didn't want an easy solution for them because it's very complex to have deep feelings – even more when it's not "normal."

Films such as those made by Obomsawin, Alliez and Delvoye have an obvious value beyond their ability to entertain. They contribute to a normalization of nonheterosexuality that, while most would have hoped to be redundant in this day and age, is still needed in a world where alarmingly large swathes of the population continue to oppress and shame what they do not understand – or are wrestling with themselves. Nobody with emotional intelligence would look at *J'aime les filles*,

Figure 2.13

Still from *Les liaisons foireuses* (Dir. Chloé Alliez, Violette Delvoye). LES LIAISONS FOIREUSES ©2022 Vivement Lundi ! / Zorobabel / ARTE France

Toutes nuancées or *Les liaisons foireuses* and interpret them as "woke" propaganda pieces; they are films about love and humanity that anyone who has ever experienced love, reciprocal or not, can relate to, regardless of their sexual orientation.

This long-overdue increase in content that might prove a comfort to struggling LGBTQIA+ young people can take on other forms than narrative shorts. The Future Youth Project,[11] an organization that facilitates creative spaces and projects for queer young voices, make use of animation in their online series *How Life Is: Queer Youth Animated*. The project, which comprise 22 episodes over two seasons, is essentially a collection of testimonials from young queer people recounting a variety of potentially daunting experiences, such as coming out as trans to family (*Cal*), code switching (*Zion*), speaking up about self-identity (*Brianna*), demonstrating affection in public (*Ken*) and enduring homophobia in school environments (*Will*). Across most of the films is a throughline of self-identity and acceptance, acknowledging that we often only truly know who we are at the end of a long journey of reflection and experience. Each film has its own look, and while they often err on the side of simplicity in the animation itself, the diversity of the design styles across the ten shorts serves as an appropriate reflection of the diversity of the testimonials themselves. While the full spectrum of sexuality and lived experience could not hope to be fully represented by 20 personal stories, the project is an earnestly conceived attempt to prompt discussions and get the ball rolling on being comfortable with these and associated topics. Similar to some of the educational resources discussed in the preceding chapter, the series also has a degree of educational value, The Future Youth Project's website providing accompanying "Action and Discussion" guides[12] for their target audience as well as parents and educators.

Coming of Age

Between establishing a reputation for her extraordinarily unique storytelling style and humor from her early shorts and embarking on the independent feature film *My Love Affair With Marriage* (discussed in the Introduction and Chapter 1, respectively), in the mid-2000s, Signe Baumane would be approached by representatives of a website looking for short form, adult animated content. In a subsequent pitch meeting, the director would quickly win them over with her disarming manner and relaxed attitude toward the comedic potential a series about developing sexuality might have.

> When I'm nervous and I have to make small talk, I always start to talk about sex. So I was talking about how guys are always obsessed with big dicks and that, in my opinion, the big dicks are really overrated. They were really having a good time, just laughing away, and then they said, "Okay. Thank you for the meeting." I said, "Wait, wait, let me start the pitch!" They said, "That was the pitch! You're gonna record yourself and make the film about that!"

While the project ultimately would not move ahead with this particular website due to limitations of budget and, more importantly, rights ownership, the seed planted from the meeting led to the development of *Teat Beat of Sex*,[13] an episodic series of one-minute anecdotes about the sexual proclivities of Cynthia, a lightly fictionalized, animated counterpart of Baumane herself (Figure 2.14). Shortly after beginning the project as a self-started, indie venture, the director would be contacted by Italian producer Pierre Poire, who was fortuitously in the market for content "about love and sex, that bridges misunderstandings between the genders." This union would properly get the ball rolling on the series, Baumane coming up with ideas for a potential 50 episodes, of which 15 were produced in 2007. Of these, the first three are perhaps the most well-known due to their festival performance and availability online as a free "trailer" for the series (the remaining 12 exclusive to DVD and Vimeo On Demand[14]).

Episode 1: Kirby directly stems from the original pitch meeting in its reflection on men's obsession with penis size, Cynthia recalling various former lovers on different ends of the endowment spectrum. Contrary to societal myth, the partners with

Figure 2.14

Stills from *Teat Beat of Sex* (Dir. Signe Baumane). ©2007 Pierre Poire / Signe Baumane. Images courtesy of Signe Baumane

above-average penises would prove less compatible, or turn her off entirely with their arrogance. In contrast, one particular companion's thorough sexual knowledge and ability would more than compensate for his relatively small member. With each episode, we learn more about Cynthia's sex-positive attitude against the backdrop of her upbringing and formative sexual experience. The series also explores her boundaries, an important factor in dispelling the myth that sex positivity might be synonymous with the idea that "anything goes." Sometimes these are practical, such as in *Episode 2: Juice*, in which Cynthia declines a former lover's suggestion that she not wear panties under her dress when they go out, something that could have visible consequences from being aroused when near him.

> It can upset me when people subscribe to a certain ideology or fashion, and they don't really think about why. For example, in *Juice*, when the lover suggests that Cynthia take off her panties for the party, she says, "Well, if you want me to be hot, the juices just flow out of me. How can I walk without panties?" But we are brought up to think a certain way, that a girl without panties is very hot. There are logistics about walking around without panties! I'm amazed about how society makes people forget the practical matters, or natural matters, or the things that are really important.

While the proposal in *Juice* does not yield the intended result for Cynthia's partner, it has a happy ending in that they blow off the party to spend an amorous evening together at home instead. Other boundaries come from personal autonomy and self-respect, such as her distaste toward a partner crowbarring in misogynistic dirty talk during sex and killing the mood (*Episode 7: Respect*) or deriding the off-putting way in which men inflict boastful, unsolicited stories of their sexual conquests (*Episode 13: Score*).

Although it is not presented chronologically, the series also lays out crucial milestones in Cynthia's sexual development. When a spell of sex deprivation over several weeks sees her climbing the walls, she reflects on her reservations toward masturbation that stemmed from childhood. She concludes that these hang ups, instilled by her mother (a character who, according to Baumane, is based more on conservative society as a whole than her own, real-life mother), were damaging, given that the alternative ultimately led to her marrying early and living in a dysfunctional relationship for years (*Episode 3: Trouble*). Breaking away from the standalone format of most of the series, episodes 8 through 11 are narratively linked, telling a story that foreshadows the early stages of protagonist Zelma's journey in *My Love Affair With Marriage*. In this run of episodes, we see a high-school-age Cynthia endure an emotional rollercoaster of initiation into love and jealousy when, at a dance, she is taken out to the parking lot by a boy and kissed for the first time (a sensation she initially finds repulsive, but quickly warms to – *Episode 8: Lizard*). They then abscond further into a nearby graveyard where their fumblings lead to Cynthia "almost" losing her virginity when he finishes prematurely (*Episode 9: Graveyard*). They return to the dance, only for Cynthia to become incensed when her suitor, about whom she had already built up fantasies of a long-term relationship, goes off with another girl who is more experienced (*Episode 10: Dawn*). Determined to learn more about sex and find enjoyment from it, over the coming months, Cynthia accrues more by way of sexual experiences but cannot find a boy prepared to go all the way. Her solution is to pick up an "old" (all of 33 years) man, lying about her age and experience to get him on board. In spite of him seemingly being able to tell that she's a virgin, nor

Figure 2.15

Stills from *Teat Beat of Sex* (Dir. Signe Baumane). ©2007 Pierre Poire / Signe Baumane. Images courtesy of Signe Baumane

her finding the act of losing her virginity especially mind-blowing, she views the encounter as a positive experience overall (*Episode 11: Puzzle*).

Of all the case studies presented in this book, there are perhaps none that represent the charm and personality of their creator more explicitly and directly than *Teat Beat of Sex* (Figure 2.15). Although semi-fictionalized, the caffeinated pacing and excitable delivery of Baumane's narration feels entirely authentic, delivered with the gleeful urgency of a close friend desperate to tell you something they have been holding on to for far too long. More often than not, it is the comedic value of her anecdotal storytelling that is the focus, especially in episodes that focus on random, standalone recollections – such as *Episode 5: Key*, in which Cynthia and her partner's waning sex life is rekindled by the sound of jangling keys, a Pavlovian reminder of when they would have sex in secret, fearful of a tyrannical college dorm supervisor bursting in. Others showcase a cheeky propensity toward feigned naivety, *Episode 4: Soul* seeing her going along with a potential suitor's interest in finding her "soul" (which remains undiscovered, despite enthusiastic exploration of every available orifice). The presentation of the series as a whole, which heavily indulges rapid-fire jump cuts and a plethora of sight gags and visual puns that sometimes warrant repeat viewing and freeze-framing to fully comprehend, makes it something of a forebear to more recent series such as Lisa Hanawalt's 2019 sitcom *Tuca and Bertie*, which boasts a similar pairing of frantic energy, quickfire pacing and sex-positive female empowerment. The unique hook that puts *Teat Beat of Sex* in a league of its own is just how intimately acquainted the viewer gets with Baumane (via Cynthia) herself. This absence of inhibition is, to the right audience, refreshing and liberating. To the easily daunted, however, it can prove intimidating.

"From day one, my films have polarized people – they're not for the faint of heart," Baumane concedes. "Some people get it, and some people don't. In person, it's different – when you meet me personally, you get exactly what I mean. I just do it for fun, to poke around and try new things."

While much of her audience will cheerfully go along for the ride, the pockets of resistance that occasionally appear in the face of such provocative work are often fascinating for the capriciousness of the logic behind them. One such instance reared its head when the now-defunct video platform AtomFilms[15] expressed interest acquiring certain penis-oriented episodes of *Teat Beat of Sex*, but balked at ones that featured depictions of vaginas.

> I was like, "Explain to me why you can show *Kirby* but you cannot show *Juice*?" They said they had very strict guidelines, where they could show penises in any form, flaccid or aroused, but couldn't possibly show female genitals in any way. My drawings of female genitals are so stylized, you wouldn't even know what they were if I didn't tell you! I just feel that female genitals are very pretty. They're like flowers. But so are male genitals. I love them. It never occurred to me that there would be a preference for one over the other. Now I know, but it doesn't stop me from drawing and addressing these subjects, because that would be some kind of censorship.

While such resistance inhibited the sales performance of the series, it undoubtedly contributed to the making of Baumane's name as an independent creator whose unique boldness would reliably translate to thoughtful and witty filmmaking. With various episodes selected for over 200 international film festivals, including Sundance, between 2007 and 2010, *Teat Beat of Sex* would pick up multiple awards, honorable mentions and help build a fanbase that has fervently supported her subsequent feature film endeavors.

As well-received as *Teat Beat of Sex* turned out to be, one wonders if it might have fared even better had the series come about on the other side of the post-2010 "sea change" we mentioned back in the introduction of this book. In more recent years, audiences have let it be known that there is a growing appetite for such warts-and-all memoirs of sexual rites of passage, one notable recent case study nudging its way enough into the elusive mainstream to earn itself an Academy Award nomination.

With an extensive career in writing for acclaimed animated features such as *Moana* (2016), *Ralph Breaks the Internet* (2018) and *Nimona* (2023), Pamela Ribon[16] is also celebrated for her work as a writer for television, comics, VR and bestselling novels, including her 2013 memoir *Notes to Boys: And Other Things I Shouldn't Share in Public.* Accrued from years of saved first drafts of love notes to the young men she found herself infatuated with throughout adolescence, the premise of Pamela as a grown woman reflecting on the teenage girl (who considered herself an old soul) she used to be would eventually get the attention of FX Vice President of Development Megan Reid and then-Director of Animation & Development John Agbaje. Recalls Ribon,

> I had been coming off of these big studio animated movies, and they suggested this book might translate to an independent, smaller animation produced with a television pipeline. That was a whole bunch of things I hadn't gotten to try yet, so it was really intriguing. I was stepping into a whole different world. Everything had a different name, every pipeline worked differently, completely in reverse to 3D animation, where you can keep changing the scripts until the very last second.

Having to adjust to the idea of her scripts being locked before production began was made easier by being paired with Sara Gunnarsdóttir,[17] a director whose track record on projects such as *The Diary of a Teenage Girl* (Dir. Marielle

Heller, 2015), *The Case Against Adnan Syed* (Dir. Amy Berg, 2016) and her own short films including *Sugarcube* (2009) and *The Pirate of Love* (2012) proved an immediate fit for the prospect of translating them to animation.

"I fell in love with Sara's work the second I saw it, and I thought *Gosh, wouldn't this be a fun, beautiful thing to get to make together, if she would say yes?*," recalls Ribon.

The enthusiasm would prove to be mutual, Gunnarsdóttir drawn to the relatability of Ribon's experiences and excited to work on a longer-form series of animated segments than the smaller-scale projects she was used to. Initially intended to be part of the FX experimental anthology series *Cake*, the production of Ribon's scripts, collectively titled *My Year of Dicks* – as well as its original plans for broadcast – would be obfuscated by the 2020 COVID-19 pandemic throwing things into disarray. Pushing through these challenges, Gunnarsdóttir, Ribon and producer Jeanette Jeanenne would ultimately steer the ship with an old school, auteur spirit evoking the 1990s indie film scene in their corralling of friends and family to bring the production together.

The stories, as adapted, focus on Ribon's 15-year-old counterpart Pam, recounting "A story from the year I was determined to lose my virginity" that spans several months in 1991. The young Pam is portrayed as relatably naive in her continued endeavors to romanticize the at-best mediocre young males in her life, as her seemingly platonic male friend Sam wearily watches on. While the stories are humorously recounted, they frequently lay bare personal and intimate incidents from Ribon's coming-of-age that most would struggle to reveal about themselves. As the writer attests:

> My superpower is a lack of dignity or shame, so oversharing is very much in my wheelhouse! And I was fortunate that Sara was a digital magpie, she just wanted anything I could share because it would help shape the world that she was creating. She definitely pushed me, as did FX, to get weirder and not worry about it being "too much."

The collaboration would yield a number of advantages as regards the visual execution of the film. Giving *My Year of Dicks* a uniquely personal flavor and highlighting its teenage-diary-cum-memoir nature is the use of authentic home movie clips of Ribon as a teenager that introduces each of the film's chapters. Though actually taken from a school Economics project, the brief moments of to-camera footage featuring the real "Pam" lend the project an extra layer of authenticity as well as contributing to the '90s tone and aesthetic. Gunnarsdóttir, who would take on the film's editing as well as directing, recalls that

> It was so much fun. Pamela gave me tons of photos and quite a lot of old VHS tapes where she was either goofing by herself or with friends. So few people were doing this at the time, yet it speaks so much to the youth of today. I thought This is gold. We have to use this. What really drew me to the writing and the project is that it is autobiographical, it's reality. When something is written personally, it just has this honesty. I felt that if we actually saw the live-action footage of Pam at this time, it would take the world to a new level.

Adds Ribon,

> One of the things that's a big difference between the book and the film is that there's no modern version of me commenting on this. It was really important to

let "Pam" be the protagonist of this film and not the butt of the joke. And when Sara put the actual me in there, it made it undeniable that you are in the head of a young woman who deserves to be the lead character of her story. So even if you might sometimes hear an audience get slightly ahead of what's going to happen to Pam – because those poor people have had something like that that's happened to them – it's a moan of recognition as opposed to waiting impatiently for her to wise up. That, I think, is what makes this such a sweetly nostalgic story; we've all just had a dick that we didn't see coming!

Pam's romantic misadventures see her hopping from crush to crush, remaining ever hopeful that the next will yield a more positive result than the one that came before; this rarely proves to be the case. Her first such infatuation, David, an uncoordinated skater whose affectatious manner prompts literary fantasy scenarios (animated by Brian Smee and Isabelle Aspin), uses her interest in him to coordinate a party at her house. Her hopes that an ex-boyfriend, also in attendance, will be tortured with jealousy at her impending loss of virginity are dashed when she learns that both of them are in a contest of who can bank the most hookups from their school's female student body. The story establishes a pattern of behavior for Pam, in which she sets herself up for disappointment not out of hopeless naivety or lack of emotional intelligence, but an earnest impulse to think the best of people. This is perhaps most catastrophically evidenced in Chapter 4, *The Horrorshow*, in which she attends a more intense house party than those she is used to and, while not in her best state of mind, misinterprets a teenage neo-Nazi's interest in her "purity" as her virginity being a desirable trait.

While the humor and relatability of the scripts would have translated to live-action well enough, it is the implementation of a variety of animation processes that truly fleshes out Pam's flights of fancy and shifting state of mind, evoking how we flit between visual and cultural interests during our teenage years. To achieve this, Gunnarsdóttir drew upon the unique and distinct talents of several animators' respective visual styles to add to the anthology feel of the piece.

I had a really wonderful team. When I was reading the script, I would think *Josh* [Shaffner,[18] *Un Gros Penis*] *would be perfect for this one*, or *Grace* [Nayoon Rhee,[19] *The Sweet One*] *would be perfect for that one*; I could just see the personal style of my friends and coworkers that I had worked with in the past. And because I knew the team so well and had worked with them before, I felt less afraid to take it on. We started out with just five extra animators, so I could give each animator a chapter to do, for when we leave the grounded style and the fantasy takes over. I said "as long as you work with me throughout and help me with the more roto-based normalcy, you get to play with some chapters," and it was really great. In the end, we ended up having seven animators, and they all just nailed it.

This approach brings out aspects of Pam's personality and interests that otherwise go unsaid, as well as communicating significant shifts in her headspace and emotional state, hopping from Nayoon Rhee's anime-informed cutesiness in one chapter (in which Pam is on cloud nine, oblivious to her current boyfriend's interest in other young men) to Amanda Bonaiuto's[20] grim, hallucinogenic horror visuals in the next (following both the breakup and a falling out with Sam). These visually disparate fantasy tangents are ultimately bound by a single throughline style for Pam's "reality," which grounds the action in a world that is relatively normal in its heavy use of live-action reference footage for a quasi-rotoscopic look. The effect is similar to the at-times uncanny approaches taken by Richard Linklater in feature films such as *Waking Life* (2001) and *Apollo 10 1/2: A Space Age Childhood* (2022) and would be achieved by recording live-action performances – of the film's voice actors, animators as well as Ribon and Gunnarsdóttir themselves – to be replicated in animation. The characters' faces would also use the likenesses of their respective voiceover artists, save for Ribon, whose real-life appearance was animated over a voice performance by Brie Tilton. As the project progressed, the approach to who precisely did what when it came to references would settle into a system that made production more consistent and easier to keep a handle on. Gunnarsdóttir:

> After that first episode we actually decided to shift it a little bit and always have the same person do references for the same character. That's when we asked a lot of the voice actors to spend a little bit of time with us, through Zoom, to record references. So a lot of the boys did their own references, Pamela and I did a lot of references for "Pam" and then my husband and I did a lot of references where two people are touching and kissing and stuff. It was a lot of mix and match and cut and paste.

As well as the general disappointments that come with common or garden-variety, one-track-minded teenage boys not having the capacity to meet the romantic expectations projected upon them, Pam also finds herself having to endure more pointed instances of cruelty. When forewarning the vampiric David that she is on her period before any intimacy begins, he responds to the information with an abrupt, wordless rejection and digs his sharpened nails into her hand in an act of physical aggression. In the second chapter, *Un Gros Penis*, Pam's *Henry & June*-inspired fantasy devotion to cinema usher Wally (Mical Trejo) builds him up in her mind as a French-accented specter of Parisian suaveness. The real-life Wally lacks the romantic flair of his imaginary counterpart, sneaking her into the cinema on his break, immediately guiding her hand into his trousers once seated and urgently insisting on oral sex, to her (and, accompanying them, fantasy Wally's) horror. Taking her to a grim supply closet, they lie on the floor as he aggressively fondles and kisses at her, oblivious to her lack of interest. In one of the film's more difficult-to-watch moments, Pam freezes into a state of tonic immobility as fantasy Wally appeals to her to remove herself from the situation while a separate, imagined incarnation of erotic author Anaïs Nin insists that she is "lucky" for the attention and that she should see it through. For Ribon, it was especially important for the closet scene to be handled with extra time and consideration:

> The closet moment did take more time than some of the others. We were really careful. One of the things that we were mindful of was that, most of the time, these boys were just bumbling around too, and making mistakes – but not some of them. Some of them are just preying on nice people and are taking advantage of a moment. We really slowed down how fast everything had to be made at that moment, to say "This one can't feel icky." I mean, it feels icky, but you can't come away feeling icky. And particularly on the other side, it's not that Sam opens that door and yanks her out of there, and it is not that this guy gives up; her fantasy says, "I am you; run!" I look back and think how lucky I was at the time, to be able to get out of there because of this weird fantasy life that I had that got me out of moments that could have destroyed me. All hail *Fleabag* for influencing what a fourth wall can do, and what your fantasy world can get you through.

Adds Gunnarsdóttir,

> When we were storyboarding that scene and working on it, right from the beginning we talked a lot about how people still have to be allowed to know that she's fine, and be allowed to laugh. I was very proud of how it turned out. It was also really important to me that the voice actors were actually young, but for Wally it was the only adult playing a boy, because we really wanted to handle it with care.

Ribon:

> [Mical] was someone I knew, for a long time. I knew how he could be funny or serious, I knew he was a very talented actor. So we were really stacking the deck on that one, too.

A heartening aspect of the film is that Pam, though proverbially beaten, is never broken – each chapter ends with a reclamation of autonomy when she snaps out of the self-inflicted fugue states and sees her prospective partners for how unremarkable they really are. When Pam musters up the reserves to reject her inner Nin's insistence that she endure Wally's frustrated gropings, she flees the supply closet, reuniting with her friends in the foyer. Sam, seeing the disheveled Wally emerge after her, hurls the group's drinks and snacks on the floor; while he was not there – or necessary – to protect or save her, the appropriately adolescent gesture represents something of a defense of her honor after the fact.

The characterization of Sam is refreshing in that he does not harbor any archetypically "friend-zoned" grudge toward Pam; he is clearly not thrilled about her quest and correctly intuits that the young men she pursues are not worth the effort on her part, yet in an era predating incel culture (and even the term "friend-zone" itself), his relatively well-rounded, emotionally mature feelings toward her do appear to be predicated primarily on friendship before anything else, only becoming incensed in this scene, when her well-being is in jeopardy. Indeed, the only real threat to their friendship comes in Chapter 3: *The Sweet One* when Pam herself comes around to the idea of Sam as a romantic prospect, albeit on the rebound following an abrupt breakup; seemingly hurt, he shuts down her advances.

Following her aforementioned neo-Nazi nadir in Chapter 4, the film's closing segment Chapter 5: *The Sex Talk* sees Pam endure further torment when, after an attempt to bond with her mother (Laura House) on the subject of sex is harshly shut down, she is redirected to her father (portrayed by Ribon's real-life cousin Chris Kelman) to hear his calamitous "wisdom" on the subject. Among objectively terrible takes on orgasm and masturbation, his and her mother's own sex life and an insistence that "women don't actually like having sex," Pam's animated inner turmoil sees her melt with embarrassment, vomiting and tearing out her ears in a sequence that would feel at home in a Bill Plympton short. As with much of the film's more cringe-inducing moments, this exchange was rooted in a real-life event, as Ribon recalls:

> [My dad] wrote about this incident as well; in his own works he was an aspiring writer and wrote about giving me this sex talk. A classmate raised his hand and said, "I'd like to be the first offer to pay for your daughter's therapy someday." So the story was a little bit open-season, I think, because of that. It was probably most uncomfortable for my cousin, of everybody, to have to record that.

Shellshocked, Pam seeks out Sam and the two mend fences. They go to his room and, in a moment reminiscent of Chris in *Mind My Mind*, Sam abruptly appears naked before her. While Chris's bluntness is borne out of pragmatism and the certainty of sex, Sam's is accompanied by self-consciousness as, in as vulnerable a way as can be imagined, he begins to deliver a prewritten speech that outlines his feelings for her. Endeared to the effort he has made, she eases his embarrassment at putting everything on the line by playfully draping clothes over him; once he is fully covered, he tells her he loves her. She crawls into the pile of clothes with him and the two embrace on the floor. Whether this marks the impending end to Pam's quest is left to the audience's imagination, though we are given the impression that the importance of losing her virginity has been put aside for a more significant connection, one rooted in friendship and real love.

While the original plans for *My Year of Dicks* as part of *Cake* never came to be, as a standalone work, it clearly held its own, receiving the Special Jury Recognition for Unique Vision in Writing and Directing at the 2022 SXSW Film Festival (South by Southwest), a positive omen of things to come. The team's intuition to gauge the film's performance via festival audiences would prove sound as *My Year of Dicks* (now reworked, with the assistance of Benoit Berthe Siward of The Animation Showcase,[21] as a standalone short film compiling the five shorts as chapters) would make significant waves, winning a coveted Cristal for a TV Production at Annecy in 2022 as well as major prizes at the Ottawa International Animation Festival, Raindance Film Festival, International Animated Film Festival Poznań and the Chicago Film Festival that same year. It would also receive praise-filled coverage in publications such as Vanity Fair and Variety, with the aforementioned Best Animated Short Film nomination at the 95th Academy Awards a welcome cherry on top. Says Ribon,

> We were grateful for that, and we were scrappy. So I remain honored and humbled that we got that far, which had everything to do with how it was being received at festivals, and got people talking and interested.

By depicting and telling stories that give such open and honest accounts of self-discovery, these filmmakers provide the viewer with an opportunity to not just further understand the emotional journeys of others, but to see themselves, explore their own stories and potentially find solace in knowing that they are not alone. Next we will explore how animation has been used to similarly bring about understanding, awareness and acceptance of the human body itself.

Notes

1. Helmed by Lise Wedlock and Daniel Scott respectively, marking one of the most vital contributions brought to the film by its co-production with the NFB.
2. www.instagram.com/veronimon_monta.
3. www.manuelaleuenberger.ch.
4. www.lukassuter.com.
5. Symbolic, perhaps, of the phenomenon of "post-nut clarity," a more palatable synonym for which unfortunately eludes us.

6 Short of the Week (2019) *The Wrong End of the Stick | Award-winning Animated Short Film | Short of the Week*. 26 August. Available at: https://www.youtube.com/watch?v=J-9MoVlHIE8.
7 www.curiouswolf.productions.
8 Though somewhat phallic in design, Adams attributes the character's appearance to economic simplicity: "It just needed to have a head and eyes and had to walk and touch things. It needed to be very quick and move more fluidly than Chris, which was easier when he was less complicated to draw."
9 In 2016 it would win several awards including FANtastischer Prize at the Stuttgart International Festival of Animated Film and Best Short Film at Toronto Queer West Film Festival.
10 www.worldinstopmotion.wordpress.com/a-propos/.
11 www.thefutureperfectproject.org.
12 www.thefutureperfectproject.org/actionguides.
13 https://www.signebaumane.com/films#/teat-beat-of-sex.
14 www.vimeo.com/ondemand/teatbeat.
15 Not to be confused with the similarly-named Irish production house Atom Films.
16 https://pamie.com/.
17 https://saragunnarsdottir.com.
18 www.joshshaffnerart.com.
19 www.vimeo.com/nayoon1212.
20 www.amandabonaiuto.biz.
21 www.animationshowcase.com.

3

The Body

It perhaps isn't hugely surprising that early instances of animation that incorporated sexual themes, whether directly or in the abstract, often used the female form as a means to get its message across. As discussed in the introduction to this book, women in many early animated films were largely created to drive the otherwise-level-headed males around them to fevered distraction through exaggeratedly curvaceous bodies and sensual mannerisms. Of all the characters in animation to exemplify this, perhaps the earliest and most enduring would be Betty Boop, who debuted in the 1930 Dave Fleischer short *Dizzy Dishes* as an anthropomorphized poodle-cum-flapper girl who enchants the nightclub's patrons via a near-infantilized performance style paired with what would then have been considered suggestive attire. Though this pairing, which would recur through her subsequent appearances (notably 1932's *Boop-Oop-a-Doop* and *Minnie the Moocher*) as a human woman, might suggest little more than an innocent undertone of sexuality to contemporary audiences, at the time such flagrant flaunting of a woman's curves and bare skin (thighs and even – contain yourselves – midriff sometimes both on display) would prove scandalous enough to provoke censorship, through the introduction of the Hays Code in 1934, which would see Betty Boop reworked as a more conservatively dressed, morally upstanding housewife-type character.[1] Though this iteration would make a far greater number of appearances across films and other media than those that preceded it, from a cultural perspective, it is her first, vampish, cocktail dress-clad incarnation that feels the most synonymous with the character and her legacy.

Stepping slightly away from this convention, the unabashed excess of Gerald Potterton's 1981 animated sci-fi fantasy feature film anthology *Heavy Metal* is

DOI: 10.1201/9781003415503-4

encapsulated by its poster image, bearing the scantily clad warrior Taarna atop a flying mount of indeterminate species, legs splayed, chest arched forward, head tilted back in a lubricious pout. While the film itself injects a fair amount of sex and sexual conquest into its stories (its first two segments, *Harry Canyon* and *Den*, both featuring scenarios in which their physically unremarkable male leads circumstantially find themselves able to bed desirable women, a prospect that would hold doubtless appeal to the film's target demographic), the actual *Taarna* segment is a more straightforward avengement tale, seeing the titular Taarakian warrior face off against a tribe of mutant barbarians who have descended upon a city, attacking and murdering its inhabitants. Other than a scene in which she is leered at in a bar, it is interesting to note that, as far as story is concerned, at no point does her practically naked body nor any implication of sexuality play a role in outwitting her would-be captors; her acrobating dueling and pained writhings are entirely for the benefit of the film's audience. One might put forward the notion that the depiction of a warrior figure with agency and skill, paired with a physical presentation that heightens her beauty, is more evolved than it first appears. This argument is somewhat undercut by the fact that she is mute throughout, or that she is initially introduced to the audience completely nude, with a full minute and a half of the film's runtime devoted to her sybaritically pulling on her skimpy battle attire.

This is not to say that autonomous female characters in contemporary animated fiction do not exist. The overt, sexually spellbinding nature of *Red Hot Riding Hood*'s titular nightclub performer made a lasting enough impression since its 1943 release to be a primary reference point in the years that followed. Aspects of films made decades later would make direct reference to it, such as a CG-assisted scene recreation in Chuck Russell's *The Mask* (1994) and, more notably, *Who Framed Roger Rabbit* (1989) animation director Richard Williams's iconic design for Jessica Rabbit, a then-contemporized hat-tip to Avery's creation.[2] This is most clearly apparent when considering her first appearance in the film as the club's very human, not-remotely leporine singer who slinks around the venue (dubbed *The Ink and Paint Club* – at which, in a story detail somewhere between affectionate and cruel, we find an obsolescent Betty Boop serving drinks, her glory years behind her) reducing each man she coquettishly interacts with into a blushing mess of slack-jawed adoration. With proportions so outlandish as to make the unrealistic beauty standards perpetuated by fashion dolls seem reasonable by comparison, Jessica Rabbit's design is so ludicrous in its tiny-waisted, large-chested proportions as to transcend misogyny into something curiously joyful, and universally loved. Indeed, there is an argument to be made (and has been)[3] for Jessica Rabbit as being something of a feminist icon in cinema.

We quickly learn that there is more to her role than the club patrons – and perhaps even the film's audience – might suspect. When we next see the character outside of a club setting, she is brutally admonishing protagonist Eddie Valiant for the role he may have played in the murder of one of her admirers. As the film continues, Jessica Rabbit's demonstrable autonomy is made clearer, with the film tropes that define her as a character expanding beyond superficial eye candy into the cunning femme fatales of the film noir era; those tropes, in turn, are subverted when it is revealed that her supposedly duplicitous nature was entirely a projection of the men around her (her suspected infidelities a misunderstanding, her role in the murder a red herring), and that she's that most unfathomable of beings to said men – a woman who simultaneously possesses both sensual beauty and decency of character.

Bill Plympton's Manhattan-based operation Plymptoons has been responsible for dozens of independent short films alongside a glut of features, commissioned work, commercials and music videos. Although it is not a constant presence in his work, sex has frequently reared its head as a subject of many projects, suited as it is to both his penchant toward comedy and exaggerated depictions of the human form. Building on the foundation of a masterful understanding of human anatomy, Plympton's works trade fluidity (often opting for lower frame-rates) for strength of draftsmanship, expression and comedic timing.

While some of the women of Bill Plympton's films are relatively conventional in appearance and realistically proportioned, others are overtly sexualized. Perhaps hinting at the notion of the Madonna–whore complex, Plympton often presents an interesting duality wherein both qualities are inherent to the same character; outwardly prim and conservatively dressed, but highly sexual when the mood and scenario is appropriate. This is seen in the protagonist of his 1997 independent feature *I Married a Strange Person*, in which young newlywed Keri navigates the consequences of a bizarre twist of fate that has seen her spouse Grant imbued with supernatural, reality-contorting powers. An early scene in the film sees Keri's attempts to seduce her husband stymied by his workaholic tendencies – in the process of breaking him down, she uses her body to remind him that she's a sensual being (Figure 3.1), her overtures becoming increasingly bizarre, in true Plympton fashion (fingering her ear canal, licking her shoe, dry-humping their sofa).

It ultimately takes a change of clothing into a negligee to wrench him away from his work (Figure 3.2), but proceedings are ground to a halt at the first use of his new superpowers – predictably, making his penis enormous – to Keri's offscreen horror. In a film that is predominantly focused on slapstick comedy and speculative fiction, the scene stands out as a moment of wry social commentary

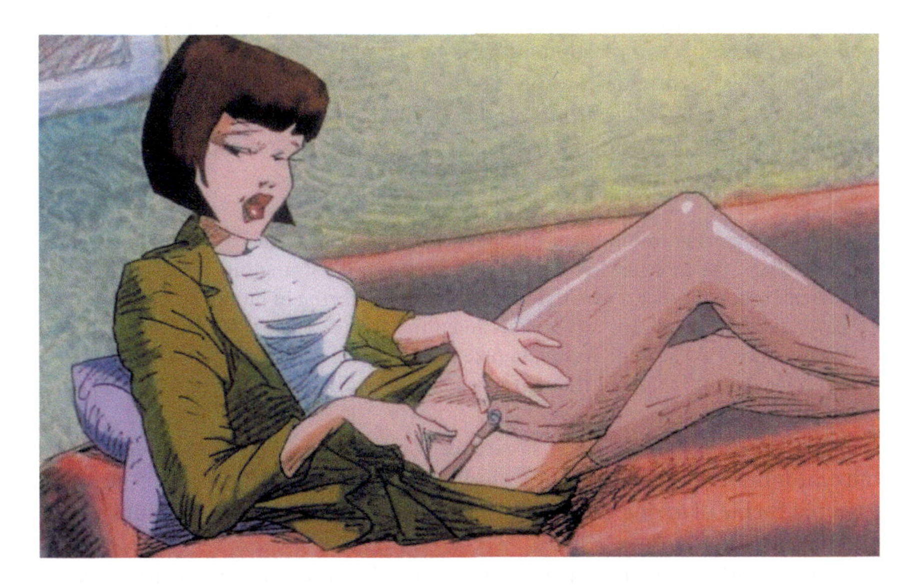

Figure 3.1

Still from *I Married a Strange Person* (Dir. Bill Plympton). ©1997 Bill Plympton

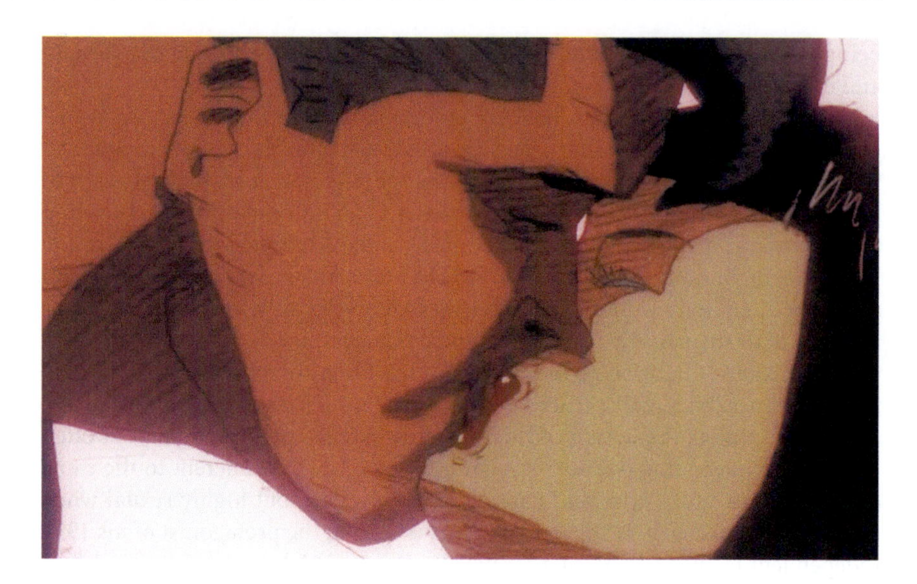

Figure 3.2

Still from *I Married a Strange Person* (Dir. Bill Plympton). ©1997 Bill Plympton

highlighting the disparity between how men and women value the importance of penis size; Grant's ideal scenario turns out to be Keri's nightmare.

A later scene in *I Married a Strange Person* pointedly addresses the issue of how our bodies change as we age, and the psychological ramifications it may have on the long-term relationships we have sustained – again, through Plymptonian horror surrealism. Countering Keri's insistence that her husband's new abilities to shape-shift himself and everything around him is not what she signed up for when she married him, Grant cites their wedding vows and analogizes that she should stay with him in spite of his change because "If you got fat and wrinkled, I'd still love you." This passively manipulative argument quickly escalates to an aggressive, literal act of manipulation as he uses his magic to make her fat and wrinkled in as nightmarish a manner as possible (conjuring a creature made entirely of fat to chase her around the house, ultimately forcing its way into her and bloating her body from the inside). When it came to the main inspiration for the sequence, Plympton recalls:

> I'd started getting into a lot of the Japanese films; a lot of the really outrageous ones, where the monster becomes a big penis, and it's strangling a woman, very surreal. I thought that it would be a great concept to bring in humor; the Japanese never did it, it was always very serious and ultra violent. That's what inspired me to make *I Married a Strange Person*, to take those strange sexual moments and try to put some humor in them. I thought it worked very well.

The Cronenberg-esque body horror of this scene sets up a relatively jaunty musical number *Would You Love Me If…?*, a song that puts forward the same essential theme of loving one's partner in spite of their idiosyncrasies and physical "defects."

While relatively sincere (at the end of the day, the film's main focus is on physical comedy) in intent, this sentiment is undermined slightly by the scenes that follow – despite insisting that he still loves the fattened/wrinkled Keri, he

Figure 3.3

Still from *How to Kiss* (Dir. Bill Plympton). ©1988 Bill Plympton

immediately returns her back to "normal." A subsequent sex scene sees Grant unable to resist the temptation to playfully change her appearance in spite of her admonishing him not to, cycling through different hairstyles, physiques and costumes, creating duplicates of her and, inevitably, enlarging her breasts to the point where they spill out of the house.

Similar themes appear in a number of Bill Plympton's short films, notably *How to Kiss* (1988) (Figure 3.3), a pastiche of the instructional guides to intimacy from the VHS-era adapted from a comic originally created for *Rolling Stone*, and its 1995 successor *How to Make Love to a Woman*. The first film serves mainly as a vehicle for his natural leanings toward surreal sight gags, in which a modestly dressed, average-looking couple perform a narrated demonstration of the mechanics of different varieties of kissing to the viewer, each resulting in some form of cartoonish, hallucinogenic mutilation to one or both partners.

The piece fits very much within a particular strand of Plympton's early films, in which the action takes place in a featureless environment inhabited by one or two characters who passively endure a succession of bizarre physical transmutations.[4] Building on this concept, *How to Make Love to a Woman* (Figure 3.4) does more with its camera angles, environments and overall presentation (making use of painted cels over its predecessor's colored pencils, combined with an organic development of Plympton's style and artistry as a whole) while retaining the same independent spirit. As its title suggests, the short is less an homage to videos targeted at couples than those for men specifically, its opening scene focusing on how "women come in all shapes and sizes" in which a garden-variety, middle-aged man scrutinizes a parade of women (all of whom appear "flawed" via tricks of perspective). Throughout the film, the female body is examined piece-by-piece – eyes, hair, neck, nostrils, mouth (one scene serving as something of a callback to *How to Kiss*) and breasts – alongside a breakdown of sexual rituals such as disrobing, hugging, caressing and incorporating "kinky accessories." Ultimately the film is more focused on the concept of the male gaze itself than

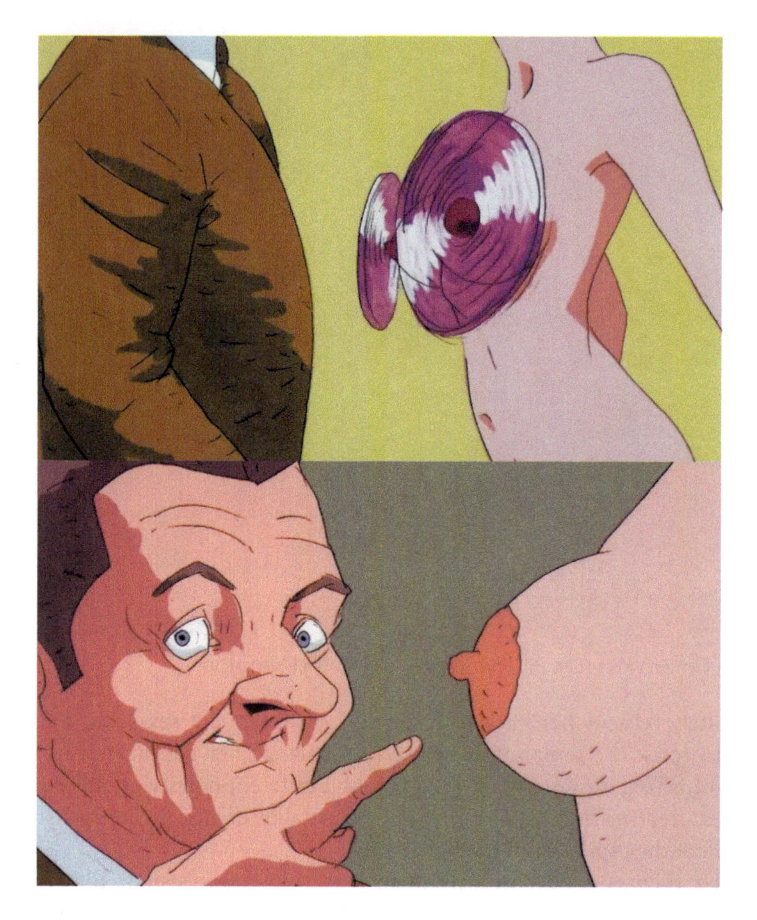

Figure 3.4

Stills from *How to Make Love to a Woman* (Dir. Bill Plympton). ©1995 Bill Plympton

the practicalities of sexual intercourse; the woman plays a passive role, standing nude and virtually motionless throughout, while her suitor fawns over each aspect of her physicality, only to be met with some kind of brutal injury when she displays any sign of arousal (the goosebumps on her neck punching him in the face, her flared nostrils engulfing and suffocating him, her spinning nipple tassels slicing of his fingers as though helicopter blades).

In spite of her evident enthusiasm and the punishments she unwittingly inflicts, the woman exists in the film as a literal sex object, whether lambasting the instructional videos the film is referencing or for the sake of simplicity in delivering its sight gags. Yet Plympton's films, by and large,[5] don't come across as overtly misogynistic, by virtue of their humor being more focused on absurdism, physical comedy and slapstick violence. When and if misogyny rears its head, it generally appears to be the punchline of the joke and, if not, the joke will be so ludicrous and surreal as to have no discernable malice behind it. While this treads a potentially dangerous line (insofar as the most common defense legitimate misogynists trot out is that they were "only joking"), the fact that Plympton is clearly in the business of creating gags as immoderately and overblown as possible serves the notion that he isn't trying to hurt the women who might be watching his films. The comedy doesn't hinge on the mere presence of a comely lady with large breasts, it comes from when she kisses her lover so violently as to eat off his face, or when her aroused nipples become so cartoonishly erect as to blind him, leaving him writhing on the floor in agony. Indeed, when overt sexuality is used as a punchline, it is more often than not the man who is the butt of the joke. While a lazier, sexist filmmaker might punch down at a woman's insecurities, Plympton instead targets his own gender, as seen at the end of *How to Make Love to a Woman* when the film's male protagonist is blighted by erectile dysfunction.

Beautiful Bodies

Ultimately what makes Bill Plympton's animated work succeed is his ability to harness an objectively high degree of artistic ability and pair it with a concept that would not be served nearly as well in live-action. By virtue of him having made as many films as he has, this inevitably works better in some than others, but when it does, the end result is exceptional. In this same respect, one would be hard-pressed to find an artist in the realm of animation whose work has done more, and with such deft wit and masterful artistry, than Joanna Quinn.

As a filmmaker of note, Quinn came out of the gates swinging with her 1987 quasi-student[6] film *Girls Night Out*, the first of several short form animated projects produced with partner and writer Les Mills centered around Beryl, a larger than life Welsh working-class factory worker and matriarch voiced by Myfanwy Talog (Menna Trussler in subsequent films) brimming with an infectious joy for life, her family, her friends and the arts. This inaugural outing would earn itself a hat trick[7] of awards at the prestigious Annecy International Animation Film Festival and is arguably the simplest in terms of concept, seeing Beryl and her friends carouse the streets of Wales, congregating at a "Ladies Only" night at their local pub and whipping themselves into a frenzy of mirthful exuberance while a male stripper performs for them. Given Quinn and Mills's propensity toward themes of body image in many of their projects, it is interesting to note that their first project focuses its attention on a mostly undressed, archetypically buff man. While the women bawdily howl in appreciation of his physique and dance moves, the true payoff comes when a devilish Beryl snatches off his posing pouch and, with it, his confidence. Growing from a comic strip, the bawdy misadventures of Beryl and her cohort came from Quinn's interest in feminist literature and an impulse to move away from a habit of solely drawing men.

> When I forced myself to draw women, it became easier to tell stories. I wanted to do an anti heroine, a middle-aged, chunky woman, one who isn't normally the star. So Beryl was sort of based on my mum, who had to put up with a lot but always seemed to be quite happy. There was also this woman in the College canteen who was a sort of mother figure to all of the students; it was quite an intimidating place, and everybody gravitated towards her. She was big and would make you cups of tea and chat, and was really nice. And so Beryl was partly her as well.

While the film demonstrates inordinate ability and filmmaking intuition, we aren't given much of a look into Beryl's life beyond a brief glimpse at her television-fixated spouse, nor her hopes and dreams. Subsequent films build on both aspects, and through each outing, we come to learn a new dimension to her, such as a passion for cinema that manifests itself chaotically when charged with filming a wedding video in *Dreams and Desires: Family Ties* (2006), or an avid enthusiasm for fine arts as seen in *Affairs of the Art* (2021). What sets

Figure 3.5

Vince design sketch by Joanna Quinn for *Body Beautiful*. ©Image courtesy of Joanna Quinn

her up as a fully rounded, lovably idiosyncratic character is her second outing *Body Beautiful* (1990), which sees her working as a circuit board constructor at Mishima, a Japanese factory in Wales among a group of similarly high-spirited female friends. Opening the film is a self-aggrandizing monologue delivered by their supervisor Vince (Figure 3.5) (an archetype of toxic masculinity performed with despicable brilliance by radio personality Rob Brydon, who would go on to achieve significant fame in the United Kingdom as a television presenter and character actor), on his physical desirability and Beryl's perceived lack thereof. The workplace environment sees her the victim of multipronged humiliation, mostly from Vince himself, that she is reluctant to raise with higher management.

> Vince was constructed from different people. But there was one particular bloke who worked at a car boot sale and could sell anything. He had a curly, Kevin Keegan hairdo and just had the gift of the gab – just incredibly funny and cheeky and awful, but you sort of loved him, because he was such a character. He wasn't so awful, he just couldn't see himself, or laugh at himself, and I think that's what we were trying to get across with Vince. I quite like Vince, really, he's just been brought up wrong, he's got the wrong morals. But within half an hour, I'd sort him out!

Mixed in with Vince's comments about Beryl's weight are ironic sexual overtures intended to deride and humiliate, earning fury from her coworkers on her behalf. The behavior is consistent with his own elevated opinion of himself as a workplace lothario, a status that gives him the right, in his own mind, to harangue without reprisal; from his perspective, women should be grateful for any attention he gives them. It is a mindset that is simultaneously archaic from an evolved social perspective, yet chillingly evergreen in that it still exists to this day.

Beryl's mistreatment is compounded by pressure from her misguided but well-meaning friends to stick to a diet that she is struggling with and be able to perform with them at a workplace cabaret contest. Their admonishments when she trips up conjure memories of being similarly belittled as a young girl, a time when, in spite of her outward joviality, some pervasive insecurities had taken root. While browsing through magazines at a newsagents, Beryl notes the disparity between the body types being reinforced by women's health magazines and those more focused on sporting activities. Bolstered by a sudden epiphany, she joins a fitness group for overweight men at a local leisure center where she is motivated, rather than ridiculed, for her efforts. Several weeks later, having bowed out of joining her friends in the chorus line, she instead participates in the social night's "Body Beautiful" contest against Vince. Her improved self-confidence and stamina blows her competition out of the water as she launches into an elaborately animated musical number extolling the virtues of loving yourself for who you are – "My body is fine, so let me be/Skinny, fat, tall or muscley" (Figure 3.6). As well as earning a personal victory against her harasser, who is left to slink off, defeated, Beryl's journey is emblematic of the best way to go down the road of self-improvement (and, ultimately, self-acceptance); appropriately motivated, and on our own terms.

> The whole point was that Beryl is so nice and, because she's a union rep, has to deal with this awful brute but doesn't know how to. She can't confront him, so she

Figure 3.6

Still from *Body Beautiful* (Dir. Joanna Quinn). ©1991 Beryl Productions / S4C / Channel 4. Image courtesy of Joanna Quinn

Figure 3.7

Stills from *Elles* (Dir. Hortense Guillemard, Joanna Quinn). ©Trans Europe Film. Image courtesy of Joanna Quinn

> challenges his masculinity. Rather than telling him not to do stuff, she just beats him at his own game of being macho.

Outside of the Beryl series of films, other work by Joanna Quinn to embrace themes around the human body include the César-nominated *Elles* (1992), a brief but exquisite study codirected by Hortense Guillemard in tribute to artist Toulouse Lautrec[8] (Figure 3.7). Taking its visual cue from his 1896 painting *Seule (Alone)* – the piece depicts a pair of the artist's models taking a break in his studio, one playfully luxuriating on the bed as the other gorges on food and prepares coffee. The pair dance and playfully tussle with one another in a scene that, while intimate and physical, does not read as sexual,[9] but rather uninhibited and carefree; in its brief three-minute runtime, we are given a thorough glimpse into their relationship predicated on being completely relaxed around one another's bodies and secure in themselves, not concerned with 19th-century society's expectations of "feminine" comportment or modesty, before the approaching footsteps of the artist prompts them, duty-bound, to resume their pose.

While perhaps not the most celebrated entry in the director's filmography, *Elles* is a particularly strong example of the separation of sexuality from the naked (or semi-naked) human body when it comes to art. Conversely, Quinn's excerpt from the BAFTA-winning[10] animated Channel 4 adaptation of Geoffrey Chaucer's *The Canterbury Tales* (Dir. Jonathan Myerson), *Wife of Bath* (1998) is very much concerned with sexuality and body. The classic tale follows one of King Arthur's knights who, having assaulted a young maiden, is sent out as punishment on a quest to learn what women most desire; if he is unable to give a satisfactory answer to Queen Guinevere within a year and a day, he will be executed for his crimes. The knight sets out, asking multiple men for the answer, to no avail. When it comes time to return, he comes across a group of dancing women who, as he approaches, transform into an elderly crone (Figure 3.8). In desperation, he asks the woman, who gives him his life-saving answer – "Women desire sovereignty over husband and lover, they desire the upper hand at all times" (Beryl Productions, 2009: 02:50) – on the condition he take her as his wife. Disgusted, he agrees, and on their wedding night, she gives him two options: to be young, attractive but potentially unfaithful, or old and plain but loyal and obedient. Tortured by the decision, he passes it over to her to choose, giving her

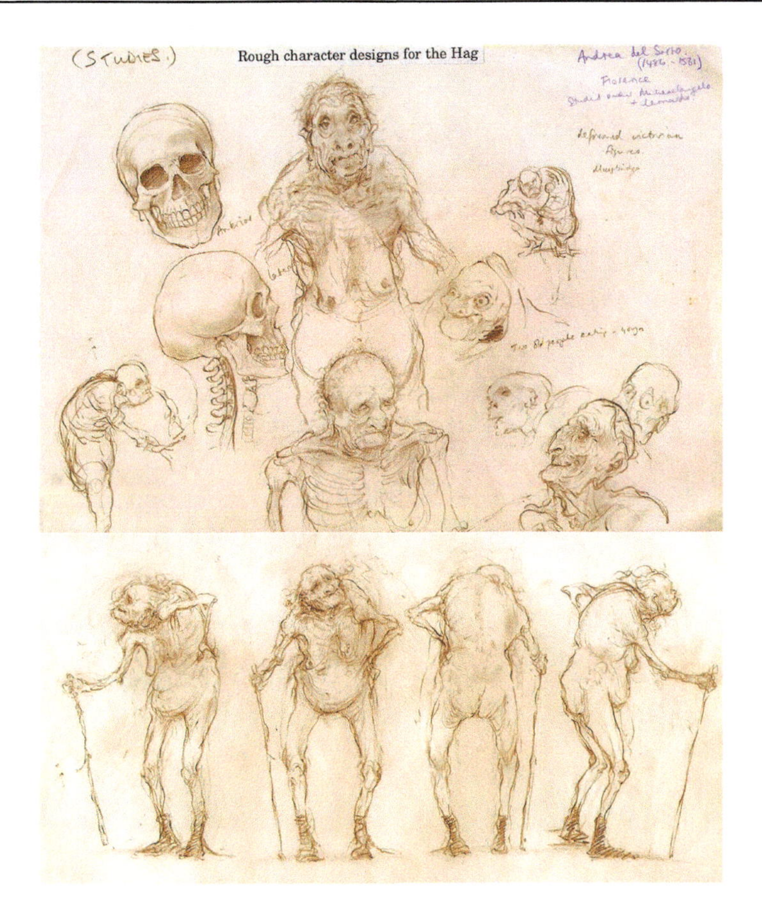

Figure 3.8

Hag design sketches by Joanna Quinn for *Wife of Bath*. ©Image courtesy of Joanna Quinn.

the upper hand; satisfied, she gives him the best of both worlds – loyalty and, to his eyes at least, beauty.

Through Quinn's soft, emotive lines and sublime movement, the film maintains a contemporary feminine energy throughout. The sexual scenes themselves are mostly alluded to and given a dreamlike quality, even the rape represented largely through the symbolism of the young maiden's flower, held aloft to show damage that repairs itself when the knight is duly punished.

While sex is certainly a component of Joanna Quinn's films, it never serves as their focus; it is simply a part of the world her characters live in. Yet when it does occur, it is not an activity reserved for the beautiful or the skinny, but something the plump, dimpled and jiggly can get in on as well. This element of her storytelling holds particular appeal as it doesn't present as preachy; while body positivity is an important and valuable message to incorporate, films like Joanna's hopefully portend a more accepting future in which there's less necessity for it.

Veljko Popović's *Cyclists* (2018), whose narrative themes we'll explore further in Chapter 6, also possesses the notable visual characteristic of presenting a world whose inhabitants are capable of being sexual beings while also being decidedly average-looking and often obese, reflective of real-life (Figure 3.9). Depicting a bike race in a quaint Mediterranean town, the men participating (two of whom

Figure 3.9

Stills from *Cyclists* (Dir. Veljko Popović). ©2018 Lemonade3D / Bagan Films. Image courtesy of Veljko Popović

pointedly in competition for the attention of one woman) are, rather than the type of wiry athletic specimens one might expect from such an event, heavy-set and paunchy. This aspect of the film is owed to its drawing visually from the illustration and sculptural work of Croatian-Yugoslavian artist Vasko Lipovac. The film essentially functions as a tribute to both Lipovac's paintings and sketches that, while not exclusively erotic, dip their toes into the waters of sexuality alongside a keen sense of national identity and the odd dose of surrealism. One such instance of the latter is demonstrated in *Cyclists* with the introduction of another male love rival, a fêted boat captain who is perpetually naked from the waist down (save for a pair of bright blue socks). Popović recalls,

> I saw an image Vasko did in one of his paintings, where this really spiffed-up, older gentleman was wearing no trousers. I thought it really had this *Monty Python*-esque quality to it, where they create something which is completely absurd and funny, but also is a really perfect metaphor or commentary to current affairs of the world. Mediterranean culture is filled with this image of these half naked men trying to impress women – it's sort of a competition that's rooted, traditionally, here in the Mediterranean countries. For me it was really funny because usually, in these kinds of images, the men are athletically built, like superheroes, but here Vasko gives these attributes to everyday people who are chubby, and out of touch. I thought the irony of it was really, really interesting.

Although Vasko Lipovac had passed away by the time *Cyclists* was made, Popović took on the project with the help and consultation of his surviving family.

> Mario Lipovac, one of [Vasko's] sons, was a consultant on the film. They were really interested and really hands-on, both when we were creating the script and creating the narrative structure – and then later on, especially when we were creating the visuals. I think on one hand they were really protective of the legacy of Vasko Lipovac, and on the other hand, they were really curious as to what would happen when the characters actually came to life.

This collaboration wasn't entirely without its bumps in the road: said protectiveness tended to be centered around the director's interest in making Lipovac's penchant toward eroticism a recurring theme within the film (indeed, sexual conquest is its primary throughline). Particular pushback came on the subject of a scene in which the cyclists approach a tunnel that, in a fantasy sequence, transforms into a giant pair of legs that spread apart as they enter.

> I was adamant to keep the scene in the film because, for me at least, it's one of the scenes that makes the film really work. So I was pushing back on their ideas to remove it, or cut it, or change it to make it less sexual, saying, "I've seen some drawings of Vasko's depicting orgies; dude-on-dude, women-on-women, crazy stuff – so I don't think he would mind!" They were skeptical with the film but I was really happy that, in the end, they were super excited and happy with it, and with how the film has been received, both locally and internationally. So that was a load off my shoulders.

The design sensibilities of Lipovac, as channeled through Popović, carry with them a certain familiarity despite being of a specific time and place. The variation in body types seen in many of the characters is, while worlds away from her drawing style, certainly reminiscent of the worlds built by Joanna Quinn. The combination of the designs' inherent "roundness" and Lipovac's painterly approach also evokes the work of British artist Beryl Cooke, whose work also saw an animated interpretation in the two-part 2004 BBC series *Bosom Pals*, sharing the key trait of a community made up of appealingly boisterous – though "average"-looking – folk. While comedic, the films come across as a celebration of differently proportioned people living their lives enthusiastically rather than making them the butt of the joke for deigning to do so.

> When you think about it, the main building blocks of the visual approach to the characters – and to the world of Vasko Lipovac – is the round ball and these basic elements. I think this approach can be seen throughout history and throughout different countries. I've been approached by a few different nationalities, and a few different artists and animators from different countries, and they find similarities with some artists from their hometown or from their countries. So it was really interesting to start conversations, in this sense, and try to remove these stereotypes you find in images of modern people, where everybody's super healthy, and super buff, super pretty. I tried to activate this image of the everyday person who is flawed, who has excess weight and just doesn't care, they're still sexy and still erotic. Today, this is an interesting topic to go into, and also it helps make the sex scenes kind of real and relatable, not vulgar – and there is a certain humor to it. So the film, although it has a lot of sex in it, some pretty explicit stuff, it doesn't go into this pornographic valley, just by how the characters are portrayed. You kind of laugh with them, and you kind of live with them through it.

The Perils of Conformity

In spite of the efforts of the filmmakers discussed in this chapter, beauty remains a constant within the film and media landscape. In turn, its elusive attainability remains a source of inordinate insecurity to many, and the rise of body positivity in films and commercial campaigns has done little to thwart the indefatigable beauty industry. Perhaps one of the most scathing and viscerally discomfiting attacks on the culture of cosmetic surgery – and the social pressures surrounding it – is Frédéric Doazan's *Supervenus* (Figure 3.10), in which an anatomical illustration of a woman is subjected to an increasingly horrific succession of "enhancements." The independent, self-initiated project was made as part of 12 fps,[11] a collective consisting of Doazan, Paul Rodrigues and Sylvain Cappelletto, originally formed in 2012 with the purpose of motivating the three artists to set themselves creative challenges separate to their professional work, with other animators coming on board as it grew. Divided into "episodes" grouping each artist's micro-shorts made with a designated theme in mind, *Supervenus* was conceived for their fourth such endeavor – *Supervixens*[12] – alongside Cappelletto's *Dead Vixen* (in which a haggard, unclothed female figure ominously lurches, zombie-like, toward the viewer from a dark void).

Doazan's film begins with a surgical-gloved hand opening a vintage book of anatomical illustrations to a page labeled "femme adulte." In a morbid spin on such meta, creator-versus-subject animated films as *Duck Amuck* (Charles M. Jones, 1953) and *Manipulation* (Daniel Greaves, 1991), the gloved hands come back into frame to interfere with the accompanying illustration, starting with the relatively innocuous removal of her pubic hair, escalating quickly to fat being transferred from her neck into her cheeks via syringe, her brown eyes plucked out and replaced with blue ones. From there, things snowball in an increasingly nightmarish manner.

Taking his inspiration from the book *Beauté Fatale* by Mona Chollet (ZONES, 2012), as well as the parade of disquieting images his online searches of "plastic surgery disasters" would yield, Doazan found himself going down an educational

Figure 3.10

Still from *Supervenus* (Dir. Frédéric Doazan). ©2013 Frédéric Doazan / 12fps.net / Autour de Minuit

rabbit hole of all the ways in which beauty-obsessed cosmetic surgery clients might wish to enhance their bodies.

> Besides breast implants, liposuction, lifting, and botox, I discovered that you can stretch your legs to be taller, remove your ribs for a smaller waist, adapt your feet to fit your shoes, and even design your vagina.

As the film progresses, all of the above are depicted in a grimly absurd manner – bones are tweezed out of open wounds akin to a game of *Operation*, fat drained in an instant by syringes, limbs extended by hand as though interacting with an app. Unresponsive throughout her ordeal, she gradually begins to conform to a notion of traditional "beauty," before being subjected to blasts of UV light to darken her skin and further mutilations that bring the film's visuals into horror movie territory. In one of the more darkly comedic moments her brain is poked at, violently removed and injected with an interminate pink, phosphorescent substance before being put back, at which she exclaims a gasp of childlike glee (the only instance in the film where she exhibits any kind of response). As the surgical processes repeat, breasts made ever-larger, hair made ever-blonder, limbs made ever-skinnier, she becomes an increasingly gruesome Frankenstein monster of overzealous "improvement" (Figure 3.11). Her belly is sliced open, and an inconvenient fetus is delivered/discarded by Cesarean section, the opportunity to

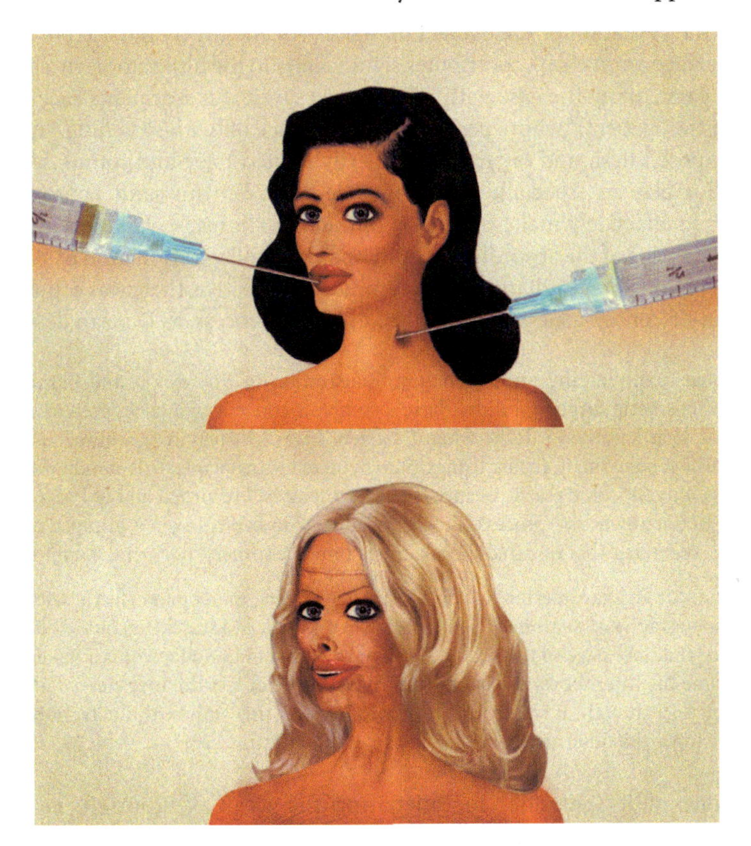

Figure 3.11

Stills from *Supervenus* (Dir. Frédéric Doazan). ©2013 Frédéric Doazan / 12fps.net / Autour de Minuit

staple her stomach taken before closing the wound. Her engorged breasts brutally reject their implants and a final blast of UV light scorches her skin with radiation burns. Finally, her smoking, grotesque corpse falls apart, sinking gracelessly into a bleak perversion of the *Venus de Milo* pose.

The graphic quality of Doazan's visuals are consistent with a natural propensity toward using gory imagery combined with humor in reaching his audience, as well as jolting the viewer awake and heightening their receptiveness to the topic at hand.

> It can be somehow gratuitous, but if you add some clever irony in the mix, provocation can reach an interesting level. For me, provocation is like shaking up the audience. It helps to make them active and raise questions. And it makes sense when you talk about cosmetic surgery. Besides the pain of the surgery, many cases involved breast implants exploding, degenerating into cancer and even causing death. Psychologically, well, it must be so strange to wake up after a surgery and not recognize yourself. Are you still yourself? When you practice extreme cosmetic surgery, it's like you were totally breaking your body away from your mind. Your body becomes akin to a showcase that you try to promote to the world. A clean, thin and busty body, forever young, led by a pinky plastic brain. Your body has become a perfect beauty product.

The animation process itself, though distinctly stylized and not photorealistic save for the pixilation of the live-action hands (essentially a digital replication of cutout/collage animation), contributes significantly to the film's stomach-churning quality; particularly the ease with which these surgical instruments slice up and mutilate the "patient," whose paper-doll layers sluice off with sickening fluidity to reveal exposed flesh and organs (the expertly crafted foley and sound design by Vandy Roc play an especially important role here). Yet this same approach also manages to effectively make the action of the film strangely playful, reminiscent in some respects of the absurdly comedic, analogue collage animation of Walerian Borowczyk and Terry Gilliam. From a technical perspective, there was some degree of stream-of-consciousness ad-lib to the animation process, as Doazan details:

> I started manipulating an old anatomy illustration in Photoshop and became a virtual cosmetic surgeon. I didn't have a complete concept or a clear, preconceived idea of what I wanted it to be when I started. I was just playing spontaneously in Photoshop, enjoying it, trying things. Step by step, I transformed this standard illustration into an iconic plastic beauty falling into pieces. I recorded all my Photoshop work to document the process like a timelapse. You can also get a glimpse of my internet searches that inspired me: anatomy, bimbos, surgery, porn and zombies...
>
> The cut-out style animation, all made in After Effects, matched perfectly with the old iconography of anatomy. I remember when I was a kid watching, out of curiosity, the anatomy page of the school dictionary with a man and a woman naked. At that time the internet wasn't around and it was more or less the first view of nudity we got. So I thought it was interesting to start with this standard illustration and evolve towards something terrible, like a new standard.

In spite of its potential for alienating the weak of stomach, as a film *Supervenus* would hit a nerve and achieve significant success, with over a million online views on the video's official upload alone[13] following a festival run of more than 130 events. While a fair amount of the audience responses comment on the grim – even paradoxically "satisfying" – nature of the visuals on a surface level, a large portion of the comments express appreciation for its resonance and overall message as a lambasting of the cosmetic industries and societal attitudes toward women (and beauty) as a whole.

> You just need to see how women are represented on TV, in magazines, advertising, fashion. It's all about beauty and we are surrounded by that. These images are either Photoshopped or transformed with cosmetic surgery to show a perfect body without any faults. When you see these images everyday and everywhere, there is an obvious impact on people, like a vicious brainwashing. Slowly this modern view of beauty is finally becoming a norm; an unattainable norm full of consequences. Women will be easily frustrated about their bodies, men will get attracted by fake beauty.
>
> This unattainable norm is here to attract people in order to sell them lipstick, shoes, boobs, dreams or whatever you could buy to fit yourself into this strange idea of beauty. And just to qualify the statement, this is not just women; men can be totally obsessed with their looks too. Women and, above all, men should question all these everyday gender clichés. We sometimes get stuck in stupid rules which are deeply rooted in our culture and society.

Pushing Back

Doazan is not the only contemporary filmmaker whose work suggests a resistance to these societal "rules." London-based filmmaker Anna Ginsburg's work has been especially noteworthy for challenging perceived standards of beauty and opening up conversations around our bodies, whether in a sexual context or otherwise.

With a particular interest in animated documentary, Ginsburg made an impact early on in her career with her 2012 micro-short *Living With Depression*, a piece crafted during her studies at Edinburgh College of Art that demonstrates a natural intuition toward conveying information about a lofty subject using brevity and judiciously selected sound bites paired with effective, hand-drawn animated visual metaphors.

> I wrote my dissertation on animated documentary because I feel that, as a genre, it has quite a lot of power in expressing and evoking empathy in real people, through universally accessible visuals, in a way that talking heads perhaps don't. It also brings subtext to the forefront that, perhaps, is quite difficult, and people may not want to be filmed talking about.

After graduation and spending several years working on various commercial projects, Ginsburg was inspired to work on something personal once again. The first germ of the idea for *Private Parts* (Figure 3.12), "an animated documentary involving vaginas and penises talking about sexual equality and masturbation," came to her in 2014, where the concept of gathering audio testimonials from roughly 40 participants (a mix of strangers and people she knew) laid the foundation for the film. The impetus to develop it further came when she was approached by It's Nice That, a creative community with whom she'd previously worked on such projects as *Living With Depression*, and Channel 4 for their short film initiative Random Acts. With five minutes of pre-edited audio to work with, Ginsburg refined her audio backdrop further to fit into the Random Acts format.

In terms of structure and concept, *Private Parts* continues a tradition of animated documentary shorts popularized by films such as Nick Park's 1989

Figure 3.12

Still from *Private Parts* (Dir. Anna Ginsburg). ©2015 It's Nice That

Oscar-winning *Creature Comforts*, in which audio snippets of tenants bemoaning their accommodation circumstances are set ingeniously to the visual of an assortment of enclosed zoo animals. Finding herself newly single following a long-term relationship, the initial impulse to pursue a project of this nature came from discussions with her own social circle.

> A lot of my peers, my female friends in their early twenties, were kind of struggling sexually; a lot of them had never had an orgasm with a sexual partner. I found this to be a revelation and I also found it deeply sad, that there was something in terms of the way they saw their own bodies, their inability to be relaxed with a sexual partner, or even their inability to masturbate and get to know their own bodies. I felt like all of these things had come from somewhere and were limiting sex for everyone. There were a lot of boys who were struggling with similar things, feeling that in some ways they were not performing, when actually a lot of it was in the women's heads, or something to do with shame surrounding the issue of masturbation. It was just really interesting. I mean, I've never felt these things but I think that's partly because of my context; I was brought up by a lesbian single mum, who's also a militant feminist, but I also feel that sexual empowerment and sexual liberation and sexual pleasure is a huge aspect of our lives that you should be able to talk about more freely if you want to, especially with your sexual partner. So it's kind of just getting the conversation started, in some respects.

Given a tight turnaround of five weeks to create all of the animation, Ginsburg drew upon her own ability as a hand-drawn animator to create the visuals for roughly half the film, the other half provided by several talented industry contemporaries she had befriended through her career. In spite of the project's modest budget, the subject matter proved a draw for everybody she approached to be involved. The end result presents a range of styles and artistic sensibilities that bring the perspectives of her interviewees to life as a community of anthropomorphized genitalia. In order to keep a level of coherency across the piece, Ginsburg set up visual rules regarding the film's color palette, which digital brushes to use and the overall animation process. These parameters gave the artists enough

Figure 3.13

Still from *Private Parts* (Dir. Anna Ginsburg). ©2015 It's Nice That

flexibility to bring their individual touch to their segments while ensuring the film retained a comfortable uniformity of presentation throughout.

> I thought it would be a bit outrageous to give them too many constraints. I also felt that, as long as there were a few rules and as long as it was 2D hand-drawn, it would work if people brought their own styles to the piece. So people were given complete creative freedom. There were two rounds of design feedback that I gave to each of the people. With Will Anderson, for example, he does the bit with the older voice, where the pubes grow as she's talking about the history of feminism. It's quite obviously him because he designs the vagina a bit more like a bird! He kept doing the lips of the vagina too much like a beak, so there was a few rounds of feedback with him. (Figure 3.13)

Alongside Anderson (whose own work will be explored further in Chapter 5), other artists involved included Moth Collective, Loup Blaster, George Wheeler, Mark Prendergast, Guy Field, Jake Evans, India Windsor-Clive and Peter Millard; an example of the effectiveness of synergy between visual and subject is evidenced in Millard's faux-naive visualization of a young girl's testimony.

While the film is populated by genitals of all varieties, it focuses on female anatomy as a discussion point; participants engage in word association with the terms "vagina," "clitoris," "pubic hair" and "masturbation" as a prompt, muse on the ways in which different vaginas can be especially complex to navigate from a partner's perspective, the gratification from pleasing someone else, questioning the necessity of constant shaving, insecurities around self-pleasure and pressures to perform. While it makes sense that the film need not bring male genitals into the discussion (being a subject that, let's face facts, is pretty much exhausted at this point in our penis-oriented culture), curiously absent is the degree to which these standards have their roots in the pornographic industry.

> Porn was something that I kind of avoided in Private Parts. Loads of people touched upon it, but I felt like it could have been its own film because it's such a vast subject in itself. Without me saying "I think porn is negative" – which I'm not sure if I do

> – loads of the men were saying that they were trying to give it up. They were trying to reclaim their own sexuality in some way, which I found really interesting – I think that that could be its own self-contained episode.
>
> When I was gathering voice recordings and talking to all these girls who had issues about their bodies, or about being unable to climax, or whatever, I was desperate to find a "nasty" man. I was actually struggling. The people who I was approaching were kind of old friends who I'd gone to school with, who I thought might have a chauvinistic mindset, and actually they were all advocates for female sexual pleasure, which was kind of heartening. Something great that came out of the process.

When expanding upon why these issues may manifest in young women, Ginsburg cites two male contributors whose perspectives, at 15 years old, represent an interesting duality in the manner that young men express themselves, where sensitivity and empathy are in conflict with a less evolved, prevailing impulse toward grandstanding. Depicted as two cheerful penises, their brief screentime represents one of the film's darker moments (wherein one demands of his partners that "they just need to shave or I tell them to put their clothes back on") before swinging starkly in a more positive direction.

> Those two have a redeeming moment at the end where they say "Just do what you wanna do girl, don't get depressed." They ended up talking to me about self-harm on social media and how widespread depression is among their female friends. At the end of the film they're saying "Don't get depressed, just do what you want to do, look after yourself," basically saying that if you want to masturbate and touch yourself, go for it, it'll make you happy. So that side of it was lovely, in terms of research, that actually the reason women are feeling the way they're feeling is perhaps a history of sexism in society and the expectations pushed onto all of us by the media, unrealistic expectations to do with what being a woman is and what it should be. But it's not coming from men to women necessarily.

While these contributors touch upon the subject of intimate grooming as a social expectation prior to their redemption, more disconcerting are the subsequent sound bites of female interviewees bemoaning that they "don't want to be seen as disgusting" should they not conform, as well as the financial expense of "being bald down there." Something of an oddly contentious subject, other animated projects to address it include fellow Strange Beast director Sacha Beeley's *The Pube Song* (2021) that sees a lachrymose, abandoned pubic hair lament her shunning from society via a Disney-esque musical number, enquiring "why the mass hysteria/about the pubic area?" While the spot (commissioned, ironically, to advertise Gillette's line of Venus women's razors) addresses the importance of personal grooming on one's own terms and to one's own preference, the notion of electing to not shave pubic hair being somehow unfeminine or – more ludicrously – unhygienic is effectively lambasted in Signe Baumane's *Teat Beat of Sex* entry *Hair* (Figure 3.14), which recounts the director's acquiescence to an insistent lover's request. While curious enough to try fully shaving her pubic hair at least once, Baumane notes with interest and concern an immediate diminishment of sensation. Valuing her physical pleasure, she grows it back and keeps it in spite of her companion's disappointment in a demonstration of simple but crucial autonomy; it can be gratifying to consider and even indulge our partners' turn-ons and preferences by doing things we otherwise wouldn't necessarily, but not at the cost of our own pleasure or comfort.

Figure 3.14

Still from *Teat Beat of Sex: Hair* (Dir. Signe Baumane). ©2007 Pierre Poire / Signe Baumane. Image courtesy of Signe Baumane

As an online release, Ginsburg's *Private Parts* is largely responded to as a positive presentation and dissemination of its subject and related societal issues – and, similar to *Living With Depression*, lauded for doing so in such a short space of time. Its visual approach is uncompromising from the start – the opening scene being of three grinning pudenda (Figure 3.15) laughing gleefully at different slang expressions for vagina – though at no point does it come across as aggressive or confrontational. One particularly important, unspoken aspect of the film is how reflective its wide variety of genital presentation is of real life, where fears surrounding the notion of "perfection" are fairly common. The only recurring

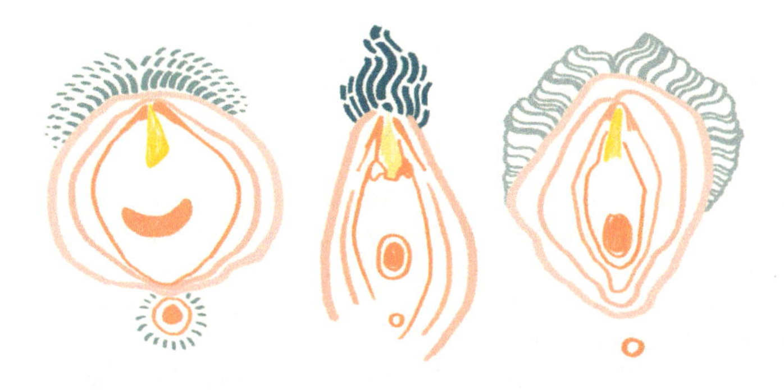

Figure 3.15

Still from *Private Parts* (Dir. Anna Ginsburg). ©2015 It's Nice That issue from international audiences cited by the director is that, having been recorded in and around boroughs of London, some of the participants' accents and verbiage become lost in translation. Within the United Kingdom, however, the piece is embraced to an extent beyond just festival programs but educational environments as well.

> Teachers have said they want it to be in the syllabus, which it will never be, but it's a nice idea! I got an email from a young girl who had started a feminist group at her secondary school that boys attend as well, and she screened it and it got a really good reaction, which is kind of my aim. It was more to get young people to kind of relax a bit, and to have conversations.
>
> I think that part of it is that "sex sells," and talking vaginas and penises get people talking, but I don't really mind if that's why they approach it because I do think the message is uplifting and positive. I feel like it's not crude, it has quite a sweet overall atmosphere.

The Road to Acceptance

While *Private Parts* is focused on specific aspects of our anatomy, Anna Ginsburg's next major project would cast a wider net in its examination of beauty standards across the ages. Commissioned by CNN for International Women's Day 2018 and produced by London-based animation production studio Strange Beast,[14] *What Is Beauty?* serves as a capsule summary of how society's attitudes toward acceptable and desirable body types have vastly changed over an extended period of time (from 28000 BC through to present day), using noteworthy art pieces and figures from/moments in popular culture as its main reference points. Less playful than *Private Parts* insofar as there is no spoken audio (until its closing entreaty to "celebrate the diversity of the female form") or range of firsthand perspectives, the film remains uniquely appealing due to Ginsburg and team's morph-heavy animation approach, bridging character animation and motion graphics together in a peaceful but eye-catching blue-on-cream color palette. We begin on an interpretation of *Venus of Willendorf*, a figurine whose plump proportions are theorized to represent fertility, before metamorphosing through a succession of similarly zaftig prehistoric sculptures that denote a body ideal that endured for thousands of years. Recognizable works of art – including Henri Matisse's *The Dance I* (1909), Pierre-Auguste Renoir's *The Bathers* (1918), Amedeo Modigliani's *Reclining Nude* (1919) and Pablo Picasso's *La Dormeuse* (1932) among others – follow in quick succession and reinforce this ideal, before the figures take on a more slender build, evoking iconic poses from the likes of 1920s Flapper Girls through to Marilyn Monroe, Twiggy, Grace Jones, Madonna and Pamela Anderson, finishing off with a brand of "acceptable" curviness as brought into vogue by such internet-breakers as Kim Kardashian and Nicki Minaj. The film closes on a nude woman in the present day, falling asleep while bathed in the light of her phone screen.

The intent behind the piece reads clearly enough – to celebrate physical diversity and prompt discussion on whether or not the general public is amenable to modifying their own perception and definition of modern beauty. By virtue of its distribution strategy incorporating the types of social media platforms that encourage unfiltered feedback, the length and breadth of this discussion proved extensive. While a fair percentage of commenters voice appreciation for the concept and execution, dissenting opinions range from the focus being strictly on feminine beauty with no consideration for male representation (evidently missing the point of the piece specifically celebrating International Women's Day), to umbrage at the notion that being overweight must be anything other than vilified.

> The reaction to *What Is Beauty* is my only experience ever of going viral; that video got over 15 million hits, and therefore it was shared on all the global CNN platforms and then started going mad on Facebook. The Spanish version alone got around 11 million hits, and if you went under the American Facebook post, loads of the comments were like "No, CNN, fat is ugly." To be honest with you, that makes me really excited, because you're not preaching to the choir anymore when people are having tangible conversations. I truly was excited about being trolled on that film, because the animation community is so elitist and pretty small, and there's not really going to be anyone at an animation festival who is throwing rotten tomatoes at a curvy woman's body on a screen, so the idea that conservative America were coming for that film, and that there were full-on debates going on in the comments section was making me so happy. I thought *They might be ridiculing it, maybe their daughter's in the room when they're watching it.* It feels like it has a life of its own when things like that happen. When that *doesn't* happen I feel a bit disappointed, almost, because it's only gotten in front of people who already feel that way.

Another Strange Beast production that continues the themes of womanhood and physicality is Ginsburg's *A Love Hate Relationship*, commissioned in 2020 for the charity Breast Cancer Now. At an especially brief one-minute in length, the film communicates an enormous amount about the complex subject of living with breasts, from initial shame and unsureness as they develop to the sudden lascivious advances they rouse from others. Mastectomies and health concerns are referenced, alongside their maternal function; a sequence that hearkens back to *Private Parts* and *What Is Beauty?* Sees a wide range of breast types morph into one another, with the film's closing message a unifying "Love Them. Hate Them. Check Them."

> It was always supposed to be two sides of the coin, to include everything: the beauty and the horror, the dislike and the love. I don't like something being *just* sad, or *just* joyful. It's a similar thing with *What Is Beauty*, where it starts with moments of real lightness and warmth, essentially being overwhelmed by how soft and amazing the referenced pieces of art are, all the fertility goddesses – and then there's a bit of a sting in the tail, when it starts being this mad consuming of the female form. In *Private Parts* there are some slightly sinister moments and there are some really uplifting moments; I never want it to preach, I never want to tell people "You should love your breasts" or "You should love your body" or "You should love sex," I want honesty and openness, to make people feel that they're not alone. I think that's the main thing of trying to pervade feelings of shame, by trying to capture something authentic. I think that's often the core motivator for me.

There are a fair few films, animated or otherwise, that keenly scrutinize breasts as their subject – such as *The Boob Fairy* (2021) by Léahn Vivier-Chapas, *Boobs* by Hannah Lau-Walker,[15] *Breast Friends* (2019) by Caitlin Young and the less-cerebral but fairly beloved *Boobies*, a viral anijam produced by Titmouse in 2013. Perhaps most thematically linked to *A Love Hate Relationship* would be *Lolos* (*Boobs*), a Canadian Screen Award nominated[16] short animated film directed

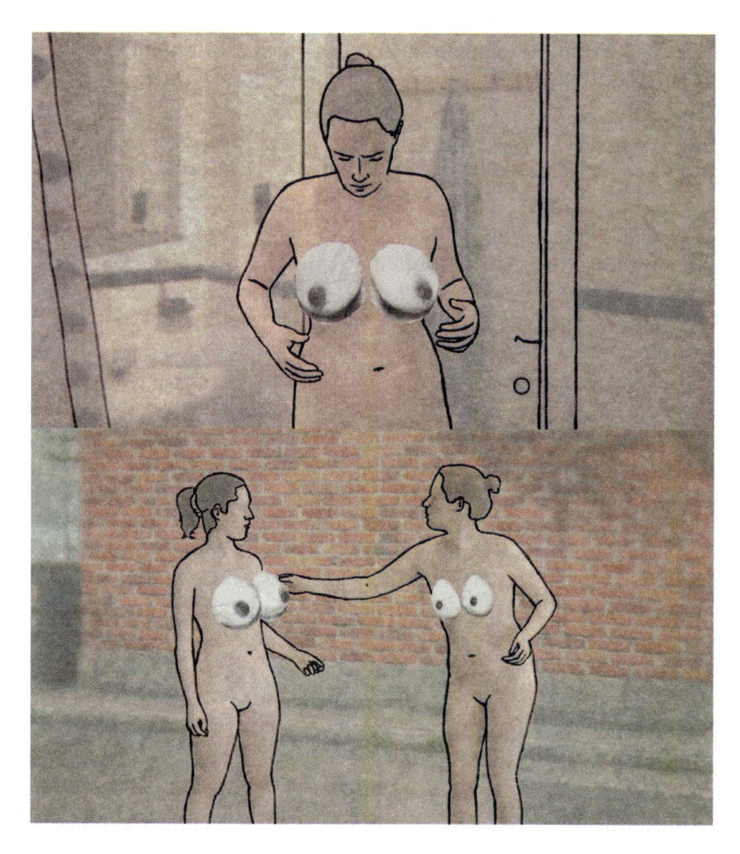

Figure 3.16

Stills from *Lolos* (Dir. Marie Valade). ©2021 9167 7286 Québec Inc. / Les Productions des Films de l'Autre. Image courtesy of Marie Valade.

by Montreal-based filmmaker and curator Marie Valade in 2021 that similarly takes on the ambivalence of a person's attitude toward their breasts, though at a more meditative pace (Figure 3.16). *Lolos* sees a young woman drawn in ink (Valade herself, rotoscoped) who is forced to come to terms with paper breasts that appear on her chest and lead her into increasingly undesirable situations. Says Valade of the impetus behind the film,

> It probably started at puberty. I just felt like boobs kind of clashed with my body, in a way. It's just generally hard to live with them, because they're so symbolic and there's so many things attached to them. There's attraction, there's feeding – there's also sickness, you can get cancer from them. So it's many things mashed up in one piece of flesh, and it's a bit of a struggle to live with that daily.

Taking place in a mixed-media world where breasts grow on trees and sprout, without warning, on the chests of their owners from crumpled paper balls, the protagonist's first encounter with her own breasts comes with pain as, touching them, she gets a paper cut, portending more trouble ahead. Going out into the world, she compares her new assets with those of another newly breasted woman she encounters in the street. Intuiting their value, she makes use of their paper form and photo-enlarges them before affixing one to a fishing line with which to catch a mate, a cleverly communicated use of meta storytelling that draws upon the paper cutout aspect of the breasts against their hand-drawn environment.

> Very early on I knew I needed something to separate from the girl and her boobs, to have something visually different, like they're coming from two different worlds. I thought of the cutouts a bit like stop-motion in a way. I needed 2D and I needed rotoscopy to have the reality aspect of it.

Initially pleased with the fish-man hybrid she snares, she finds herself put off by his groping insistence, marking the first of numerous disadvantages that breast ownership has brought to her life. The film goes on to present symbolic depictions of the concerns that swirl around cosmetic enhancement, breastfeeding (depicted through a darkly comedic visual of the woman, now a mother, detaching a breast and draining its contents like a grapefruit over a citrus juicer) and sickness, a crab appearing in her bed, auguring the loss of both breasts to cancer.

> I think it's based mostly on myself and my anxiety of the next steps of my life – what is it to be able to breastfeed? What is it to have cancer? What is it to lose your boobs or to have surgery? Of course, I read a lot about boobs in general and, through working on the film, I had some people come up to me and talk about their own relationship with their boobs. I even met a woman that had a mastectomy, she showed me the scar and told me everything about how she needed to massage it, and how it was hard for her to lose that part of herself, and how much she loved her boobs. That was really touching, to open up that door with the project.

Found near-death in the street, the woman is operated on by a group of tiny figures who save her life and reconstruct her breasts, perhaps as a literal representation of post-surgery reconstruction or as an indication that she has come to accept her anatomy and all it represents, both good and bad. Against a film landscape largely dominated (as explored in the Introduction) by male filmmakers who regard breasts as either a comedic device or as strictly objects of desire, the value of films such as *Lolos* and *A Love Hate Relationship* adds dimension to the subject and discussion points, due to their distinctly female viewpoints. Says Valade,

> I think it's important to have this female perspective on boobs. I wanted to have something similar to Eve Ensler's *Vagina Monologues*, but for boobs, because I felt that we didn't talk about it much. People do tell me that they reflect about their own relationship with boobs. I think women relate to it on a more personal level, but I did speak with some men who reflected on it as well. One of the most satisfying comments I got is that someone told me he wanted to speak with women about. If the film can achieve that, then that's perfect.

Mass Consumption

Moving away from shorts and features to consider the landscape of adult animated series, some progressive strides have been made, or at least attempted. Building on the foundations laid by trailblazing shows such as *The Simpsons* and its 1990s cohort (including *The Critic, Bob and Margaret, King of the Hill* and *South Park*) that would, by and large, make only passing references to their characters' sex lives and infrequently focus an episode on them, adult animation pushed through an "edgy" adolescence in the 2000s (where an onslaught of shows – *Stripperella*, *Drawn Together*, *Ren and Stimpy: Adult Party Cartoon* and the multitudinous offerings of Seth MacFarlane – seemed dedicated to rubbing "adult" themes and visuals in their audience's faces) before settling into the calmer 2010s where TV shows would present sex with a touch more complexity than the odd sight gag or one-liner.

Despite proving controversial in its handling of certain topics, the objective success of Andrew Goldberg, Nick Kroll, Mark Levin and Jennifer Flackett's Netflix series *Big Mouth* (and, by extension, its spinoff *Human Resources*) is owed in part to being a sincere attempt on the part of its creators to put something out into the world that helps teenagers realize they are not alone in their struggles against the miasma of emotional turmoil that puberty brings with it. While it flaunts a similar breed of overstated, genitals and bodily functions-focused vulgarity that its noughties predecessors thrived on, its basic premise of a group of high school students navigating adolescence opens the door to a number of difficult subjects rarely tackled by mainstream television. Certainly the criticisms leveled against its mis-steps (notably dialogue that was scrutinized for fundamentally misrepresenting the concept of pansexuality as opposed to bisexuality[17]) are valid, though an argument could be made that such blunders are afforded to it by virtue of how few shows have attempted to present these issues in earnest. While *South Park* would occasionally address them – such as in the season 5 episode *Proper Condom Use* that sees the parents and school faculty at odds with how sex education might best be incorporated into a curriculum, or season 6's *Bebe's Boobs Destroy Society* that sees a young female student simultaneously deified by the boys and ostracized by the girls when she starts to develop breasts before anyone else in her grade – its overall remit as a show that alternates between blatant silliness and indiscriminately satirizing all walks of life inevitably makes them less of a focus. Similarly, Mike Judge's *Beavis and Butt-Head* would infrequently touch upon real issues that affect teenagers (sex education, pregnancy, peer pressure), but through the lens of two characters so dimwitted that no discernible lesson or message has any hope of being gleaned.

Big Mouth's menagerie of metaphorical characters could not be accused of being subtle or cerebral in their conception – raging hormones take the form of furry, horned beasts; shame manifested as a wizard that flits from child to child, validating their insecurities and self-loathing; anxiety a swarm of identical mosquitos that buzz around them until they are overwhelmed, and so on. Yet they are effective enough for the format and easily relatable, perhaps more to older viewers looking back on that time in their lives. The dialogue and scenarios are often crude in a manner consistent with just how feral young teenagers wrestling their newly discovered libidos under control tend to be. Yet in spite of its caustic presentation, the takehomes are generally positive and reassuring. The show's attitudes toward body positivity are best encapsulated during a musical number *I Love My Body* during the second season episode *What Is It About Boobs?*, in which Maya Rudolph's hormone monstress Connie waxes rhapsodic in a health spa changing room about the enormous variety of human body types the world has to offer, bolstering the self-confidence of the two adolescent girls in her proverbial charge.

Presenting this type of message to a potentially young and impressionable audience is not without its pitfalls, and regardless of its clear intent to propagate the idea that our bodies and developing sexual urges are nothing to be ashamed of, the show's use of underage characters and cartoon nudity to carry across its points would earn itself some hand-wringing and histrionics from conservative viewers (social media outcry would include comparing the show's audience to "border line [sic] pedophile(s)" and likening it to Maïmouna Doucouré's live-action feature *Mignonnes*, another contentious Netflix offering that earned critical and political furore for its depiction of minors dressing and dancing provocatively[18]).

While more focused on interpersonal relationships as a whole than sexual politics, another animated Netflix series[19] that matches – and often exceeds – the manic energy of *Big Mouth* is Lisa Hanawalt's *Tuca and Bertie*. Following in the wake of the adult sitcom *BoJack Horseman* (on which Hanawalt was Production Designer), the series is focused on two young adults who are best friends in spite of a distinctly different approach to life. Living in a *BoJack*-esque world of animal/plant-human hybrids, "wearer of short shorts" Tuca is an uninhibited, highly personable but unreliable toucan recovering from alcoholism, while Bertie is a cautious, anxiety-ridden song thrush grappling with childhood trauma. As with *Big Mouth*, the show embraces its "cartoon" format in that its world is unrestricted and peppered with surreal interludes and meta fourth-wall breaks, though its approach differs entirely. The series has a hyperactive joyfulness to its energy, frequently freeing itself from the shackles of its character rigs to indulge moments of dynamic, model-breaking character animation, as well as delivering an onslaught of split-second sight gags, puns and mixed-media cutaways. Amidst this energy are refreshingly honest themes of body and sex positivity from a female perspective, sometimes direct and explicit (the first season's opening credits declare the show's playfully absurd intentions by greeting the viewer with a gyrating apartment building that bears a set of jiggling breasts) though oftentimes woven into the overall fabric of the show. Draca, an inordinately tall, casually topless neighbor of Tuca and Bertie's, is idolized for her relaxed lifestyle and comfortability in her own skin. Tuca, to a similar extent, expresses a degree of body confidence, though it is impeded by occasional blows to her self-esteem; in an early episode, *The Deli Guy*, we see her struggling to make a good impression on a date with a prospective partner (her first since becoming sober), becoming self-conscious about her beak and shrinking it with concealer. During the date she leans into her "wild, impulsive, very scary at times" nature, and while her uninhibited personality is endearing to a point, she eventually sabotages the date by taking off her top on a fairground ride, tipping it over into impropriety.

Bertie, by contrast, is less outgoing and more reserved about her own body, to the point that her breast literally detaches from the rest of her in umbrage at being objectified by the misogynistic rooster Dirk, a work colleague, in season one's *The Promotion*. With echoes of the dynamic between Vince and Beryl in Joanna Quinn's *Body Beautiful*, the episode explores the seemingly no-win situation this harassment puts our protagonist in. While Beryl is reluctant to raise the issue with higher management in a late-1980s working environment (presuming that it would only yield trouble), *The Promotion* demonstrates just how little has changed in the decades since, Bertie's female HR manager dismissing her complaints and urging her to take Dirk's remarks as a compliment. As with Beryl's predicament, the solution comes by taking the matter into Bertie's own hands, aided by Tuca who becomes an office temp and motivates her to assert herself. A resulting sexual harassment seminar emboldens the other women in the company to speak out against Dirk, bolstering Bertie's self-worth and ultimately giving her the confidence to put herself forward for promotion.

The storyline serves as a prime example of what the show succeeds at, insofar as it raises important issues as regards workplace harassment without breaking its stride of dynamic, irreverent sight gags and quick-witted dialogue. The series should also be credited for not drawing a line under these issues as though resolved. The dearth of support from the HR representative nods to the pernicious culture of women not supporting women, as well as a misaligned sense of propriety as regards gender and sexual politics. Yet it portends a later scenario in the episode *Plumage* that sees Bertie, now apprenticing at a bakery, respond to another, more physical instance of sexually charged workplace harassment with desire, retreating to the bathroom to aggressively masturbate. In a later episode, *The New Bird*, the same aggressor is reprimanded by another young apprentice, who calls the behavior out as problematic when he attempts the same on her; she admonishes Bertie for neither warning her nor comprehending her outrage.

Although they are worlds apart in many respects, among the main takehomes of both *Tuca and Bertie* and *Big Mouth* is that our bodies and all their perceived strengths and flaws are an incontrovertible fact of life, to be discussed and normalized to the point where nudity might not always have to constitute sexuality. Most importantly, it is that our bodies are our own and do not deserve or warrant any unsolicited attention, physical or otherwise. It is a simple message, but one especially valuable to the inevitable percentage of its audience that will likely be teenagers – even children – and, as such, be the most susceptible to the conflicting but highly pushed narrative that their bodies must be a root source of their insecurities.

With all of the case studies discussed in this chapter, it is their shared trait of being animated that makes them stand out and prompt discussion. As to why, precisely, that is, director Anna Ginsburg's thoughts on the matter hold significant weight:

> Animation is always going to have this innocence to it, and this accessibility that enables difficult subjects – issues that still lay on the lines of taboo, and are still so shrouded in guilt, shame, disdain – to be welcomed into the consciousness of people that you wouldn't expect. I think that is what gives animation its power. In animated documentaries especially, I always say that animation is like a protective layer that you can use to cover a subject, therefore everything is more able to flow because you're not actually seeing human beings, so there's less judgment; the drawing can protect the person.

Notes

1 Cohen, Karl F. (2004) *Forbidden Animation: Censored Cartoons and Blacklisted Animators in America*. US: McFarland & Co Inc., p. 20.
2 Davies, J. (1996) *Interesting Roger Rabbit Facts*. Available at: http://www.jimdavies.org/roger-rabbit/roger_rabbit_facts.html.
3 Loughrey, C. (2018) *Who Framed Roger Rabbit? at 30: The Feminist Appeal of Jessica Rabbit*. Available at: https://www.independent.co.uk/arts-entertainment/films/features/who-framed-roger-rabbit-30th-anniversary-jessica-feminism-appeal-a8411501.html.
4 Others in this vein include the Academy Award-nominated *Your Face* (1987), the similarly "instructional" *How to Quit Smoking* (1989), *Plymptoons* (1990) and *Push Comes to Shove* (1991).

5 Amongst criticisms made against Plympton's work is a noteworthy moment in the 2011 documentary *Adventures in Plymptoons!* (Dir. Alexia Anastasio) where his protégé Signe Baumane condemns a scene in his short film *The Date* as "disgusting" in its implication that a woman should be expected to perform oral sex on a first date.
6 *Girls Night Out* was produced at Middlesex University London (then Middlesex Polytechnic) with assistance from Channel 4 and S4C.
7 Special Jury Prize, Ufoleis Prize and Mellow Manor Award.
8 The film is one of several animated shorts that make up *Cabaret*, a Toulouse Lautrec-themed anthology made for an exhibition of his work at Musée d'Orsay, Paris in1992.
9 It is interesting to note that, behind the scenes, scriptwriter Guillemard would push Quinn out of her comfort zone by insisting on incorporating some degree of sexual openness, including a moment in which one model playfully slaps the other's rear-end, a sequence Quinn would concede as being "quite liberating" to animate.
10 Short Animation, 1999.
11 www.12fps.net.
12 A reference to Russ Meyer's 1975 erotic comedy feature film of the same name.
13 As is often the case with viral videos, its overall aggregated view count across hundreds of unofficial reposts would far exceed this number; many such copies would be from a Arte television broadcast rip where the original uploader edited the ending so as to leave Doazan uncredited.
14 www.strangebeast.tv.
15 Created for a 2021 crowdfunding campaign in aid of the charity art book *Boobs*.
16 Best Animated Short, 2022.
17 Ferguson, L. (2019) *"Big Mouth" Co-Creators Apologize for Inaccurate Pansexuality Scene*. Available at: https://www.indiewire.com/features/general/netflix-big-mouth-co-creators-apologize-pansexual-bisexual-transgender-1202179923.
18 Lewis, R. (2020) "DISGUSTING" Netflix's Big Mouth blasted for "glorifying paedophilia and underaged sex" as series branded "as bad as Cuties." Available at: https://www.thesun.co.uk/tv/13535523/netflixs-big-mouth-blasted-glorifying-paedophilia/.
19 Although its first season debuted on Netflix, it would ultimately find a home on Cartoon Network's programming block Adult Swim after not getting picked up by the streaming platform for its second season.

4

Lust

In this chapter, we will take a more pointed look at sex as an act of libido that is based on personal carnal desire; as with the previous chapters, we will do this through subthemes and case studies. Speaking with key filmmakers, we will explore how themes of arousal and sensual exploration – spanning sexual play, fetishism, masturbation and sexual liberation – are paired with and conveyed through animation in thought-provoking ways.

An artist who encapsulates all of these themes, as well as others discussed elsewhere in this book, is Sawako Kabuki,[1] a Japanese animator and illustrator who has made a name for herself through her fun-filled and often erotically charged anarchic short film projects that bring a burst of energy to any screening. We first came across Kabuki's work at Annecy in 2017 where she received the Jury Award for *Summer's Puke Is Winter's Delight* (2016),[2] a film based on a chapter of her own life that shows a character attempting to keep her lover's affection by purging food to lose weight. Kabuki's acceptance speech was the concise but definitive statement "Thank you so much, I feel so good. I wanna fuck everyone," a sentiment that perfectly complements the immediacy, humor and daring nature of her work.

Kabuki's website showcases an eclectic range of films, idents, GIFs and illustrations that share a common visual identity and focus on humanoid forms and sexual imagery. Her work is hypnotic with its use of patterns and repeated imagery that continuously morphs, often to the beat of high-energy musical accompaniment. The films themselves offer an onslaught to the senses made up of kaleidoscopic strobing colors, bodily fluids, naked dancers and disembodied body parts – such as lips and tongues – which lick, suck and

DOI: 10.1201/9781003415503-5

probe one another. According to Kabuki, such themes have been part of her work from a young age.

> I've been making works on the theme of "sexuality" since I was little, as part of the "interesting topic" like "poop." As I grow older, many things gradually accumulate in my mind and I get tired from them. I guess "sensation of pleasure" has been added there to try to decompress it? There was a time when I used to watch ASMR videos every night, with a pretty Korean girl talking to me gently, and I really loved it. She gave me a "sensation of pleasure" a lot. I feel like I tried to make something like that in my style at that time.

Sexuality is often explored at a young age, as discussed in both the sex education and self-discovery chapters, and can offer a foundational understanding of sex and pleasure. Kabuki explores this in her pro-masturbation film *Don't Tell Mom* (2015)[3] (Figure 4.1), framed as a children's educational film with songs and innocent, child-like testimonials, parodying the Japanese educational program *Okaasan to Issho* (roughly translated as *With Mother*). According to Kabuki, the original show consisted of multiple songs and various styles of animations that she used as the basis for the film, which she came up with while drinking and talking with friends from university. The film follows interconnecting sections that include parental sex, frottage on a bicycle and burdock root, bondage and the unusual use of an aubergine that is inserted into the bottom of the mother before later being eaten in a family meal. Hosted by a blue, penis-headed mascot, the scenarios are set against a sing-song musical number and employ various animation styles ranging from Kabuki's flat line style, *faux naïf* children-styled drawings and clay animation, all of which coming together to create a comically convincing pastiche of sex education media.

This continued exploration of the "sensation of pleasure" flows into various projects and seems to be at the heart of much of her work. A focus on things that cause arousal and pleasure can be seen in her music video for 1980 YEN,[4] *Takoyaki Story* (2018)[5] (Figure 4.2), which follows the arousal and growing

Figure 4.1

Still from *Don't Tell Mom* (Dir. Sawako Kabuki). ©2015 Sawako Kabuki

Figure 4.2

Still from *Takoyaki Story* (Dir. Sawako Kabuki). ©2018 Sawako Kabuki

attraction of a woman to the famous Japanese food Takoyaki, a ball-shaped snack made from batter filled with octopus. Although Kabuki herself is not a fan of the dish, due to childhood memories of the food scorching her mouth, it was the lyrics for the song that served as the inspiration for the film. Alongside the visual motifs and recurring themes of her work, music plays a pivotal role in much of Kabuki's work, as she explains:

> It's easier to make visuals if the music is first. For the most part, the music comes first and then I animate to it. The people who do the music are generally my friends, so I trust them from the beginning to the end with no particular demands.

Kabuki's sense of rhythm makes her an ideal candidate for directing music videos, as seen in her work for musical artist THE POTONE! on *Nou Nen feat. Utae* (2015).[6] The music video was inspired by an episode of the heartbreak of a male friend, a decision Kabuki explains further as having wanted to make an animation from a man's point of view for a change. On reflection, Kabuki feels she wasn't overly successful in her original intention of wanting "to portray a painful sadness of men in the midst of ideals and reality." However, the film remains a powerful visualization of various aspects of relationships such as lust, infatuation, obsession, distance and eventual heartbreak, set to an upbeat electronic track.

As seen in the previous film, another key theme in her work is love in all of its forms including a kind of all-encompassing love, verging on the obsessional (obsessive love is explored further in Chapter 6). This theme is perhaps most clearly seen in her film *Master Blaster* (2015), in which girls hide in their lovers' rectums, showing a desire to be as close as possible to the person they love.

"This animation expresses my desire to hide in the butt hole of someone I love," elaborates Kabuki. "Like people who hide illegal drugs in their butt hole when flying. I wanted to be carried like that by someone I loved. Then you would only have to pay for one plane ticket for two people."

Similarly, her earlier film *Ici, là et partout* (2013)[7] has a parallel but slightly calmer tone. If *Master Blaster* can be seen to show the early stages of infatuation,

Figure 4.3

Still from *ANAL JUKE – anal juice* (Dir. Sawako Kabuki). ©2013 Sawako Kabuki

Ici, là et partout evokes the growing, maturing love of long-term commitment that, as Kabuki suggests, may be due to her being "in a longer relationship" when she made the film. However, as often comes with love, comes heartbreak; having touched upon this in *Nou Nen feat. Utae*, Kabuki's 2012 film *ANAL JUKE – anal juice*[8] (Figure 4.3) – also explores the demise of a relationship.

Kabuki's Vimeo description of the film states that it was made after breaking up with her boyfriend and is based on a dream she had of him. Aside from the sadness felt due to this parting of ways, the film is also set in the context of the earthquake that took place on March 11, 2011 and the mounting tensions regarding nuclear power in Japan. Her ex's penchant for enemas was combined into the imagery, as a character (who presumably represents Kabuki herself) is shown interacting with a male character bearing a set of buttocks for a head, this also resolved her inability to see his face in the dream (Sawako Kabuki, 2014). The frenetic intensity of the film depicts both the emotional rawness of a breakup and the incomprehensible fluidity of dreams, as the filmmaker explains:

> My graduation project should have been just one animation, but I misunderstood and made two animations. For *Ici, là et partout*, at this time I had a boyfriend, so I made an animation full of love. And when I was thinking about what to make for the second animation, I was dumped by my boyfriend, and I had a crazy dream. I immediately jotted down a note about the dream after I woke up. This work is based on that dream. I animated that dream almost exactly as it was.

It is clear that Kabuki's work has at least a semi-improvisational style, which affords her a level of self-reflection and infuses her work with a high level of energy and freshness. When discussing her working practice, the director says that when she starts a project,

> I have some kind of idea and start drawing animation based on it. I like to think about details and stuff while drawing animation. The process of making animation becomes "work" if I make a storyboard or animatic and it's not my favorite way to make animation.

If required for a client brief, however, Kabuki will incorporate these stages of production, having lent her unique style to multiple commercials and idents which, while understandably more subdued relative to her personal projects, still retain her signature esoteric style. One commercial that retains those knowing visual motifs is a set of short commercials created for the toothpaste company Marvis for their *Marvel Your Routine* campaign.[9] Kabuki created two 10-second segments with English talent agency Pocko,[10] which feature nude or semi-nude female characters in morphing snapshots of dental hygiene among other pleasurable activities, such as sleeping in a plush, screen-wide bed and an expansive bubble bath after dropping from a pearly moon. It is clear to see why Kabuki's bold style and audacious approach to filmmaking have led to her being screened, awarded and exhibited internationally. Her overall body of work serves as a model representation of how and why much of the powerful, female-led content explored in this book is so effective, in its seemingly effortless combination of unique, engaging, daring and often comedic takes on sexuality and sexual pleasure in the modern day.

What Lies Beneath: Sexual Liberation and Fantasy

Kabuki's work lends itself to interpretations and discussions of symbolism due to its often poetic nature and construction. For the filmmaker, such approaches to filmmaking are surely liberating when examining the somewhat nebulous sensation of arousal and can prove incredibly useful when combined with music, lyrics or indeed more poetic/descriptive testimonials. Another example of this approach to visuals can be seen in the work of noted filmmaker and academic Ruth Lingford is one of several women animators whose work blazed something of a trail in the 1990s and early 2000s. Having initially trained as an occupational therapist, Lingford discovered a passion for art, something she'd previously only dabbled in while at secondary school, through attending life drawing classes, leading her to study part-time at Middlesex University. There she would in turn develop a fascination with the addictive process of animation and the advantages it had over static painting and sculpture.

Particularly inspired by such films as Andy Stavely's Royal College of Art (RCA) graduation film *Strangers in Paradise* (1987), Lingford would also look to the work of Yuri Norstein and Caroline Leaf as she developed her own animator's voice.

> They were very influential in terms of the humanism of their work. Neither of them were obsessed with technical bravura, they were interested in the minutiae of what people were like, how people behave, how people's behavior illuminates their interior lives. I guess interiority is important for me in relation to animation.

Going on to graduate from the RCA herself, Lingford would find herself struggling to find a place in an industry whose job market was still a relatively analogue world of painting and tracing roles ("One place apparently kept the cels I'd painted as an example of what *not* to do for the next people; it was clear I wasn't going to make a living in that part of the animation industry"). In a stroke of cosmic fortune, on the day of being fired from one such job, she would receive a grant from Animate Projects, an organization with whom she'd work on numerous films over the subsequent decade, beginning with *What She Wants* in 1994. Leaving paint and trace behind, Lingford would soon begin implementing digital processes in her work, a practice not especially common in the early-to-mid-1990s, ultimately coming up with her own experimental animation process using her home computer ("an Amiga with half a megabyte of memory; we had to upgrade to a full megabyte") and the now-discontinued software Deluxe Paint. The result gives her work a truly unique feel, pairing the analogue sensibilities of straight-ahead, paint or sand-on-glass animation with a mid-1990s pixelated aesthetic evocative of that era's video games. Her boldness of expression shines through in the film, which follows a nondescript woman as she travels across a city by subway, increasingly subsumed by intense sexual desire.

Set to a freeform saxophone solo score by Lol Coxhill, the film incrementally introduces suggestive imagery, beginning with the woman cradling and caressing the inside and pudenda-esque opening of her handbag, rummaging through it sensually to retrieve her change. The visuals – and sound design – quickly escalate as we travel through throbbing subway tunnels that undulate like vaginal walls, a train sliding into and through them as though lubricated. By and large, the depiction of the subway station seems almost tainted by her presence, projections of her headspace contorting the mundane reality around her; vending machines pout as she passes by them, ticket barrier gates groping at her like hands as she passes through.

It is within the train carriage that things tip over into explicit sexual fantasy, as the woman again contemplates her open purse and imagines an oversized tongue emerging from it, wrapping around her and dwelling on her erogenous zones as her clothes melt away. Rather than a standard fantasy with any kind of linear narrative, what ensues is an abstract succession of vignettes that morph into one another, suggesting a relinquishing of rational thought reminiscent of hypnagogic hallucinations that play out in our mind's eye when on the verge of losing consciousness. Using mostly white line-art against a black void, the woman imagines herself being examined, possibly in some kind of medical setting, leading to a series of tableaus and digitally recreated artworks that become increasingly more graphic and beholden to a certain dream logic. Among them is a particularly striking sequence in which a woman's mouth fellating a penis transmutes into Francisco Goya's *Saturno devorando a su hijo* (*Saturn Devouring His Son*), which in turn becomes a baby suckling on a breast.

At the conclusion of this section of the film, it initially seems as though the fantasy visuals have concluded as we return to the woman in the carriage. Before disembarking, however, things take an especially hallucinogenic turn as she disrobes and her lips, nipples and genitals briefly engorge into a grotesque caricature of womanhood (Figure 4.4); a fellow commuter watches on, his head extending to resemble a phallus unsheathing itself. When she arrives at her destination, the woman removes her clothes, followed by her skin, revealing a winged, emaciated creature that circles above the city (whose erect, high-rise buildings shrink and become flaccid underneath her).

The uncompromising visuals of *What She Wants* establish a precedent for Lingford's subsequent work. Alongside a career in filmmaking that would bring about several loose, sometimes sexually charged adaptations of existing texts[11] and an award-winning commercial music video,[12] Lingford would come to teach at various prestigious arts institutions including the Royal College of Art and the National Film and Television School, eventually finding herself at Harvard University at which she remains as a Senior Lecturer on Art, Film, and Visual Studies.[13] Off the back of contributing animated segments to Harvard colleagues Peter Galison and Robb Moss's 2008 documentary *Secrecy*, Lingford became interested in developing a new film project of her own, using unused footage

Figure 4.4

Still from *What She Wants* (Dir. Ruth Lingford). ©1994 Ruth Lingford

from the documentary as a springboard. Aided by a Harvard Film Study Center Fellowship, the resulting project was 2010's *Little Deaths* (Figure 4.5), an exploration of the experience of orgasm through recorded interviews set to interpretive, experimental animation.

The title, a reference to the French expression for orgasm "*La petit morts*," is set up by the first testimony of the film referencing a deceased partner's final moments as being reminiscent of how they appeared during orgasm. The film's structure, and the interviews compiled for it, would be predicated on informal conversations that incorporated certain specific questions. While participants proved eager to participate and generally did not hold back, this resulted in the champagne problem of often having too much material to work with, the director frequently having to jettison interesting – but overlong – sections of audio in favor of those that would translate best to edited sound bites. The insights into such an ostensibly universal experience are demonstrative of just how unique and personal our individual relationships with orgasm can be, its participants (among which are fellow case study directors Signe Baumane and Andreas Hykade) presenting a broad variety of physical, emotional and mental responses to achieving climax. While being able to turn to a group of interviewees largely composed of her own – surprisingly open – peers does result in a fairly diverse range of perspectives, a minor regret for Lingford is that said diversity could not have been broadened further.

> There was a lot of pressure to be more multicultural, which would have been great if I'd had more time and more money. I'd have loved to have gone to the Muslim countries and asked people, but basically the people I asked were either people I knew or friends of friends, so in a way they were slightly pre-selected. Within

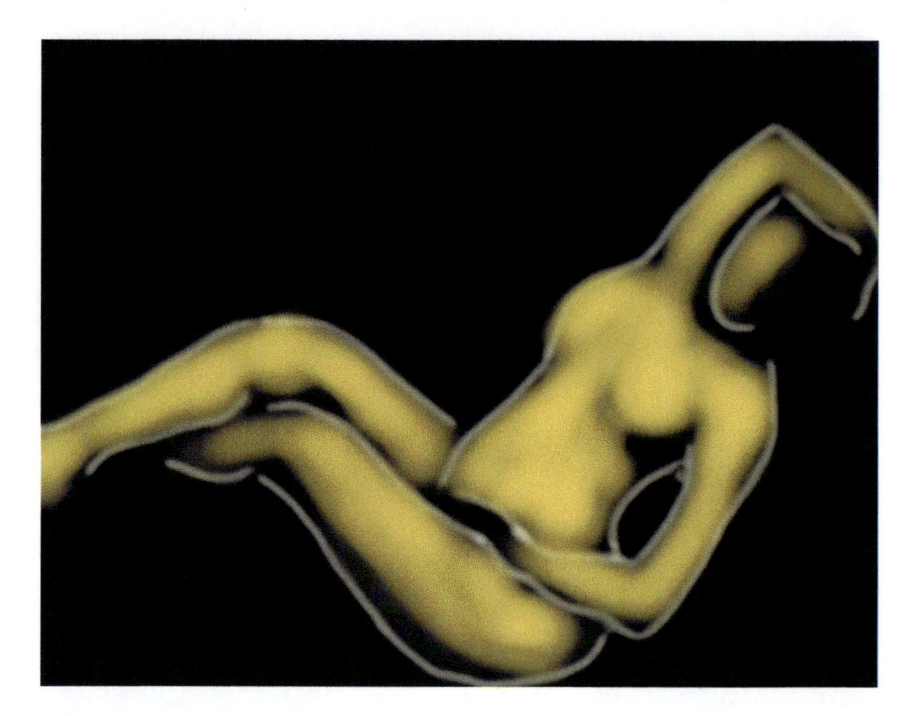

Figure 4.5

Still from *Little Deaths* (Dir. Ruth Lingford). ©2010 Ruth Lingford

> that there was a wide range of people – male, female, gay, straight and one male-to-female transsexual – though not such a wide range of ages. Probably the oldest would've been late-fifties, and they were all American or European.

The opening question "What's it like?" invites comparisons reminiscent of the types of stock footage montages old movies and shows would indulge to represent the occurrence of sex – such as rollercoasters, gates opening, guns being shot, bombs being dropped and – somewhat out of left field – Daffy Duck. The follow-up question "What do you see?" elicits a fascinating array of responses that span visuals conjured in one's mind's eye, memories of specific places or events, synaesthesia and hallucinations, light being a recurring theme. This segment is, understandably, the stretch of the film most directly reflected by the animation. Calling back to the intense fantasy sequence of *What She Wants*, *Little Deaths* uses a similarly hypnagogic, freeform visual approach to its abstract interpretations of each interviewee's contribution. Much of the visuals are similarly made up of white or colored line-art against an expanse of black, though while the sequence of images in *What She Wants* feel more rooted in explicit fantasy, *Little Deaths* takes its abstract approach a little further, fluidly blending coherent visuals with stream-of-consciousness experimentation, evoking concepts such as ideas association, the Tetris effect, retinal bleaching and the lightshow of phosphenes we sometimes see against the *eigengrau* of our closed eyes. All of these phenomena feel thematically appropriate given that they are often physical effects of – or exacerbated by – orgasm itself. Among the parade of images are enmeshed, intertwined human forms, droplets, neurons, barbed wire and kaleidoscopic, orgiastic limbs (Figure 4.6). While largely using similar digital animation processes to those of *What She Wants* (though produced on hardware

Figure 4.6

Still from *Little Deaths* (Dir. Ruth Lingford). ©2010 Ruth Lingford

significantly more advanced than the Amiga 1500), mixed-media approaches are also used, such as MRI footage paralleled with abstract strata-cut, both of which resulting in a shared visual of traveling through the inner workings of a structure that would otherwise be impossible to explore.

"What's it like after?" is perhaps the most interesting segment from a psychological perspective in consideration of the vulnerability of the interviewees – and how comfortable they are with being vulnerable. In a moment that foreshadows her own exploration of the biological processes behind what governs love and sex in the film *My Love Affair With Marriage* (as discussed in Chapter 2), director Signe Baumane reflects on how a gratifying sexual experience and the ensuing rush of hormones can be crucial to developing attachment and falling in love. Others are more nihilistic, speaking of postcoital comedowns, regret and melancholia, one in particular regarding sexual pleasure as "the illusion of not being alone," a fleeting distraction from the otherwise solitary journey of their life.

> Maybe one of my surprises about the film is how sad it is, in a way. There's a melancholy in the film which I wasn't necessarily expecting. It fascinates me that the way people generally describe orgasm is as an absence, an absence of experience, a temporary absence of self, almost a negation of the self in those moments. A ceasing to be, and yet for most people it's an overwhelmingly positive experience. That seems kind of odd for such a non-experience in a way, that it was so valued while at the same time having very melancholy overtones.

Little Deaths also incorporates elements of humor, generally through the more bizarre and random associations its contributors find themselves coming up with, and the juxtaposition of concepts that feel wholly universal against those that are hyper-specific to an individual's experience. In the final segment, "What does it mean to you?" philosophical musings on orgasm as a weighty and spiritual aspect of the grand human experience are met with deadpan deliveries of "It's about impregnating a woman" and likening it to "needing to pee really badly."

> Those sorts of juxtapositions I'd found very interesting and potentially funny, so I wanted to have those. But [for] some things, the humor almost comes out of surprise. I also wanted to capture the pathos – people can get quite grandiose talking about their orgasms but then there are moments where that's punctured.

Little Deaths would largely do its festival rounds in the early 2010s, winning several awards at events including the Ottawa International Animation Festival and Vienna Independent Shorts Festival. As witnessed firsthand when it played at the 2011 Stuttgart International Festival of Animated Film, the film would spark excited conversations among young, largely female students and upcoming filmmakers about the effectiveness of animation and sex as a pairing. Through her position as an educator, Lingford has been able to directly inspire noteworthy new voices in animation. One such filmmaker whose uniquely wonderful artistic voice lends itself well to some of the more ineffable aspects of desire and libido is Houston, Texas-born Renee Zhan. Prior to an established career as a commercial director, Zhan came into animation from an initial interest in painting at a young age, paired with a desire to make films on her own in her bedroom. She attended and graduated from Harvard University, where she produced the films *Pidge* and *Hold Me (Ca Caw Ca Caw)* (Figure 4.7) under the tutelage of Ruth Lingford, someone in whom she saw a guru, mentor and friend.

> She taught me everything I know. The only animation I was familiar with was Pixar, so it was quite a shock, going to her first screening – I really expected to be watching *Finding Nemo*! And then she showed Suzan Pitt's *Asparagus* and Michèle Cournoyer's *Le Chapeau (The Hat)*. It was really eye opening, realizing what animation could be, what it could say and show and how powerful and effective it could be.

Figure 4.7

Still from *Hold Me (Ca Caw Ca Caw)* (Dir. Renee Zhan). ©2016 Harvard VES / Renee Zhan. Image courtesy of Renee Zhan

With her horizons further expanded by lecturers including Robb Moss as well as the late Chris Killip and Paul Bush, Zhan's first Harvard film *Pidge*, a dark comedy about a suicidal pigeon who jumps off a building and changes his mind on the way down (only for fate to ultimately make the decision for him), showcases an innate and unique gift for character design and performance, as well as an inclination toward incorporating birds in her work.

"My dad kept like 10 cockatoos in our house when I was growing up, and I think I really inherited that love of birds. There's something really weird and scary and also beautiful about them," says Zhan.

All of these qualities are keenly observed in Zhan's follow-up film *Hold Me (Ca Caw Ca Caw)*, in which a giant bird shares an apartment with a naked man (or "a small boy," as per the film's official synopsis). The pair coexists in something that approximates a romantic relationship, albeit a wholly unnatural one – they eat together grotesquely, have aggressive sex and hold one another in bed at night. It is clear, however, that the bird feels simultaneously trapped within the confines of their home, yet daunted by what might lie outside its walls. When she lays an egg and prioritizes it over her partner's sexual needs, his cruelly unthinking retaliation sends her into a tailspin.

> All of my films came from personal experience or a feeling I had – or at least they started from there, and then sort of grew into characters. Now I'm trying to look more at the world and other sources as well, because I'm running out of things to say about myself. That film, in particular, was sort of based on a relationship I was in at the time and then exited, but still very much was thinking about. I actually made three films about one relationship; it's great that I was able to milk so much material out of it! So it started there, then once I was writing the film, the characters took on their own story.

As with *Pidge*, *Hold Me* demonstrates not just an assured grasp of the main tenets of animation for an artist at such an early stage in their career, but also a gift for comedic writing and carrying out its execution well.

"I was involved with the Harvard Lampoon. So I was really interested in comedy, but then I started to think about other uses for animation or other things that could be expressed through animation," says Zhan.

In terms of her physical characteristics, the first impressions one gleans from the main character of *Hold Me* feel rooted in comedy, especially her lopsided, bumbling movements that at times feel not so much birdlike as mammalian, her and her nude human companion chaotically lurching around the apartment like inelegant walruses. As we spend more time with her, however, we come to realize that there is a certain tragic helplessness to her existence, one that grows increasingly hard to watch as her empty life is finally given some purpose, knowing on some level that it is likely to be unfairly snatched away. The perhaps unexpected dimensions to a character that might initially read as silly, or mere comedy fodder, are qualities attributed to Zhan's appreciation for certain, potentially contentious depictions of women in cinema.

> I looked a lot at live-action films. I really love Lars von Trier, which I think is a controversial opinion; people say that he's sexist because he creates these "weak" female characters, but I don't really think they are weak – or I don't think a female character needs to be strong in order to be...well, in order to *be*. I really liked his female characters. I sort of identified with them, and the bird in *Hold Me*, I thought

of her as someone in that group. I also really love Björk and her commitment to being herself. She's really weird, but somehow people really identify with that. I've heard a lot recently that my work is very weird, and often that's said in a negative way. Sometimes it's hard to take that as a compliment, but I think I probably should try to.

After graduating from Harvard and producing the interim film *Reneepoptosis* (a Sundance award-winning[14] piece described by the director as "a bunch of Renees who go on a quest to find God, who's also me") as part of a traveling fellowship that saw her spend a year in Japan, Zhan would continue her animation journey in the United Kingdom at the National Film and Television School, an environment where she knew she would be pushed to work with others and direct a team, a significant shift away from her comfort zone of going solo, and where she would further explore "issues of the body, nature, and sexuality – all things beautiful, ugly, and squishy." While these sensibilities are evidenced to varying degrees in all her work to date, including her final NFTS musical, mixed-media, mini-epic *O Black Hole!* (a much-loved darling of the festival scene that sees a woman so aggrieved by the prospect of her own mortality that she transforms into a black hole, absorbing all she holds dear to "protect" them from the same passage of time that she so fears), they are perhaps at their most concentrated in what began as a first-year project *Soft Animals*, a densely packed three minutes of fraught emotions, tensions and lustful urges (Figure 4.8).

Figure 4.8

Creating *Soft Animals*. ©Photo courtesy of Renee Zhan

Against a faded backdrop of a train station, we're presented with the ostensibly straightforward scenario of two acquaintances happening upon one another by chance. It becomes quickly apparent that they are former lovers doing their best to maintain a cordial dialogue; through the animation visualization of their inner impulses, however, we find that their civility is at odds with their still-raw recollections of the passion they once felt for each other.

> I think it's something that happens – somebody that you were really close with, and then you leave each other. But then, if you run into them again, it's very awkward. The audio of the film is this kind of surface level encounter, where they're just saying, "Hi, you look great." But then the second level of that is the way that the body feels and responds and remembers, separately from the mind. So the visuals of the film are what they're imagining, what their more animal instincts are expressing, which is lust and, and missing each other in some way.

Though not pigeons, their physical forms are almost inhuman, the young man lumbering and grotesque with what seem to be large black caverns for eyes, while the woman is featureless (her face essentially a giant lipstick smear), squat and angular. It's a design approach that well-serves their transmutations into prowling creatures; as they go through the motions of polite small-talk, we see their inner thoughts and urges play out as a dance of almost baleful, libidinous desire. To anyone who has experienced such an encounter, it is pointedly relatable; mature comportment dictates outward civility when unexpectedly happening across someone we were once intimate with, yet our shared recollections of one another's most personal and private details make it a struggle. In some respects being able to share that experience can be affirming and even comforting, though in the moment the onslaught of memories are chaotic and jarring.

This chaos is brilliantly conveyed through manic charcoal strokes, brutally animalistic character performance and globular, flesh-toned expulsions of paint evocative of such artists as Lucien Freud and Francis Bacon.

> I think, for me, the texture, dampness and "squishiness" of paint is really tied in heavily to bodies touching each other, and sweat, and the kind of visceral "gross"-ness of it all. The other thing about the technique was that I used this draw-erase approach with the charcoal. I like the traces that it leaves behind, and I thought that tied in as well with the memories; the traces and the imprints that people leave on each other.

As their encounter continues, they appear naked before each other to expose lolling genitals and tongues, their faces fusing together into something approximating a licentious kiss before tearing off one another's limbs and leaping into one another to form a writhing, carnal sludge (leading to one of the most visually appealing shots in the film as their internal struggles manifest as a fleshy sea of breasts, legs and buttocks). They watch one another's faces melt away (Figure 4.9) as sounds of simultaneous orgasms can be heard, reemerging back in the train station as their charcoal outlined selves, separate from a painted, frozen-in-time moment of intimacy that hangs, distended, over them. Wearied from the strain of the encounter, they part ways again, still metaphorically unclothed.

Through its effective juxtaposition of loose (yet disciplined) character design against the tactility of the materials used, the short effectively conveys how the ghosts of lovers' past can sometimes haunt us in spite of ourselves, and the bittersweet ambivalence that comes from memories of intimacy.

Figure 4.9

Stills from *Soft Animals* (Dir. Renee Zhan). ©2021 National Film and Television School. Images courtesy of Renee Zhan

Such brief but erotically charged instances of connection can also be seen in celebrated Czech director Michaela Pavlátová's 2012 film *Tram* (Figure 4.10), a snapshot of the life of a female tram conductress as she goes about yet another potentially boring work day. As the vibration of her tram combines with her drifting thoughts, she is led to distraction as her regular route becomes a rhythmic, erotic journey into her internal desires, turning mundane activities into lustful fantasies. As previously mentioned, Pavlátová is a key figure in the exploration of sexual themes and the roles that relationships play in our daily lives through the medium of animation. *Tram* was originally commissioned by French production company Sacrebleu Productions[15] as a pilot for The Sexperiences Project, a series of short films conceived by producer Sandra Schultze about female erotic fantasies created by female filmmakers.

"She came up with the idea of making erotic animated films about female sexuality and came to Annecy to ask people to work on her idea," recalls Pavlátová. "As a producer, she thought using animation would be better as she believed that

Figure 4.10

Stills from *Tram* (Dir. Michaela Pavlátová). ©2012 Sacrebleu Productions, Negativ Film Productions

if it was in live-action no one would want to see it. After this, the head director of Sacrebleu became interested in buying the idea."

As with many of Pavlátová's other works, music was to prove an integral part of the film. Says Pavlátová of the process behind the film's development:

> Inspiration came from them to create something about female erotic fantasies, which sounds fun, but it's not very easy to come up with a story. I came up with many ideas, but to make a story that would last five minutes was much harder. I didn't know what to do, so I turned to the music. Often for me the music is the inspiration, I'll close my eyes and listen to it in my head. I knew I wanted to create something more funny than erotic, so I was listening to some of my favorite soundtracks for inspiration, whilst listening to a particular track I got the idea for the tram and its driver.

The plump, rosy-cheeked tram conductress is an instantly lovable character who, according to the director, "is just symbolic of normal ordinary people. She isn't directly inspired by anybody but most of the tram drivers I've encountered normally seem to look the same – middle-aged women who are perhaps a little overweight – and you think to yourself what joy they could have in their minds with their fantasies."

While much of Pavlátová's prior filmography uses the hand-drawn, analogue production methods of their era, *Tram* would translate her endearing visual sensibilities to a digital pipeline, created using Adobe Flash, with textural elements brought in using After Effects.

> At first I thought that this would be quick, as there is only one character and all the men look the same. But then I realized that everything is moving and bopping, all the movements happening one after the other. Her body, for instance, is separated into different parts – her first breast, second breast, legs et cetera – and they all work off each other. It was difficult to sequence and still get that feeling of bouncing on the tram, even though it was only one woman and the same men being driven along.

The playful boil of the character's line work, along with the continuous movement of the film described above, is perfectly matched to the rhythm of the music. The relatable daily grind falls into a rhythmic pattern, reminiscent of the eb and flow of sex or masturbation. As the engine hums and a succession of indistinct businessmen board her tram, amusingly unsubtle visual symbolism is indulged as they dip their bright pink tickets into her empty slot. As the music swells, her pleasure mounts, the ticket slot reappearing between her thighs as she gleefully accepts their tickets, leading her to climax to comical effect. The design of her character is simple but playful, the vivid use of color leading the eye to connect the mundanity of her gray surroundings with the erotic imagery that springs from her own mind. The rosy flush of her cheek and the pink of her brassiere are also mimicked in a bright pink button that throbs to be pressed, and the vivid magenta that fills the screen as her sexual fantasies take over the film. The conductress's red lipstick is also later mirrored in the red "glandes" of the penis-like totems her male passengers morph into, which becomes a recurring image in her fantasies. As the beat continues, her control of her gear sticks becomes masturbatory, as she imagines them protruding from behind her passenger's newspapers; she eventually finds herself in a forest of gear stick-shaped penises, dancing joyously among them (Figure 4.11). When she eventually snaps out of her orgasmic fugue, she spots that one commuter has been watching her, evidenced by her color-theory spilling over into his. The tram empties, briefly leaving just the two kindred spirits behind before he sets off on his work day. At the end of her shift, he reappears and the two board an empty tram, ardor clearly ignited.

As an indication of its popularity within the industry, *Tram* won the Annecy Crystal for Short Film and Fipresci Award in 2012, later finding itself shortlisted for an Academy award (prompting an interactive comic book on Facebook tracking the tram conductress on her route to Los Angeles). In spite of racking up further awards and being regularly selected for festivals including such heavy-hitters as Cannes (where it premiered), Clermont-Ferrand and Sundance, amidst its generally positive reception the film would also cause a stir with some viewers.

> I started to get questions and complaints or comments about its sexuality. I was shocked as I had forgotten that it was sexual; to me, it was rhythmical and funny. In France, people are much more open to these themes, as they're all part of their culture. I have noticed the people who don't appreciate it generally are young people, especially young males or young girls between 11-20 years old because, at that point in their life, sexuality is the most important thing to them. They are somewhat unable to poke fun at it. In fact, our daughter was watching it with her friends and I was in a separate room listening in; I knew the reactions to the film, and what part they were at, but there was silence. When they were leaving the room they were all trying not to look at me. My daughter explained it was difficult for them as I seemed

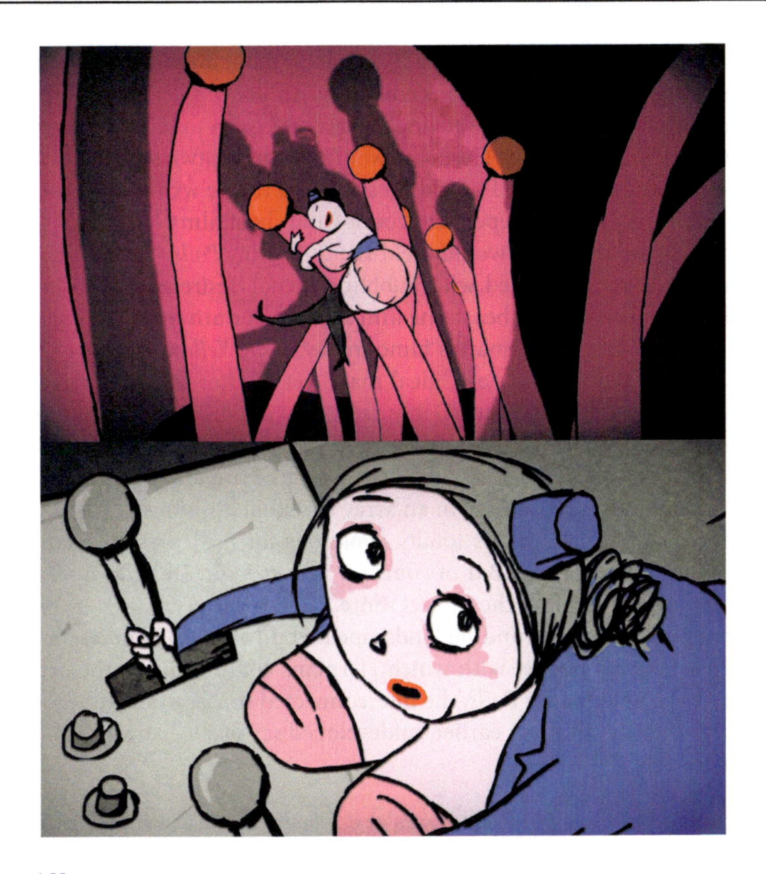

Figure 4.11

Stills from *Tram* (Dir. Michaela Pavlátová). ©2012 Sacrebleu Productions, Negativ Film Productions

> to be ridiculing something they took seriously. Of course, sometimes older people are offended, but then again sometimes the oldest people are the biggest fans.

This reaction reminds us just how evocative these themes can be for different people and age groups. Sex and sexuality are often portrayed in general media as a very important and "grown up" part of life and, generally speaking, they are. Learning about what arouses us as individuals, however, are distinctly personal journeys; as evidenced in the case studies of Chapter 2, the path to determining what is (and, crucially, what is not) acceptable to us as regards sex will not necessarily be a laughing matter before it is complete. For many others, however, the conductress and the film itself shine a joyful light on the role that the mind and fantasy plays in arousal and sexual pleasure.

Fetishism as a Way of Life

At this point, we turn our attention to the role of animation in discussing and destigmatizing fringe or otherwise alternative sexual practices that sit outside of perceived social norms. One such example can be found in the work of Belgian director Delphine Hermans, who would study for five years at La Cambre in Brussels before moving to Liège in 2006. There she would begin a working relationship with local studio Camera-etc., at which she has since remained.

Alongside opportunities to internally produce their own film projects when funding opportunities arise, the studio runs an array of creative filmmaking and animation workshops for varying age groups, open to the local community and beyond. Through these, Hermans would meet scriptwriting teacher Michel Vandam, in whom she found a kindred spirit and future writing partner on creative projects including independent comics and short films.

One such collaboration would yield the 2013 film *Poils* (*Hair*), a characterful snapshot of a city riddled with bubbling sexual desire among its populace. Though very much its own beast, the film shares a certain thematic quality with its two predecessors in Hermans's filmography – *The Yellow Envelope* (2008), in which a lonely woman buys an "ideal man" via mail order who arrives in the form of a blow-up doll (that unreliably deflates when she attempts to bring their relationship into the bedroom), and the more overtly frivolous *La vie sexuelle des dinosaures* (*Sex Life of Dinosaurs*, 2012), a parade of fun animated loops of various dinosaur species copulating in an array of sexual positions.

"I'm not sure everything is totally conscious for me," says Hermans of the throughlines in her work. "But of course it interests me. I like to find different points of views, to dig into the subject more."

Although the Belgian funding landscape is competitive, Camera-etc. eventually secured a solid budget with which Hermans could dedicate the better part of a year to production on *Poils*, the interconnected stories of the (often literally) naked city built up from an earlier, undeveloped script she had worked on some time previously.

> That script had a lot of different stories also. One of them had someone hearing a scream and being curious about it. When he looked in the windows, he could see a woman removing all of someone's hair. That was the beginning of the script for *Poils*. I had this idea that the hair could be a metaphor for desire, because hair is always growing, and then sometimes you cut everything off, and then it regrows again. So I started with this first idea of a woman taking all the hair of her lover, then tried to find other stories where the parallels between hair and desire would be central.

This binding premise would make its way into the final film, more or less as originally envisioned, presenting a dominant woman intimately plucking out the body hairs of her supplicant male companion (Figure 4.12). As hairs float out of their bedroom window, we follow them out into the city, meeting several lust-struck residents along the way.

The men among these eccentric citizens include one who appears to be collecting and cataloging found strands of hair in the hope that they will somehow cure his erectile dysfunction, as well as another who, seeing a topless sex worker exhibiting her wares in a window, fantasizes about dangling from her armpit hair and falling into a river that leads to a hirsute, cave-like vaginal opening; she rejects his interest in favor of other patrons who boast full heads of hair, while he himself is bald. The two men's stories converge when, upon spying the first man's collection, the follically challenged man swipes it to fashion a makeshift wig and thus be granted time with the object of his desires; the ruse succeeds. Meanwhile, the collector, initially panicked and bereft without his accrued hairs, attempts suicide by hanging, discovering that autoerotic asphyxiation is the cure-all for his impotence.

Elsewhere, an office worker fantasizes about the physique of the male window washer outside, setting out to seduce him. Initially not realizing he is blind, she

Figure 4.12

Still from *Poils* (Dir. Delphine Hermans). ©2013 Camera-etc

strikes a series of provocative poses to no avail (Figure 4.13). After she eventually wins his interest, the pair head out into the street, but his attention is taken by a more fragrant woman passing by. The intertwined stories that make up *Poils*, though fairly loose in their execution, are cleverly assembled together in a way that does not alienate the audience. This assemblage is attributable to the unique working relationship between Hermans and Vandam, which saw them develop ideas as they went along.

> For *Poils* we had text, but we also figured out together what the narration would be. When we agree on what will happen, Michel puts it into words and I come up with the drawings and we combine everything. So it's complicated for us to convince a

Figure 4.13

Still from *Poils* (Dir. Delphine Hermans). ©2013 Camera-etc

> film commission, because at the beginning, we don't know what the film will be! It's really being constructed piece by piece.

The overall look of the film feels very much rooted in the traditions of Belgium's strong comics scene, especially those that exhibit more of a bold, underground edge. Hermans's use of color is especially attention-grabbing, indulging an unnaturalistic palette of rich, hyper-saturated hues that give the piece a heavy and sometimes oppressive vibe. This atmosphere, which complements the notion that the characters of *Poils* are enduring a particularly hot day (a possibly culprit as to why they are all so concupiscent), is owed in part to the bold color theory seen in comics Hermans admired, chief among them Marko Turunen's *De la viande de chien au kilo.*

> I think I always have influences from the comic book world, but animation can also influence my work in comics. For *Poils*, at the beginning, the colors were not so wild. When I did the paperwork to apply for the money, the colors were more "normal." When I started animating, I had the feeling it was too flat and not intense enough.

As the film progresses, we periodically return to the hair-plucker, who throws herself into the act with increasing abandon. She conjures a fantasy scenario in which she scythes, saws and mows huge thickets of her lover's body hair (Figure 4.14), his body a sprawling terrain she is traversing to reach the final "summit" of his penis, envisioned as a grand, Mayan temple-esque structure. When he is rendered fully hairless, she appears to be satisfied, dismounting him to light a cigarette. Desperate for more intimacy, he lies on his back and forces himself to grow more body hair by sheer strength of will; she is delighted when he succeeds. While this moment functions effectively as a punchline for the film to end on, it can also be read as symbolic of something deeper.

> When you start a relationship with someone, you don't know how long it will last, and you don't know how long your desire will remain alive. That was the point of this hair coming back at the end of the film; that even with someone who you know by heart, for so many years, some surprises can come and it can restart.

Figure 4.14

Still from *Poils* (Dir. Delphine Hermans). ©2013 Camera-etc

Using the potentially taboo topic of fetishism as such a prominent theme to carry both its gags and its overall message did not do much to hinder the public enthusiasm for *Poils* (save for one instance Hermans recalls of it being denied a screening in Morocco), with Annecy, Fantoche and GLAS among the 50+ events it would screen at. Certainly, the strength of its comedy beats does a great deal to put potentially guarded audiences at ease, perhaps even bringing them around to the idea of learning more about the subject. Other films that help bridge this gap include Dario van Vree's *Tabook* (2016),[16] in which a young woman peruses a selection of adult literature while fending off the judgmental glares of the bookstore's other customers, eventually working through her feelings of embarrassment and sauntering out with a book on bondage. *Symbiosis* (Dir. Nadja Andrasev, 2019) and *Toomas Beneath the Valley of the Wild Wolves* (Dir. Chintis Lundgren/ Draško Ivezić, 2018), both discussed in Chapter 5, incorporate story elements in which women, neglected in their primary relationships, are introduced to aspects of the BDSM scene that appeal to their curiosity. The aesthetics of sexual kinks and fetishes, while undoubtedly being fun to draw, also have comedic potential (in the laughing-with sense), such as in Kilian Feusi, Jessica Meier and Sujanth Ravichandran's *Pipes* (2023) that sees an ursine plumber amusingly out of his depth when called to do maintenance work on a busy night at a gay fetish club.

Looking back to some years prior, we find Matt Oxborrow's *The Banjo String* (2011),[17] which interprets a conversation about an intimate personal injury as an exchange between a dominatrix and her client (Figure 4.15). Created at the now-defunct London studio 12foot6, Oxborrow now works more as an art director and designer on well-known IPs such as *Headspace* and *Teach Your Monster*, which retains some of the slick, shape-based design found in *The Banjo String*, albeit with more color. The film was part of a series of shorts called *Get Well Soon*, based on recorded conversations with people about their real illnesses and injuries. Artists at the studio were given pieces of audio, recorded by Lucy Izzard, who also took on the role of interviewer. Oxborrow reminisces:

> We recorded them all as sort of *ad hoc* recordings in the back room of this pub. I latched on to that one in particular because it was a funny story and had a lot of comedy value. I just kind of listened to the audio. Almost trying to negate the fact that I knew Lucy, look at it blindly and picture these two characters in a sex dungeon somewhere.

The interviewee, a friend of another animator at the studio, volunteered his story: "I was very lucky to get a funny – and grim – one; some people wince and some people laugh when they see it."

Within the film, the submissive client recounts how a sex injury he sustained with his partner, now wife, led to him snapping his frenulum, colloquially known as a "banjo string" (setting up a wryly comedic banjo solo that accompanies the end credits). From the recording, Oxborrow created a list of sections he found interesting or funny and would "elicit a reaction," after repeatedly listening to the piece he was able to uncover the beats of the film.

> It wrote itself really, once I decided that it was taking place in a dungeon. Lucy had this very authoritarian interview style and was very good at sort of drawing this stuff out with people. I knew her quite well, so I just thought *Right, I'm doing you as a dominatrix, this guy's gonna be chained up from his legs*. That was a big decision. Then I think the only sound effects we added were the crack of the paddle and the winch going up.

Figure 4.15

Stills from *Get Well Soon: The Banjo String* (Dir. Matt Oxborrow). ©2011 12foot6 / Matt Oxborrow. Image courtesy of Matt Oxborrow

The setting required some research on the director's behalf, as Oxborrow explains:

> You just go down a rabbit hole on the web and it's quite weird, sitting in a studio, people around you, researching BDSM outfits and gimp masks and stuff. But I think that's literally what I did. I looked at sites for what sort of equipment was for sale, whatever BDSM sites were *kind of* safe for work at the time. I didn't go too deep, I just had this vision of leather, and rubber, and it had to be in a weird brick dungeon somewhere. I didn't visit any BDSM dungeons – I probably wasn't given the budget to do that!

From this point, Oxborrow's love for character design took over, resulting in multiple iterations of the characters, particularly that of Lucy's, the brilliantly named Polly Vinyl (Figure 4.16). As well as being selected for festivals, the short would go on to be screened on Channel 4 in the United Kingdom; Oxborrow recollects people calling him to say "I've just seen your name on that really weird film on Channel 4" and that it was well received by those who saw it. Although his work is now far more family-oriented, Oxborrow remains proud of the film.

> It's one of those things that I've done that has endured longer than a lot of my other work. I'm glad that people still like it and want to talk about it...but I wouldn't necessarily put it up alongside my more family-friendly work.

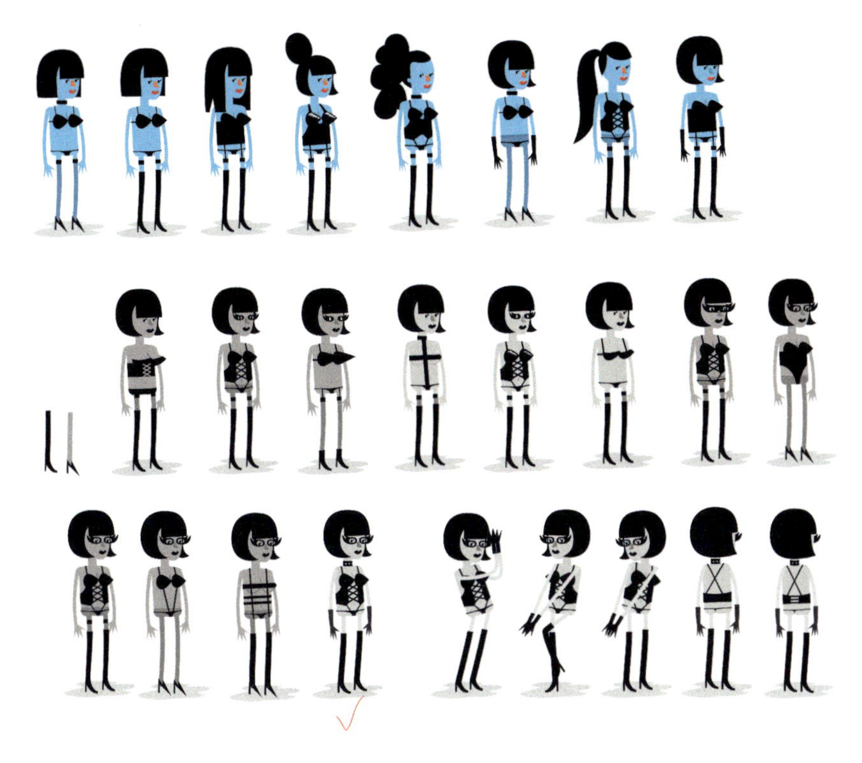

Figure 4.16

Get Well Soon: The Banjo String character design sheet by Matt Oxborrow. ©Image courtesy of Matt Oxborrow

This speaks to the United Kingdom's national tradition of comedic and esoteric animation being, if not at odds, amusingly juxtaposed against its history of producing beloved children's media, and the inevitably of overlap among some of the industry's talents. Lucy Izzard, who lent her voice and interview skills to *The Banjo String*, is now perhaps best known as the creator and series director for Aardman's *Morph* preschool spin-off series *The Very Small Creatures* (2021). Other fêted children's creators of note whose earlier work proved a touch more risqué include *Hey Duggee* (2014) creator Grant Orchard (director of the sexually suggestive mograph onedotzero piece *Yeah Just There* in 2012) and Bob Godfrey who, some years after the ribald works discussed in the Introduction, would become known for a number of children's series including *Roobarb* (1974) and *Henry's Cat* (1983–1993).

The exploration of a fetish, when you can truly let loose and freely explore yourself and your desires, can be a truly gratifying and self-actualizing endeavor. As seen in *The Wrong End of the Stick* (Chapter 2), it can also have a direct and not-always-positive impact on your romantic life. In an ideal world, of course, our lovers accept us for who we are, perhaps even able to share in our kinks. In Tobias Rud's self-initiated film, *I'll Be Your Kettle* (2021), we witness a story of love, struggle, sadness and, for one character at least, the need to let go. The film follows a young woman who tries to compete with her partner's ever-growing interest in household objects and her desire to maintain his attention. On the surface, this is a film about objectum sexuality (the sexual or romantic attraction to inanimate objects), but in reality, it is a far more relatable story about loving someone who is unable to love you back. For Rud, this central theme of the film

Figure 4.17

Still from *I'll Be Your Kettle* (Dir. Tobias Rud). ©2021 Tobias Rud. Image courtesy of Tobias Rud

was something he had also experienced himself; while not based on any one specific relationship, the film looks at "the extreme of how messy this whole thing called love and relationships is" and "the frustration of why it's so damn hard for two people to just love each other."

I'll Be Your Kettle combines composited, digital frame-by-frame 2D animation with live-action shooting and cardboard sets (Figure 4.17). This decision was partially owed to Rud wanting time away from the computer during production, as he was also working full-time as an animator in the industry. It was also to create an aesthetic that lent further credence to the object-centered focus of the characters.

"I generally find myself attracted to lo-fi, DIY looking animation," explains Rud. "Animation as a medium has this great potential of being and feeling truly personal. When I watch something that is clearly the creation of one human, I feel very connected to it."

This DIY approach was also used in the recording of the characters' voices, for which Rud would have friend Courtney Louise record herself on her phone under a blanket, making the sounds of an "emotionally broken washing machine" as well as others. The lo-fi feel of the film also adds further intimacy to the world of these two characters. The male character at the center of the film initially finds himself, as the title denotes, aroused by a kettle. As it boils, his pupils dilate, he bites his lip and sweats profusely before abruptly climaxing. His euphoria is short-lived as he quickly realizes he is being watched by his girlfriend, standing in the doorway to their kitchen. Overcome with fear and shame, he hides away.

Initially unsure of how to proceed, his girlfriend assumes that his new, unusual desire has more to do with her than him. She disposes of the kettle before donning a saucepan as a hat and gargling water atop their kitchen counter in the hope of meeting his needs. Her willingness to participate initially brings them closer together, but as his eye wanders to other house items (including a fan, broom, windscreen wiper, hoover, washing machine, alarm, lamp, car, chair, bicycle, clock, basketball and hat among others), she systematically removes each item from the house so that she might take their place (Figure 4.18), often twisting herself into ludicrous positions and behaviors. In the end, their home – and

Figure 4.18

Still from *I'll Be Your Kettle* (Dir. Tobias Rud). ©2021 Tobias Rud. Image courtesy of Tobias Rud

their relationship – are stripped bare, the girlfriend reduced to tears as she imitates some Frankenstein-esque, indeterminable combination of objects. As his eye once again wanders, this time to a lone paperclip, it dawns on her that nothing she will do will ever be enough.

After resigning herself to the mounting pile of items outside that symbolically represents their discarded life together, she ultimately finds freedom, alone on the trash collection truck, as she leaves their home – and him – behind (Figure 4.19).

The initial inspiration behind *I'll Be Your Kettle* came from Rud's interest in capturing a love story between someone and something incapable of romantic feeling, as well as the obsessive nature of falling in love.

> There are a few other stories with similar themes, but I never really felt like they fully got to the core of what my fascination was. I remember watching Don Hertzfeldt's *World of Tomorrow*, where a character briefly falls in love with a rock. It's such an

Figure 4.19

Still from *I'll Be Your Kettle* (Dir. Tobias Rud). ©2021 Tobias Rud. Image courtesy of Tobias Rud

> insignificant anecdote in the film, and it never really gets into that "relationship," but I kinda wished that it would have.

Rud's film started by exploring what would happen if such a relationship was followed further. Although objectum sexuality is a real thing, the film itself was not intended to comment or pass any judgment on the proclivity specifically (although some research was done on the subject); for Rud, this was far more of a playful love story with symbolism, rather than a true depiction of the phenomena of object-sexuality. Ultimately, the story would go on to focus far more on the female partner than the male character's relationship with these objects, as Rud explains:

> I realized that if the female character actively tried to keep her partner engaged, that would open up a whole other level of story and character arcs for her. She became the most interesting character in the process and the one with the strongest "plot," and I think it ultimately made a better film focusing on her desperate journey of molding herself to fit his desires. That desperate need to feel loved and wanted, to the point of being willing to lose yourself completely, was a strong theme that started showing itself, once I focused more on her.

Despite this, the male character's struggle remains very much part of the story, as seen in the penultimate shot of the film, where we see him alone with his paperclip, looking rejected.

> I have been both of these characters, but I mostly identify with the guy in the film. The one who struggles to feel stable and at ease with someone. The first draft was much more about his relationship with the kettle and the inner chaos of losing feelings, then finding them again in places where they shouldn't be; the story of a character's emotional instability hurting those close to him.

On one level, the male character's inability to see the harm he is causing seems cruel, though in reality, he too is struggling to identify in himself who and what he wants.

> I think the guy is as much, if not more, a victim of his own instability as we see in the end. She is finally able to free herself, but he will never find whatever it is that he needs to be satisfied.

Ultimately, the film focuses far more on the feelings and reactions of its female character. Throughout the film, we see her bend herself to better suit his wants, and through her story we are asked

> How much we are willing to compromise ourselves in order to live up to others' expectations of us – especially in the context of relationships. She tries so desperately to keep up with his desires that, by the end of it, she has completely lost herself and has become this nonsensical mix of objects without function. So her journey is one of letting go, and ultimately finding her way back to some core part of what she is. That's also why I wanted her to shed herself of all her exteriors and be naked in the last shot.

Rud also maintains that she is not completely innocent in the breakdown of the relationship, although

> It's mostly him being the issue. She doesn't manage to show any attempt at understanding or trying to embrace his unusual desires, and who knows what could have happened if she hadn't gone to war with the objects in this way because of jealousy.

From the start, the female character seems threatened by these objects, as seen in an early scene that takes place on a subway platform in which she holds her flat breasts aloft while looking at an amorous couple and an advertisement for kitchenware (Tobias Rud, 2021, 02:13). Her inability to let him explore these feelings uninterrupted leads her to try and replace them, potentially seeing his fascination as a form of infidelity, but as Rud explains,

> I think the guy deep down really wants to love her and hopes that every new attempt she makes will finally be the right one. He isn't deliberately cruel, but I think we can agree he isn't a good partner. Better she join the trash party than stay with him.

While fetishistic inclinations often push boundaries and entice us out of our comfort zones, the places they can take us are sometimes dark and troubling. Yet in darkness, there is the potential to learn more about ourselves than we might otherwise have been able to. Certainly dipping our toes in uncertain waters can help us establish boundaries and determine what lines we absolutely will not cross. In the case of filmmaker Shoko Hara, curiosity took her to an unexpected place as both a woman and an artist when she read Philip Carlo's *The Nightstalker* and developed an interest in convicted serial killer Richard Ramirez. More specifically, it was a fascination with the allure he seemed to possess in spite of his monstrous acts that earned him so many female admirers. To learn more about this seeming incongruity of common sense versus attraction, Hara sought out Eva O (of the deathrock bands Christian Death and Shadow Project), Ramirez's first post-infamy girlfriend, as well as being encouraged to contact Ramirez himself by Sarah, a personal associate the director had known since the age of 15. Hara recalls,

> He had this aura, or this energy. It felt more like contacting a celebrity, because he really looked like a rock star and had this evil soul. Additionally, Sarah is sexually submissive, so she wanted to have someone who tells her what to do and controls her. She didn't buy that kind of role play with normal guys, so she chose Richard Ramirez to get that real thrill.

Having been drafted in by Sarah (Figure 4.20), a self-described "death row inmate supporter," to take photos with her "because she knew that he had a fetish for feet and Asian girls," Hara indulged the morbid whim of printing them out and sending them, unexpectedly receiving a reply back, but ultimately choosing not to carry on an epistolary relationship.

> Richard Ramirez sent the letter first to Sarah and she gave it to me. Sarah pushed me to respond, but I was too scared because that would mean that he had my real address and I thought he might know someone else outside who could kidnap me, or something like that. I also had a boyfriend at the time. He called me sick when I told him about it. He said he didn't want to be with someone who was in touch with a serial killer. So I didn't write to him.

Instead Hara channeled her curiosities into a stop-motion short film documentary project, *Just a Guy* (a term Ramirez had once referred to himself as when interviewed) that endeavors to examine the man's inscrutable appeal. Though a compelling and fascinating work, whose end result performed very strongly throughout the world, the reality of laying down the groundwork and truly

Figure 4.20

Still from *Just a Guy* (Dir. Shoko Hara). ©2020 Studio Seufz. Image courtesy of Shoko Hara

getting into the weeds of who precisely Ramirez was – and what he was capable of – proved emotionally draining.

> It was really hard to deal with that. During the research, pre-production, I switched between the two sides, the victims and the murderer. I considered the research from both directions. I am compassionate to the relatives of the victims, of course, but I also do understand the women who stand behind the murderer, somehow. So, it was really important to me to not glorify Richard Ramirez and to show the women as authentically as possible, without any judgment. This film is about the women who fall in love with serial killers, and not about the crime or the murderers themselves.

What mainly set Hara herself apart from these women was a basic lack of physical attraction due to their age difference, as well as being fairly nonplussed with a seeming dearth of intellect or charisma on Ramirez's part.

> When I decided to make a film about it, I researched a lot. I watched a lot of documentaries and read a lot about him. I also tried to contact his niece and his other girlfriends, but I really got to know him through the many original letters Eva brought from California to Germany when I interviewed her, and I figured out that he wasn't as smart as he looked, he was not well educated, which was also a turn-off for me. Actually, he was a poor, lonely guy with almost normal feelings. He cried, for example, when Eva left or when he missed her, but when it came to his crimes he didn't have any regrets or compassion. So I tried to show those sides of him in my film, too.

Indeed, the childish qualities to his writings are seen onscreen in the letters themselves. From the glimpsed petty jealousies and malapropisms, Ramirez cuts an oddly pathetic, emotionally stunted figure. In spite of not falling under the same spell as others had, including herself in the story was an important part of the process for the director.

> I wanted to include myself in the film to create a dialogue; I didn't want to say all these women are crazy, I wanted to show the different intentions for contacting a

serial killer. For Eva, it was real love. For Sarah, it was more for her sexual benefit and for me, it was more out of curiosity and naivety. So, before people put a label on these women who contacted him, we have to differentiate their intentions. Before I started to make the film I was already open to and interested in unconventional relationships, or sexuality, but since I interviewed the women I got more into the psychology and understood even better why specific women feel attracted to murderers. I also understood that every woman has their individual and comprehensible reason why they felt attracted to murderers, and you cannot lump them together.

One interesting moment in the film references Hara's attempts to include a woman known only as "Doreen," who had taken the step of marrying Ramirez while he was incarcerated. With one of the original plans for the film to be more focused on this particular relationship, the hiring of a private investigator and attempts to contact relatives all led to dead-ends, and in the film, we briefly glimpse a message from "Doreen" appealing to no longer be contacted.

I think she doesn't want to have anything to do with this topic because there was a big shitstorm in the past and she lost family and friends because of it. She grew up in a very Catholic family and she's living somewhere anonymously now, perhaps even a lonely life somewhere with a new face. I wanted to give her the opportunity to share her own story and view without any judgment, but she didn't want to, and I had to accept that.

The assemblage of the film is, appropriately enough, a brutal and sometimes messy combination of archival materials (a labor in and of itself for producer Stefan Michel as far as securing the licenses for everything they wanted to use), abstract/experimental clay animation helmed by Valentin Kemmner and inspired, in part, by the collage work of David Lynch, as well as articulated puppets representing Sarah, Eva O and Hara, each designed on their real-life counterparts, thanks to the masterful fabrication of Eliott Deshusses (Figure 4.21).

Figure 4.21

Just a Guy (Dir. Shoko Hara) Title Graphic. ©2020 Studio Seufz. Image courtesy of Shoko Hara

The trio's animated representatives stand out as being more naturalistic in their design and performance, a quality reflective of their present-day humanity.

> The sequences are visualizations of the present, so the women share the view of the relationship with Richard Ramirez from today's point of view. The thoughts are more clear and reflective when talking about memories of the past, so I decided to show the women also as clear and realistic puppets. Also, these sequences have been animated in 24 frames per second instead of 12, as with the other sequences, when it's about the past and memories. I thought it was also important and interesting to show what they looked like for the audience, to show what kind of woman they were. Because of that I decided to design them as lookalikes, or as realistic as possible. They also have their original eyes tracked onto their puppet faces, and I think eyes are really important, to express emotions.

The process of compositing live-action footage of eyes onto a puppet's head gives the characters an uncanny edge that fits in well with the discomfiting nature of the piece. Another contributor to the naturalism of their performances was their being animated to live-action reference footage Hara shot of herself, miming to the audio recordings that would be used in each of their shots. Other characters that appear in the film include clay depictions of Ramirez himself, a suitably grotesque, demonic manifestation of the evil he represents, prone to bursts of anger and sexual aggression. Also among the clay menagerie of background characters are a group of unnerving, spider-like creatures comprised entirely of limbs (Figure 4.22).

> They represent the groupies of Richard Ramirez. Since he had a fetish for feet with painted toenails, I made them out of limbs with red painted toenails. I assumed he didn't care about the personality or faces or bodies of the groupies, so I thought faces or bodies were not necessary to show. And groupies were like spiders, they literally wanted to own Richard Ramirez and be the special one for him as well, so I created them like spiders.

While the experimental approaches with the visuals help wedge a bit of comfortable distance between the viewer and the grim reality of the film's subject, Hara never shies away from opportunities to incorporate explicit imagery, such as Ramirez's wielding of an oversized penis in impotent rage, or grimly ejaculating on the photos he is sent. While some of the film's more overtly extreme

Figure 4.22

Still from *Just a Guy* (Dir. Shoko Hara). ©2020 Studio Seufz. Image courtesy of Shoko Hara

moments actually proved enjoyable to create, others rooted less in abstraction and more in real-life materials would take more of a toll.

> I've seen so many explicit films and not many can shock me so easily, but dealing with the original drawings and letters by Richard Ramirez was more challenging and disturbing for me, I think because I knew that they were "real" real and original, by Richard Ramirez.
>
> We got a few critics, especially from people who felt very disturbed by the topic in combination with these explicit and ugly and weird visuals. And some misunderstood the film as a glorification of Richard Ramirez, which I don't understand, to be honest, because we didn't give him any platform. The film is actually about the women and not about himself. We were also criticized by his groupies – they found it very disrespectful to "make money" with letters from a dead person without any permission; they can relax, because we didn't make money! And in the end some of them reported our Instagram account, so it got banned because of this explicit content.

Although the notion of supporting someone as objectively evil as Ramirez while still maintaining a moral high ground holds some fascination of its own from a psychological perspective, the film's detractors fall by the wayside when evaluating its overall success. Among its many international festival screenings were official selections at Annecy, ITFS Stuttgart and Ottawa, and it would win major awards at Animafest Zagreb and the Krakow Film Festival. Most importantly, it prompted conversations and discourse from its audiences.

> I was really glad to receive so much positive feedback, because I was really worried about it. I think there was a huge true crime hype when the film was released, back then, but *Just a Guy* stood out because it was told from another perspective, which was really rare in this genre. Some people also told us that they can relate to Eva and even liked her, and seeing the original letters by Richard Ramirez is both creepy and fascinating at the same time, I guess.

Going Solo

Our relationship with masturbation, and the role it plays as we become increasingly realized sexual beings, is imbued with immeasurable, complex importance and associations – perhaps disproportionately so, given the mechanical simplicity of the act. Simply providing our own physical and emotional pleasure for the sake of growth and developing a sense of comfort in our own skin remains a curiously taboo subject across the globe. It can be powerful, but it need not be threatening, and film is as good a medium as any to instigate conversations about it. Animation has been particularly successful in demystifying masturbation, stripping it of shame and normalizing it.

This concept is demonstrated with skill and humor in animator and cartoonist Renata Gąsiorowska's 2016 tribute to female masturbation. Hailing from Kraków, it was during her studies at The Leon Schiller Polish National Film, Television and Theatre School in Łódź that her fourth-year project (of a five-year course), *Cipka* (*Pussy*) would be made (Figure 4.23).

> I wanted to make a film about sexuality or sex, basically an erotic movie, and I thought if it was about masturbation then I would only have to animate one person! I thought I was very smart, although it ended up being two characters, even three characters at one point. It turned out that actually masturbation was a much more interesting idea.

Figure 4.23

Still from *Cipka* (Dir. Renata Gąsiorowska). ©2016 PWSFTviT. Image courtesy of Renata Gąsiorowska

While brainstorming and sketching out ideas, she would come up with a doodled character of a mischievous, disembodied vulva, seeing potential for a film to be built around it. Encouraged by her professors to lean into the explicit absurdity of the concept, another primary inspiration for the film came from the culture of sex and body positivity that had become more prevalent in the types of media Gąsiorowska consumed.

> I knew Signe Baumane's movies, of course. This kind of freedom with talking about sex and sexuality seemed really cool and refreshing to me – and of course, she uses her voice, so it has another layer of humor. But I think I was more inspired by general body positivity and sex positivity themes that were coming into mainstream discussion. Suddenly I found myself reading blogs for women about sex positivity, and they were often talking about masturbation in a way that was a little bit like self-help. I don't want to be mean, because I think it was very cool, but I thought the way they were talking about reclaiming your sexuality – "have a masturbation session," "have a good time with yourself," "light a candle," "treat it like a date with yourself" – had comedy potential.

The film sees a young woman's attempt at one such solo "date night" continually disrupted; slipping underwater while attempting to pleasure herself, stoned, in the bath; other locations prove equally unsuccessful, seeing her bombarded with aural distractions such as ringing telephones and outside traffic noise. The endearingly playful visuals of the film are, for the most part, suggestive of its sketchbook origins, with a scratchy black-and-white line style (one that proved tricky to make look suitably rough using Toon Boom's naturally smooth brush strokes) and loose models for its characters, against similarly minimalistic, red and blue felt-tip rendered backdrops.

> I wanted the characters to be as expressive as I could make them, and have these boiling lines with everything moving all the time. I knew [making the film] would be a lot of work, so I decided to use minimal color and I didn't want backgrounds

> to distract from the characters. I was actually inspired by the Ikea brochure, where everything is simplified. I thought *Okay, I can do something like this very bare bones background, just to ground her in an apartment that has some kind of topology and some plan to it, but it's just gonna be blue and red, with straight lines, very minimalistic.*

While Gąsiorowska (and coanimator Agnieszka Borowa) err on the side of simplicity for much of the film, a lot is demonstrated in terms of attention to detail and comedic interplay between sound (handled by Ewa Bogusz and Wiesław Nowak) and visual gags. One notable scene perfectly depicts the protagonist's struggle to get purchase when trying to watch herself masturbate while perched on a sliding office chair in front of a wall mirror. Her battle with kinetic friction drives her to despair until she gives up, defeated, the pattern of the seat mesh visibly indented in her bare buttocks. When she is finally able to achieve some level of peace and comfort while touching herself on the sofa, the film takes a turn for the surreal as her genitals come alive, sprout limbs and scamper away.[18]

The anthropomorphized vulva (Figure 4.24) is similar in concept and execution to Lori Malépart-Traversy's characterization of the titular Clitoris from *Le Clitoris* (discussed in Chapter 1), another breakout student film that was being produced at the same time. In a noteworthy instance of parallel thinking (the directors would become friends on the festival circuit, but did not know one another at the time their films were being made), both films use charmingly *faux naïf* animation and comics/illustration-inspired design to present female anatomy as mischievous, cute and inquisitive, like something approximating a beloved pet.

> The Pussy character just appeared in one of my sketches suddenly, as a random idea, and I thought *Okay, let's do something with that.* I brought the idea to school and I was really lucky that my professors liked it and encouraged me to be even more explicit if I wanted. I thought *What if her vulva just detaches, grows legs and goes around rubbing itself on different items in the house? Maybe then she can fall on the cacti, or get stuck somewhere or pour ice cubes on herself, or whatever.* It was really funny because [Lori] made *Le Clitoris* in exactly the same period as I made *Cipka*, on

Figure 4.24

Still from *Cipka* (Dir. Renata Gąsiorowska). ©2016 PWSFTviT. Image courtesy of Renata Gąsiorowska

> the other side of the world. Of course her film is different, it's more like a documentary, but the Clitoris character is a similar concept. It was just something in the air!

Another shared trait of the Pussy of *Cipka* and the Clitoris of *Le Clitoris* is a certain autonomy within themselves. In the first half of the film, the woman's futile search for sexual release is observed by a voyeuristic raccoon neighbor from across the street, who scurries over to her apartment building only to be scared away by her Pussy, who has slid under her front door into the hallway, where it transforms into a large, menacing creature that frightens her stalker away. The scene evokes a similar moment in *Le Clitoris*, in which the usually friendly organ bares its teeth menacingly at the prodding finger of its arch-nemesis Sigmund Freud, himself intent on bringing about "a wave of clitoral obscurantism" through his ignorance of the specifics of female pleasure. In *Cipka*, the Pussy acts as its owner's protector, like a guard dog warding off a potential attacker, its toothy transformation intended as a nod to the myth of vagina dentata and the fear it instills in men. While it is a moment that nods toward a certain real-life threat element, the scene plays out with the same playful absurdity as demonstrated throughout the film.

> At the very beginning of my concept work, I thought there would maybe be a sequence where her boyfriend is leaving for some job trip, but then we decided that we didn't need that, she could just be alone in the flat for whatever reason. But then I thought I could do something to represent the "pervy" male gaze. The film is very light and cutesy, so I didn't want it to be too creepy or too serious, so I made him into this raccoon character, munching on a sandwich with this ridiculous telescope, so he's funny – but it's still creepy, he's still violating her privacy. It was very interesting to notice how different audiences reacted – sometimes the whole cinema would laugh their ass off during this scene, and sometimes there was dead silence. Super serious. It was always really interesting to see such wildly different reactions. Then he was also there as an excuse for the pussy character to get all big and scary and show teeth.

Having fended off any potential intrusion, the Pussy shrinks back to its original form, returns to the apartment where its owner, at first wary, starts to pet it (Figure 4.25). When she briefly stops, the Pussy gambols around the room, indulging in all the sensations it can find from its surroundings by rubbing itself against a variety of objects with different textures. Although woman and Pussy are separated, she is able to feel its pleasure, the ensuing montage boasting more precision-honed comedy beats as we cut back and forth between her sensual writhings and the Pussy's frottage experiments against her various furnishings, accessories and *objets d'art*. Inevitably, the sequence culminates in a depiction of orgasm that marks a significant style shift in the film's presentation; we leave behind the loose, minimal design and neutral color palette to enter an abstract, experimental fugue of colorful textures, overlaid film processes and swirling inks and paints. While the film prior takes more influence from the aforementioned Signe Baumane and, on a semi-conscious level, artists such as Polish painter Maja Berezowska, Japanese comics artist Kyoko Okazaki and French illustrator duo Mrzyk & Moriceau, *Cipka*'s orgasm sequence draws more from the vanguards of experimental film and animation, chiefly Norman McLaren.

> I didn't want to be literal in that moment. I guess it's something else, experiencing pleasure like this, so I decided to just finish with this completely abstract scene. Of course, I didn't do it on film, it was all done on a computer. It would have been

Figure 4.25

Still from *Cipka* (Dir. Renata Gąsiorowska). ©2016 PWSFTviT. Image courtesy of Renata Gąsiorowska

> much more lavish and amazing if I had more time and money. So I did it as best as I could with what I had.

Certainly it works well as an effective juxtaposition against what had come before, while addressing the same intangibility of the nature of orgasm as explored in Ruth Lingford's *Little Deaths*. As we return to the living room scene, woman and Pussy are reunited, finally satisfied.

To say *Cipka* was a hit would be a massive understatement; over 240 international festivals would include it in their programs between 2016 and 2019 alone, with awards rolling in from Clermont-Ferrand International Short Film Festival, DOK Leipzig, AFI FEST, Filmfest Dresden, Animafest Zagreb and International Animated Film Festival Animator, among others.

> It's one thing to have someone write you a comment on the internet and something else for someone to actually come to you in person after a screening and say what they thought about it. It's definitely a confidence boost!

Another project that delves further into the subject of masturbation from a wide variety of perspectives is 2022's *Caresses magiques* (*Magical Caresses*), a five-film series of animated documentaries for the National Film Board of Canada directed by Lori Malépart-Traversy that humorously present a range of testimonials and historical facts to illuminate the subject of female sexuality and masturbation.

Beginning in the Fall of 2016 as part of a writing residency at Montreal's Cinémathèque québécoise film conservatory under the mentorship of Academy Award-winning[19] director Torill Kove in Montreal, Malépart-Traversy was steered toward bringing *Caresses magiques* to the NFB as her first professional film project. Following a successful meeting with then-producer Julie Roy (later appointed Executive Director of Telefilm Canada), development of the project started in 2017. It quickly grew from a conceived standalone film to a multipart series based on four accounts from Sarah Gagnon-Piché and Sara

Hébert's *Caresses magiques* independent book series, initially a website that grouped together anonymous stories from French-Canadian women about their experiences of – and relationship with – masturbation. As Malépart-Traversy recalls:

> I just wanted to use some of the stories, but I didn't know how, or which ones. I tried to see if I could fit all of those stories into one, but it felt more natural to just divide them into different short films.

Rather than lifting the text from the books verbatim, Malépart-Traversy elected to focus in on elements of each story that had explicit potential for an animated adaptation, conducting new interviews with the original contributors so that their accounts could be more clearly visualized.

> I'd pinpoint some stuff that I liked – for example, one of my shorts is about a little girl who liked to think about a fish when she masturbated when she was young. So I just asked more questions about that, like "Can you tell me more about the fish?" "What did it look like?" "What did the other fishes look like?" so I could have more details than there were in the story. But for people who have access to those books, it's still interesting to compare, because there's some stuff I didn't put in my film that could be interesting to read. When I interviewed them, they were very open to come to my place, sit on my couch and talk to me about masturbation, considering they were all people I never knew before.
>
> The voices that we hear in the shorts are the real voices of the authors of the texts. I interviewed them based on their texts and asked them to speak in their own words, or to go deeper into some of the subjects that I liked. I wanted to make sure that they were comfortable with it, because it's their voice. There was only one of them who wanted to have her voice modified. It's really subtle, and I don't think we can even tell. But the others were fine with just having their first name, and their real voice, but no last name.

This process would ultimately yield four uniquely distinct accounts of the role masturbation played in each of the participants' lives. In *Turquoise Fish*, "Charlotte" recounts how her ability to achieve orgasm began in early childhood, with her earliest memory of the experience of masturbation going back to the age of three when she would straddle her bunched-up duvet and conjure the image of a turquoise fish. This fantasy would ultimately extend to an aquatic world, populated with other aquamarine life, until she reached an older age where the importance of the imagined visuals was replaced with the physical sensation itself, and the inclination to experiment with different surfaces, textures and household objects. As an adult, she credits this openness in her formative years as being an important contributor to being comfortable with her body and sex life as an adult, something she concedes isn't the norm when comparing herself to other women who have grown up more inhibited. Among the accounts provided, this opening episode proved one of the easiest to translate to animation while helping set up the overall style and tone of the series.

> *Turquoise Fish* was so visual already, the story was about different types of fish that all related to something sensual, but for a kid it was something I had never heard about before. So it was really the first one that gave me the idea that I could do something interesting visually with this. After that, the others were a bit harder to find what would be interesting visually.

The other films delve into trickier and more psychologically complex subject matter, such as *Big Bang* that sees 23-year-old "Laurence" – who had previously written off the concept of the female orgasm as a myth – decide to take charge and overcome her issues. Identifying that the primary inhibitors to her self-satisfaction are an overall lack of arousal throughout her young adulthood, the lack of direct conversation and instruction regarding female self-pleasure (relative to the common knowledge of the mechanics of male masturbation) and the textural quality of her genitals that she likens to raw meat, she perseveres, bolstered by a sense of "feminist obligation." Ultimately, she determines that she suffers from vaginismus, an involuntary tightening of the vaginal muscles that makes penetration and any inherent pleasure from it near impossible. With the aid of a sex therapist, she is finally able to achieve orgasm through a combination of sex toys (crucially the external stimulation of a Hitachi wand), a breakthrough that opens the floodgates to a sexual awakening and an ability to be intimate with others as well as herself. She concludes: "Masturbation changed my life!"

Other areas covered include the role religion plays in our attitude toward masturbation and its potential to cultivate ambivalence about the subject. In a story both reminiscent of Andreas Hykade's *Altötting* and Signe Baumane's *Teat Beat of Sex* episode *Trouble* (both discussed in Chapter 2), *Sweet Jesus* tells the story of "Sarah" who, coming from a relatively devout Catholic background, develops a relationship with Jesus to that of an imaginary best friend and confidante with whom she can share her secrets. Her standard evening prayers extend to conversations about boys from school she feels attraction toward, culminating in frottage with a stuffed rabbit. She is able to continue this relationship with her body without any shame, until being reprimanded for doing so in the communal setting of scout camp, from which point an enormous sense of guilt at being judged by Jesus takes hold. Forcing herself to stop masturbating and instead focus on being virtuous, with adolescence comes a new development in which a "hot Jesus" becomes the focus of her fantasies alongside the reemergence of her libido; ultimately, these fantasies inform her taste in men as she gets older. In spite of eventually embracing masturbation as a positive force in her life, "Sarah" admits that, even as an adult, the imbued feelings of shame and fear of negative consequences have never fully left her.

While some of these accounts have traces of sadness and mixed emotion, Malépart-Traversy does an admirably consistent job of keeping the tone light; in a manner similar to Diane Obomsawin's approach with her own anthology of sexual awakening *J'aime les filles* (Chapter 2), there are no curveballs or arbitrary attempts to shock the audience; masturbation is presented as a wholly normal, positive aspect of life, though the more conservative attitudes of others to the contrary are not hidden away either. This is best exemplified in the final testimonials *Playhouse* where, as someone for whom viewing pornography plays a vital role in masturbation, "Roxane" dissects the aspects of it that appeal to her as well as those that come under scrutiny, such as the disparity between the realities of lesbian sexual intercourse and the fantasy version that porn perpetuates. In contrast, male-on-male porn, by virtue of being distanced from her own lived experience, is a far more effective and gratifying proposition. In particular, "Roxane" cites the use of language, especially relating to BDSM scenarios, being the more significant turn-on than the visuals themselves.

> I think *Playhouse* was the trickiest, because it was the one where the descriptions were the most graphic and I was wondering how far I could go with that. Being at

the NFB, I was thinking *Is there a limit?* In the end, because the narration was quite graphic, the visuals didn't have to be; I could do something more like an interpretation, a bit light or humorous, because there was already this description that the people would have in their heads. I didn't need to represent that.

Other areas that prove effective to "Roxane," as someone more inclined toward monogamy in real life, are fantasy scenarios involving first encounters and the thrill of sex with a new partner, as well as receiving anal sex and owning a penis (neither prospect holding any appeal in her real life). She concludes that the functionality of these fantasies is purely to assist the achievement of orgasm through the cleansing act of masturbation, and their effectiveness comes from just how far removed they are from her real-life sexual wants.

A large contributor to the consistency of the series is owed to the harmonious relationship between Malépart-Traversy and fellow animator Keyu Chen, who replicates the director's established style seamlessly, in spite of being separated for much of the production due to pandemic lockdowns. A positive outcome of the project's sometimes-overwhelming nature (being essentially five films in one) came in the form of the director alighting upon the idea of bringing in her mother, illustrator Céline Malépart, to assist on the film's backgrounds that, by virtue of being created with ink and watercolors against digital character animation created in TV Paint, proved a vital contributor to the film's aesthetic.

It made the last bit of the production much easier for me. I already have a super great relationship with her, but we'd never worked together, even though we're both artists. She's not shy about sexuality either, so she brought very nice ideas. Even in one of the five shorts that is a bit more graphic, she was not shy at all. So that was really fun.

The four short, animated testimonials of *Caresses magiques* are rounded out with a fifth original short documentary *Masturbation: A Short History of a Great Taboo* which serves as something of a companion piece to *Le Clitoris* in presenting a historical breakdown of societal attitudes to – and subjugations of – taboo discussion points around sex and anatomy. This final entry differs from the others in the *Caresses magiques* series by virtue of being an independently written mini-documentary drawing on the research findings of anthropology researcher Xavier Robillard-Martel. Sharing *Le Clitoris*'s inherent potential for educational use, the film sees Malépart-Traversy narrate a potted history of masturbation through an anthropological lens, identifying early evidence of the practice in the discovery of prehistoric stone dildos and depictions seen on ancient Greek amphoras.

Following a period of societal indifference, by the early eighteenth-century dissenting attitudes manifested themselves in such texts as *Onania: or, the heinous sin of self-pollution*[20] which in turn would influence the writing of Samuel-Auguste Tissot's *L'Onanisme*. In tandem with religious piety, the medical professionals of the time would be inclined toward dissuading masturbation in favor of exercise, medical intervention (from treating women suffering from "hysteria" with genital stimulation to, more alarmingly, institutionalization and clitoral removal) and a bland diet, as pushed by such culinary luminaries as Reverend Sylvester Graham and John Harvey Kellogg.

Malépart-Traversy identifies the 1960s as a key cultural turning point in the West, with the rise of feminism, the LGBTQ+ movements and sex positivity as a whole. With modern attitudes being far more evolved and relaxed, masturbation is today regarded by many as a valuable activity for equilibrium of body and mind though, as the other films in the series attest, there remain stigmas and taboos across different cultural and religious backgrounds to this day.

While the series as a whole did not achieve the same extreme virality that *Le clitoris* enjoyed, it has performed well in the world, *Masturbation: A Short History of a Great Taboo* notably winning the Award for Best Education Film at Montreal's own Sommets du cinéma d'animation, an indicator of its potential value as an educational tool, much like its predecessor. Elsewhere, *Sweet Jesus* would see itself officially selected for Annecy in 2022, with other episodes doing the rounds at events across the world. Crucially, it is the response from the project's originators and contributors that proved especially valuable to Malépart-Traversy.

> At the beginning, I was worried that I didn't know how they would react, having their real voice in the public like that, because with the original text it was all anonymous. But they were really happy to see the project continue to live, and I think they appreciated the way I interpreted the stories also. During production, I had them listen to my first sound editing of their interviews, to make sure that they agreed with it. And even when I did my first animatics I also showed them, because I wanted to make sure that the visuals were pretty accurate.
>
> *Le Clitoris* really launched my career; even though it was a student film, it really was a great opportunity to make myself known in the animation world. With *Caresses magiques* it was also another launch, in a way, because it was my first experience with the NFB and it's also another big way of being seen and being known. I wouldn't say that I will never do another project about sexuality, but I feel that I've done a large amount, for now, about sexual education. I hope it was – and is going to be – helpful for some people. I feel that I did a bit of that job from the comments I've received, that some people felt that they learned stuff, or they felt more seen, in the way they approach their sexuality. So I think I can be proud of what I did.

While their focus is more on pleasure and carnal desire, the films discussed in this chapter do not forego the concept of romance and love entirely. In the final and most extensive chapter of this book, we will turn our attention to how love and relationships can yield wildly diverse approaches to story and artistic expression.

Notes

1 www.sawako-kabuki.com.
2 www.sawako-kabuki.com/summers-puke-is-winters-delight.
3 www.sawako-kabuki.com/dont-tell-mom.
4 https://1980yen.com/.
5 www.sawako-kabuki.com/tako.
6 www.sawako-kabuki.com/the-potone-nou-nen-featutae-mv.
7 www.sawako-kabuki.com/ici-la-et-partout.
8 www.sawako-kabuki.com/anal-juke-anal-juice.
9 www.sawako-kabuki.com/marvis.
10 www.pocko.com.
11 1997's *Death and the Mother*, based on Hans Christian Andersen's *The Story of a Mother*; 1998's *Pleasures of War*, based on the Old Testament *Book of*

Judith; and 2002's *The Old Fools*, set to the poem of the same name by Philip Larkin.

12 UNKLE: An Eye for an Eye, co-directed with Shynola, winner of the McLaren Award at the 2002 Edinburgh International Film Festival.

13 www.afvs.fas.harvard.edu/people/ruth-lingford.

14 Jury Prize for Animated Short, 2019.

15 www.sacrebleuprod.com.

16 www.studiopupil.com/tabook.

17 Heartshapes (2011) *The Banjo String*. 10 November. Available at: https://vimeo.com/31914238.

18 This prompts another unique comedic moment in which, at the near-halfway point of the film, the title card finally appears.

19 Animated Short Film, 2007 – *The Danish Poet*.

20 1712, author unknown – a widely-circulated pamphlet pushing the religiously-charged narrative that masturbation is sinful and will yield dire, potentially fatal physical and spiritual consequences.

5

Love

It is a testament to the universal relatability of love as a subject that so many established filmmakers have touched upon it in their formative work. The roots of Don Hertzfeldt's[1] enormously successful career as a figurehead of independent animation[2] go all the way back to his 1997 student film *Lily and Jim*, a mockumentary documenting two strangers who embark on a doomed blind date plagued by awkward small talk, violent allergies and self-sabotage. *Summer Camp Island* (Cartoon Network/MAX) creator Julia Pott,[3] also fêted for films including her Royal College of Art short *Belly* (2011) and *The Event* (2013) for Channel 4's Random Acts, would similarly make a mark on the animation world with her Kingston University student film *My First Crush* (2007). Prior to a wide-ranging career spanning film, television, celebrated shorts such as *The External World* (2010) and the video games *Mountain* (2014) and *Everything* (2017), animator David OReilly[4] established his unique fusion of minimal CG with darkly comic storytelling in *Please Say Something* (2008), a brutal tale of relationship toxicity. Kirsten Lepore,[5] later known for the viral sensation *Hi Stranger* (2016) as well as her work on the Marvel TV series *I Am Groot* and live-action/animation hybrid feature film *Marcel the Shell with Shoes On* (Dir. Dean Fleischer Camp, 2021), initially grabbed the attention of festival juries and audiences alike with *Bottle* (2010), a stop-motion tale of two characters divided by the ocean – one made of sand, the other snow – who develop a relationship by sending messages to one another, eventually journeying to meet one another on the ocean floor. In this chapter, we will look at other filmmakers whose unique approaches make a case for animation as an exciting medium through which stories of modern love can be told.

DOI: 10.1201/9781003415503-6

Uncharted Waters

Two starkly different – but equally appealing – films share a specific narrative trait of placing their protagonists at sea for much of their respective durations. The first of these, Cardiff animator Efa Blosse-Mason's[6] *Cwch Deilen* (*Leaf Boat*), explores the early phases of a romantic relationship and how the crucial foundations on which it can be built, chiefly trust and mutual support, are laid (Figure 5.1). During her studies at the University of the West of England (UWE)'s Bristol School of Animation in the United Kingdom, Blosse-Mason would take a year further afield at Hungary's Moholy-Nagy University of Art and Design (MOME) in Budapest, where she found herself developing an appreciation for the visual and storytelling approaches of Eastern European animation. While some of this influence can be seen in her Royal Television Society Award-winning[7] 2018 UWE graduation film *Earthly Delights*[8] (in which a voyeuristic gardener incites the wrath of the forces of nature), the Ffilm Cymru funded *Cwch Deilen* (*Leaf Boat*, 2020), produced by Cardiff's Winding Snake Productions[9] as part of the BFI Network's Beacons scheme, makes use of a variety of styles and approaches as we follow the journey of two women at a crucial stage in their developing romance.

The dynamic of the pair is strongly communicated from the beginning; visiting a beach on a windy day, Celyn imparts a story of how a terrible storm had once wrought havoc on her family's home. Heledd, the more assured and free-spirited of the two, responds by comforting Celyn briefly before skipping off into the ocean. Says Blosse-Mason:

> [Celyn's story] was meant to show that she has past trauma, which then affects this new relationship where she's very scared of things going wrong; it kind of stops her from fully putting herself into it.

Although Celyn doesn't demonstrate a complete dependency on her partner, these apprehensions threaten to skew the balance of their relationship; Heledd frequently relied on to assuage her existing concerns while unintentionally

Figure 5.1

Still from *Cwch Deilen* (Dir. Efa Blosse-Mason). ©2020 Winding Snake Productions

nurturing new ones. While the premise of the film has roots in Blosse-Mason's lived experiences, the couple themselves are more representative of her own duality than a specific relationship ("They're both a bit inside my head, often fighting with each other, or tugging in opposite directions"). As the pair sit on a pier and enjoy the scenery, Heledd comments on finding the idea of life in a small coastal town, such as the one they're presently visiting, restricting. Celyn constructs a boat-sized leaf with a lamppost for a mast, on which the pair trepidatiously take to the water, beginning a sequence that could equally be read as an in-universe fantasy scenario or an actual event in a world that possesses a certain degree of magical realism and dream logic. The decision to pursue the angle of having the boat and journey be symbolic of their relationship ultimately came from the idea of the film using animation as its storytelling medium.

> It went through quite a lot of transformation. It started off as just two women sat on a boat having a conversation. But then I thought *Well, if I'm going to animate it, it might as well have some sort of magical realism in it*; if they were just sat there and nothing magical happened, it may as well have been live-action.

As night falls, their boat's lamp illuminates, casting them in a romantic light. Celyn voices her concerns over the journey ahead, Heledd attempting to reassure her; they suddenly find themselves unmoored and lost at sea in the dead of night. Celyn's anxieties ramp up, their environment reflecting her state of mind as the weather gets increasingly choppy and a tentacled creature emerges from the depths, scooping up the boat.

> Celyn starts it off with imagining that they have a boat, but then she also is what makes things go wrong. Whenever she worries about something going wrong, like if there might be a monster, the next thing that happens is the monster appears. So it's about how those types of anxieties can almost manifest themselves, or they can be contagious – but I think the joy can also be contagious, it's quite powerful.
>
> The monster is kind of a version of Celyn that's almost like her subconscious. It comes out from the deep and it's quite scary and big at first, but Heledd diffuses the fear by just saying "Do you want a cuppa?" If someone has big, scary emotions, sometimes you just need to be calm and talk it out.

The creature (whose design is evocative of Celyn's, with a lobster body symbolizing a tarot symbol for the subconscious rising from the deep) comes aboard the boat and shrinks in size, pacified by Heledd and no longer a threat. The three enjoy a moment of calm as they drink together, before Celyn, in a callback to her opening monologue, voices her fears of a storm destroying their comfortable vessel. For the first time, we see Heledd grow concerned as, on cue, a storm rolls in and jostles them aggressively on the water. As they struggle to hold on, the line work becomes choppier and less defined, the mounting chaos reflected in one of the film's more artistically compelling moments (taking inspiration from the masterful artistry of Kilkenny, Ireland's Cartoon Saloon) until a rolling wave eventually separates them from one another (Figure 5.2).

> Then it's up to Celyn to actually save herself. It's about strength coming from within; you can't just be saved by another character. That's what I try to do with all my storytelling, have it come from the character, not from an external force.

This speaks to the heart of what the film communicates so well, in its navigating the delicate balance of a couple bringing out the best in one another through

Figure 5.2

Still from *Cwch Deilen* (Dir. Efa Blosse-Mason). ©2020 Winding Snake Productions

motivation, support and a strengthening of self-confidence, without tipping over into unsustainable emotional dependencies. As Heledd drifts away, Celyn voices aloud her biggest fears – of their relationship one day ending, being left on her own and losing her sense of self in the process. Emboldened and with an enormous emotional weight lifted, she jumps into the water and the pair reunite. As the sun rises, they bring themselves back on board their boat and steer it toward the shore. In an epilogue, we flash forward to their life together on the boat. Celyn rediscovers her subconscious creature (who had stowed away in a teapot before the storm hit) and, no longer threatened, welcomes it.

> They have both changed by the end. Time has gone past and they've built up the leaf boat now and it's a lot more stable. It's got a house on it and a kitchen, and they've worked on their relationship and made it more secure.

The three head off to sea in the boat together, Celyn and Heledd clearly in a more stable place and in a relationship no longer clouded by uncertainty; one in which they are content to move forward into the unknown, knowing that they have one another. For a relatively modest production, the film would make a sizable mark, festival screenings including the London International Animation Festival, Cardiff Animation Festival and an animation program curated by Whoopi Goldberg at New York's prestigious Tribeca Film Festival in 2021. *Cwch Deilen* would also be broadcast in the United Kingdom on the BBC alongside five other Beacons films, as well as on Channel 4 as part of a selection of the 2021 Iris Prize LGBT+ Film Festival (at which the film was Highly Commended). The warmth of its reception speaks to a growing public interest in queer storytelling – or, perhaps more accurately, a growing rate at which the public's preexisting interest is being satisfied.

> I think [queer representation] is definitely getting better. It's quite exciting. There's a queer character in *The Mitchells Vs. the Machines*, for example, which is a huge film. It wasn't in-your-face or anything, she's just queer and it's not a big deal. I thought that was just nice. For a long time, LGBT films were all about coming out, but I'm hoping now that it starts just to be a bit more about life. I really hope that

> *Cwch Deilen* is a bit like that. It's got queer characters in it, but I mostly hope that anyone in a relationship can relate to it.

If *Cwch Deilen* can be seen to depict the beginning of a relationship that matures and flourishes at sea, *Drijf* (*Drift*, 2023), written and directed by Levi Stoops, does an equally effective job of depicting the cracks that show in a long-term relationship as it begins to flounder. After graduating from an animation course at Belgium's Royal Institute for Theatre, Cinema and Sound, Stoops would write the early drafts of what would go on to become *Drijf* while working as a professional cook. Having never directed or worked in a studio before, Stoops contacted a previous teacher, Ben Tesseur, who introduced him to Annemie Degryse, senior producer at Lunanime who expressed an interest in producing his film. Securing a budget for *Drijf* – primarily government-funded by The Flanders Audiovisual Fund (VAF) and the Belgian Tax Shelter For Film Financing as well as private funders – was aided through bringing on board well-known actress Anemone Valcke who, along with performing in the film, also contributed to the development of the characters and story.

In the film (whose accolades include a Jury Award win at Annecy and New Talent prize at Fantoche in 2023), we join Aurora (Valcke) and Jeremy (Stoops), a young, nude couple paddling on a log in the middle of an endless ocean on a dolphin-watching excursion (Figure 5.3). Finding no animal life, save for a swooping seagull Jeremy impulsively attacks and is unable to euthanize (leaving Aurora, the more headstrong of the pair, to finish the job), they attempt to find their way back to shore and get lost. As their panic mounts, their already frayed relationship begins to unravel. The complex dynamic at the heart of the film came from both the director and Valcke's own lives, as Stoops explains:

> Both Anemone and I decided at some point that it was going to be about our own dynamics in long-term relationships. It was a very good point to start from. Then at some point, of course, we had to let go of the idea that it was about us, because otherwise we couldn't take it far enough.

Figure 5.3

Still from *Drijf* (Dir. Levi Stoops). ©2023 Lunanime

Although the outline of the story was there, it was Valcke's contributions that helped further develop the fine points of Aurora and Jeremy's relationship. While writing contributions from the actors on an animated production is a relatively rare occurrence, for *Drijf*, Valcke's input proved crucial in developing the complexity and nuance to the characters and their motivations. Says Stoops:

> [Anemone] had a huge impact on the movie. The way I work is that I have a lot of ideas, but it's while working with people that they really crystallize. I have the feeling that it doesn't happen a lot in animation, and it's something I was always a bit afraid of, that there's this kind of organic way of working that's not really present in animation because everything's so planned out, every step takes a long time and costs a lot of money. So during production I'm looking for ways to bypass that and let the project grow.

Things go from bad to worse for the couple; hunger sets in and tempers flare before the heat of the day gives way to the darkness of night. On waking to find her masturbating, in an act of reconciliation, Jeremy enters the water and delights Aurora with a deft impression of a dolphin (Figure 5.4). This moment of calm is short-lived, his antics attracting a shark that drags Aurora under the water as he watches on, helpless. Forced to kill the shark herself, a wounded Aurora brings it back to the surface, resourcefully creating a shelter from its carcass as a new day brings with it further scorching heat.

When the rising temperatures cause the shark's bloated corpse to explode, the couple are left exposed, Aurora's leg now black and clearly infected. She insists that the cowardly Jeremy amputate it using a makeshift saw from an oar and the shark's teeth. The procedure leaves Aurora unconscious and, as a storm abruptly rages, he finally demonstrates some tenacity by tying them both to the log and navigating the storm alone.

> The whole sequence where Aurora is in a coma, and he becomes himself, actually *enjoying* himself even, is grotesque in a way. She's almost dead, yet he's actually okay on his own; that's what he needs, probably, to be on his own for a while and

Figure 5.4

Still from *Drijf* (Dir. Levi Stoops). ©2023 Lunanime

figure things out. I sometimes have the feeling that it comes across as either super funny or really harsh because of that. For me, it's really recognizable to settle in a role when someone else is around, and then when the other person is away, you become yourself again. But in the context of a relationship, it's not really fair to the other person to not really be honest about what you want.

On exiting the storm unscathed, a newly emboldened Jeremy masturbates, spears fish and attempts to feed the still-comatose Aurora, before eventually bringing them both ashore.[10] On land, Jeremy reveals his newfound strength to the disdain of his now single-legged partner; although a transformational experience, Jeremy has grown in confidence but not empathy. Stoops considered having the couple break up following their ordeal but felt it unrealistic that such a momentous decision would be made within the confines of the film's relatively short run time. While the director maintains that there is potential for the couple to work it out, ultimately the film ends with them having return to their familiar dynamic; after Aurora belts Jeremy for his blithe self-aggrandizement, the two walk down the shore together, not necessarily stronger but with more familiar baggage to bind them.

As originally envisioned, the film would have started on an island stripped of its resources, the couple taking the last tree and fleeing. The lack of a destination created complications in the writing of the script, Valcke ultimately coming up with a solution that would steer the film.

"Anemone was improvising at some point, and she said something like 'Oh, it's a pity we haven't seen any dolphins yet' – it was such a small thing in the moment," as Stoops recalls.

This crucial story amendment in which Aurora has convinced Jeremy to paddle out and look for dolphins together, despite his reservations, was key to setting up their dynamic throughout the film.

I don't really know how long they've been together, but I think they've definitely settled into a dynamic where she takes care of him a lot of the time. She's also a very dominant person, so Jeremy himself kind of disappears when she's present. For a long time, while I was writing on my own, you really had to start asking the question *Why is she still with him?* I wrote him as this guy with no chance of redemption in the relationship because he leaves everything up to her. Then, at some point, I realized that if it was Aurora's decision to go out at sea to spot dolphins – which is actually a pretty dangerous idea, especially with someone like Jeremy – then it's also kind of her fault that they're there. A lot of people come to me and they say "I really recognize this character of Jeremy, a guy who just takes advantage of the goodwill of his girlfriend." I understand that, because that's part of the dynamic, but for me it's also important to see that it's really about two people who don't really know each other that well or don't really listen to each other that well.

Although the original context for both the tree they are paddling on and their lack of clothes (another resource that had perished on the unlivable island) are absent from the final film, they help amplify their vulnerability in the face of the story's mounting threats (Figure 5.5), as well as the overall absurdity and humor of the film – "It just started making sense in a way that was not planned at all from the beginning." The comedy beats of *Drijf* allow it to deal with harsher topics, as Stoop reflects:

You're already tapping into an emotion with people – they will feel something, and if you succeed in telling the underlying story as well, then you've done a good job.

Figure 5.5

Still from *Drijf* (Dir. Levi Stoops). ©2023 Lunanime

In attempting to do something exciting with her partner and continuously take the lead in the relationship, Aurora loses part of herself – both physically, in her leg, but also mentally, through her continued need to press him into action. For audiences, these facets of the characters are what make the film not just a vehicle for solid gags, but a recognizable and relatable allegory for both the challenges of modern relationships and expectations of gender roles within them.

> It's really a movie about this millennial couple, this guy who's not macho (because we're kind of past that in this kind of relationship), but then it becomes another difficult dynamic. And I think that people really like that this is something that's explored, the "nice guy" who's being analyzed in a critical way.

Ribald Rivalries

Having previously delved into the importance of the Shrine of Our Lady of Altötting to Andreas Hykade's early cultural development in Chapter 2, other formative influences on his art and storytelling would be at some distance remove from the Holy Mother, his mind opened by the game-changing musicianship of New York art rock band The Velvet Underground, the caustic irreverence of underground comic artist and satirist Robert Crumb and the writings of crime fiction novelist Jim Thompson, all of which a stark cultural contrast to the blandness of his folksy Bavarian surroundings.

The uncompromising nature of Crumb's work in particular would determine a similar intransigence in Hykade's early projects, his route to animation beginning with a school art project for which he chose to adapt an acerbic comic of his own, titled *Jochem In Search Of His Face*. Spending four months on the five-minute film (which tells the story of a young man looking, as the title suggests, for a face, ultimately finding an audience with the Pope who is aggressively masturbated by a harem of faceless prostitutes), young Hykade was spurred on by the surprising encouragement of his art teacher – until the comic book it originated from would circulate among the community, stirring outrage. Fearing what the exhibition of an incendiary animated version of the comic might do for the school's reputation – and his own plans for retirement – the previously supportive teacher would swap the film out at the last minute for a selection of Hykade's self-portraits. The months spent on *Jochem In Search Of His Face* would not be all for naught, however, ultimately succeeding as a portfolio piece to earn him a place at the Academy of Fine Arts in Stuttgart. It was during his subsequent studies that Hykade's frame of reference for the animation world as a whole was truly broadened.

> [I] didn't have [my] act together yet. On the one side there was Robert Crumb, and on the other side I thought I'd go to Disney, because in those days, animation and Disney were synonymous. So that was originally my goal, to do some animated films and then go over to Disney, but while I was studying, I discovered animation for grown up audiences – Phil Mulloy, the Quay brothers, the English crowd, what Clare Kitson did with Channel Four, and what Peter Dougherty did with all those MTV idents. That, I suppose, was the time I lost interest in Disney.

Following his art school film *The King Is Dead* ("About the last half hour before Elvis's final performance"), Hykade would move on to the Filmakademie Baden-Württemberg in Ludwigsburg where he would produce *We Lived in Grass* (1995), a project of particular importance as it represented his artistic "coming out," in a manner of speaking.

> That was the moment where things came together for me. Until then, it was all bits and pieces, a little bit of Disney here, a little bit of Crumb there, but with *We Lived in Grass* I could connect with a very simple style, a solvable style where you don't need an army of people – you could do it alone, if necessary. I took great joy from drawing these stick figures, and I discovered that, with these simple forms, I could go into any field – tragedy, if necessary, or comedy.

This "reduced mindset" has been present in all of Hykade's subsequent work, generally manifesting in a lack of extraneous detail in the characters of his films – while not purely "stick figures," as he describes, there is a certain minimalism in their approach that, being rooted in the conventions of contemporary design, do not detract from the bigger themes and stories being told; truth be told, the viciousness and occasional brutality of his stories is heightened by the way they look. *We Lived in Grass*, a snapshot of a son's rejection of his ailing father's (an archetype of toxic masculinity) "wisdom," packs more of a punch in its execution that leans into absurdism and even cartoonish physical comedy; similarly, *The Runt* (2005), which sees the same overbearing patriarch spare the life of the runt of a rabbit litter on the condition his nephew care for it and kill it after one year, is made all the more poignant for a tranquil, child-friendly aesthetic in the lead-up to its inevitably grisly conclusion. Made over a decade apart from one another, both films bookend what Hykade refers to as his "Country Trilogy," named for their narratives all being rooted in his own childhood experience of the Bavarian countryside. While the production of *The Runt* would benefit from his own experience as a teacher in the intervening years, chiefly an impulse to self-enforce the same production mindset expected of his students, the trilogy's second entry *Ring of Fire* (2000) was an altogether different, more emotionally fraught experience.

> [*Ring of Fire*] brought me to my limit, because I could not work the same way as I used to. All the old tricks would not work anymore. With *We Lived in Grass*, it was

> an unconscious process. The strength of the whole thing lies in the unconsciousness. It lies in intuition. So with *Ring of Fire*, I was a young man with his first little success, but I felt like a man walking the moon. Some journalists came along and said, "What are you going to do next?" I said, "I'm going to do a Western!"

Indeed, the film is steeped in Spaghetti Western tropes from the word go, from its cinematic aspect ratio, Sergio Leone-esque cinematography, drawling narration and – crucially – its rich musical score courtesy of Steffen Kahles that makes the effort to draw upon run-down, honky-tonk pianos and a singing saw among its instrumentation. The actual premise of *Ring of Fire* is a little less traditional, drawing not just from Hykade's childhood but also specific relationships in his adult life. Basing the dynamic of the film's two leads on his own debauched carousings with one particular acquaintance (a friendship that would see itself complicated by a real-life love triangle), *Ring of Fire* begins with two young cowboys swaggering into a surreal land of abstract, sexual imagery (Figure 5.6). The sequence is rife with unfettered depictions of impossible creatures comprising only of orifices, tongues, legs and breasts, anything identifiably human engaged in explicit sexual acts, rolling across the landscape like fleshy tumbleweeds. The sheer excess of the film's opening minutes owes a debt to a unique "workshopping" approach taken by the director:

> I'd wanted that whole sexual bazaar world to be as rich as possible, so I wrote these ads to art schools and prisons and said "send me your pictures of your sexual desires." I would try to distillate about 30 or 40 characters based on those descriptions, and in the end that made up this bazaar of sexual fantasies.

While the charged sexual energy of the film and its setting could easily make it a viable case study for the preceding chapter of this book, it is the tragic love story at its heart that burns through the cloud cover of carnal desire. It becomes quickly apparent that the two cowboys moseying their way through this carnival of excess are not on equal footing, the alpha of the pair grabbing two naked women, having his lascivious way with them before discarding them, while his companion looks on, struggling to keep up. This dynamic is further reinforced by the lead cowboy's ability to impress a prostitute with his gunslinging. Once separated, the meeker cowboy runs off, out of his depth, eventually encountering

Figure 5.6

Still from *Ring of Fire* (Dir. Andreas Hykade). ©2000 Jungfleisch / Hykade. Image courtesy of Andreas Hykade

the Water Woman. Reminiscent of *We Lived in Grass*'s Dandelion Girl (a mythical specter of femininity who steers the young boy of that film's views on love and women away from those of his father's) and, as mentioned prior, strikingly similar to Hykade's visual depiction of the Virgin Mary in his later film *Altötting*, the serenity of the character – a nude lady with flowing water for hair, presented in a recognizable style of Hykade's, both breasts jutting, Picasso-esque, from one side of her body, her coffee-bean vagina placed, accessibly, above her pubis – and her presence in this intimidating land, brings the cowboy solace. Smitten as she bathes him, his peace is cut short by the return of his aggressive companion. Intuiting an inevitable rivalry, one in which he is doomed to be a passive observer, his attempts to lure his confederate back to the temptations of the bazaar prove futile. He watches in vain as his friend initiates the Water Woman in the ways of gunplay and drinking to excess, briefly emboldened to keep a watchful eye on the situation until distracted by the prostitute he had previously failed to impress. While in her thrall, he allows the Water Woman to be preyed upon by his bellicose companion, who grotesquely laps up all the water spilling out of her head, leaving her a dried, violated and symbolically beaten husk.

While the less extreme aspects of the film's story would, in part, take their cues from the real-life romantic entanglements that were playing out in Hykade's life, finding a cohesive throughline – or any kind of finish line, for that matter – was not a smooth ride.

> I tried to put my real life problems into the narrative, but after two years, I ended up in a complete, absolute mess. I had no story and no concept. The whole process of working intuitively definitely came to a limit. As the stuff is so personal, I *took* it really personally and it led into a downward spiral. I would wake up in the morning, eight o'clock, and after one and a half hours of running in circles and not being able to sort it out, I was so powerless that I'd go back to bed. This would go on for a long while, for half a year. So one night, my producer phoned me up and said "I'll tell you what, you can drop this movie now and do it in five years if you want to, I'll be there. But I gotta know by tomorrow morning, because we cannot go on like this." I seriously considered dropping the thing, and I thought about all the alternatives – but none of them were better than finishing the movie. From then on, it became very simple, very pragmatic. I thought *I will not do a big masterpiece now, I won't change the world, this film won't save my life, I'll just do it the best way I can.*

The refocused narrative of *Ring of Fire* seems to have benefited from the artistic crisis, in that what might easily have turned out a sprawling (if visually captivating) mess is, in its final form, a modern-day parable that speaks to the momentary pleasures and ultimate futility of strictly carnal pursuits and the folly of hotheaded youth. In the wake of both cowboys' dubious decision-making, all parties find themselves at a loss, the alpha seemingly robbed of his prior abilities and rebuffed by the prostitute when he attempts to force himself upon her. Meanwhile, his meek companion is unable to save the Water Woman, feebly offering his jacket for comfort when, all too late, he happens upon her in her ravaged state. A sliver of hope presents itself in the film's closing moments as, in a callback to their first encounter, he reciprocates by bathing her, seemingly undoing some of the damage she has endured. She allows herself to be bathed further and puts her arms around him, suggesting a future that holds, if not a traditional happy-ever-after love story ending, then at least some degree of redemption.

I took the best ending I could find, because it was all lying around for years. And everything was smooth from then on. I tried to do consciously what I used to do unconsciously which, if you look at other people, seems to be quite normal.

When the film came out, it had an effect, it created some sort of "Wow," but it also created a "What the fuck?" I got many nasty letters, especially from feminists, but then there were other feminists who really loved the film, saying it was quite a sensitive treatment of women. So you had both sides. Usually when you run around the festivals, you just meet people who like your stuff, but there are many more people who you *don't* meet, who *don't* like your stuff, and I'm very aware of that. It's always been like that, it will probably never change.

Whether or not *Ring of Fire* might have served as Hykade's hypothetical masterpiece that changed the world or saved his life, the film as made has earned itself a reputation of cultural significance, its initial run snagging a Cartoon d'Or nomination and top prizes at events including Ottawa, Melbourne International Film Festival and Catalonia's Sitges Film Festival.

A film that also takes on the raw and wrathful emotions that a love triangle can incur is *SH_T HAPPENS* (2019) by filmmaking duo Michaela Mihalyi and David Stumpf. The pair initially met at the Academy of Performing Arts in Bratislava, Slovakia, where they were both studying animation, one year apart. After working on a handful of small projects together, they continued their studies at the Film and TV School of the Academy of Performing Arts in Prague (FAMU) where their first major collaboration, a whimsical tale of biblical cuckolding, took shape. Having begun work on the basic idea (that, according to Mihalyi, was "Inspired by living in small, closed spaces, and how that can provoke a lot of different interactions or strange relationships") between universities, the pair took it on as a full, "semi-professional" film with the assistance of FAMU and mentor Michaela Pavlátová (whose own work we discussed in the preceding chapter). Bolstered by a successful pitch at the Annecy short film market MIFA that brought French coproducers Bagan Films on board,[11] the duo established a working dynamic that saw Mihalyi taking on design with Stumpf handling the animation and post-production. As Mihalyi explains:

For us, we have different skill sets, so we can use both, and when we combine them I think it makes the work much better. We're also less scared to do stuff, to start new projects or attend pitching forums. Something that really interests us is to create a contrast between very colorful – and, maybe sometimes a bit naive-looking – visuals with a bit of boldness somehow, opening up some sexual themes or more adult themes, visually. This contrast is something that I really liked to do, and we try to find references for color palettes or visual influences anywhere, but mostly from illustration or contemporary graphic design.

Adds Stumpf,

When we combine our abilities, which are a bit different, we can achieve more complex things. Also we talk about these things a lot, so that means that we can intersect with each other better, like when Michaela's designing something, she's thinking about how I will animate it, and we discuss it. So it's a good system to come up with some complex solutions for stuff.

The result reads as an extremely assured film that boasts appealing, contemporary character design and a textural quality blending analogue risograph techniques with digital images to create an appealingly "imperfect" effect of overlapping colors over the line work. Taking initial inspiration from the design sensibilities of Nicolas Ménard as well as the playfully ribald, "in-your-face" work of Pavlátová, Renata Gąsiorowska and Lori Malépart-Traversy, the story itself plays cleverly with time and narrative flow, taking inspiration from filmmakers such as Gus van Sant, Quentin Tarantino, Charlie Kaufman and Damián Szifron (in particular his darkly comedic 2014 anthology film *Wild Tales*).

The inciting incident slaps the audience awake out of the gate; in a pre-titles sequence, we see two anthropomorphized deer lovers gambol toward one another across a rooftop garden in anticipation of a loving embrace. Before they connect, the female deer is incinerated by a sudden burst of lightning, leaving her aghast mate widowed in an instant. The sequence, which also serves as the focus of the film's trailer, was among the first visual concepts the pair came up with, and sets up a chain of events that the audience are shown across four nonchronological chapters.

In *1: A Caretaker*, we find that the world in which the deer inhabits is an isolated apartment building populated by couples of various animal species and built atop an arc that floats in an endless ocean; a contemporary reconceptualization of the Genesis flood narrative. Mihalyi explains,

> The basis was Noah's arc. For some people it's clear in the film, for some it isn't, but I feel that you can interpret it in both ways. We initially wanted to have the structure of a certain kind of society and then see what roles that society would need to have, and how it could be disrupted. It's not necessarily to be transgressive just for the sake of being transgressive, it's just that we both share certain interests in how to approach certain sexual topics, because it's such a fundamental part of existence. So we felt that there is a certain marriage between the biblical themes and these existential topics. It wasn't necessarily a deep dive into the roots of those things. It was just to poke somewhere that we felt needed some poking.

Adds Stumpf,

> It's also connected to the first scene. Because there are two of each animal, so when the deer's wife dies, whether he loves her or not, she's the last one, so now he's in trouble. That's why he's miserable and depressed and will eventually escalate things.

Some time later, the building's human caretaker – essentially representing this scenario's Noah – goes about his day's work, contending with the raucous tenants who urinate in the lobby and throw debauched parties in his maintenance room. After ushering them out, he notes water on the floor, coming in through mysterious holes in the adjacent room's walls. He hammers in corks to stem the flow and, exhausted, returns home to find his wife spread-eagled atop their dining room table, presenting herself for him sexually (Figure 5.7). To her visible disappointment, he declines – or perhaps doesn't even notice – the offer in favor of going to sleep. While much of the film is more overtly comedic and absurd, the vulnerability of being rejected is a story beat that comes through as being uniquely poignant and relatable, in a similar vein to *Mind My Mind*'s rejection scene discussed in Chapter 2. Mihalyi:

> I think in a way it's about not communicating with each other, not meeting in the middle, and then just passing by. The film is not autobiographical, but there are certain moments that we were pulling from; in a way it kind of fascinates us, how to communicate, and as the tone is more darkly comedic than human, we wanted

Figure 5.7

Still from *SH_T HAPPENS* (Dir. Michaela Mihalyi, David Stumpf). ©2019 BFILM s.r.o. / Bagan Films / BFILM.cz s.r.o. / FAMU. Image courtesy of Michaela Mihalyi and David Stumpf

> to put in some relatability. I felt as though a moment like this could achieve that. It doesn't necessarily mean that those people don't like each other, they just don't communicate well and they're both kind of in their heads. So it creates this weird moment that is interpreted differently from all sides.

The second chapter, *2: His Wife*, takes us back to earlier in the evening, where the depth of the wife's hurt feelings is more fully contextualized as we see the preceding moments in which she makes the effort to sensually prepare a romantic meal. In the aftermath of his disinterest, which leaves her frustrated and near tears, she walks through the building, distributing food to its other tenants, all couples who seem to be in harmonious relationships, many of which are sexually charged. She arrives at the bereaved deer's apartment who, upon opening his door, lunges at her amorously (Figure 5.8). This moment of inter-species amore is among many in the film that hinges on the value of animation in keeping the audience on board.

"When you get rid of 'real' people, and you somehow replace them with – or interpret them as – different characters, in animation you have this freedom of showing these types of things in a more complex way," says Mihalyi of the inherent freedoms the medium allows.

> You can show sex, but it can be done in a really gentle way, because in animation it's not "real" objects or "real" people. You don't see real things in front of you, you see the interpretation of it, maybe in a more abstract way. I also enjoy these themes in live-action, but I feel that in animation, they're interpreted more in a joyful way; it's more fun to watch, and it's more poetic sometimes.

In *3: A Widower*, we again flashback to earlier in the evening, wherein the widower had been attempting to join in the frivolities of the raucous basement party but, being surrounded by other couples, is left drunk and depressed. He wanders into the adjacent room, banging his antlers against the wall in despair, puncturing it. He flees at the arrival of the caretaker and, crawling through the building's

Figure 5.8

Stills from *SH_T HAPPENS* (Dir. Michaela Mihalyi, David Stumpf). ©2019 BFILM s.r.o. / Bagan Films / BFILM.cz s.r.o. / FAMU. Images courtesy of Michaela Mihalyi and David Stumpf

ventilation system, stops over a grate that looks into the caretaker and wife's apartment. Turned on by the sight of her pleasuring herself on the table in anticipation of her husband's return, the deer returns to his own apartment and passes out. Upon the wife's arrival, he lustfully embraces her; she gleefully reciprocates his advances.

Although their tryst is morally questionable, in the context of the story and how effectively their mutual loneliness has been conveyed, the audience feels less compelled to judge their actions; while in some respects it might play as analogous to the self-justification and moral acrobatics people who embark on affairs manifest to justify their behavior to themselves, the love triangle of *SH_T HAPPENS* is curiously sympathetic and palatable. As Mihalyi notes,

> They're an unlikely pair, but sometimes when everything goes to shit, you just find a closeness somewhere else, where you would not necessarily expect it. From the outside, it can look like something that you shouldn't do – it's an affair, it's cheating – but everything has its reasons. So the audience isn't on anyone's side, because there's no right side to be on. It's just that one shitty thing can change a lot and move you somewhere that you don't expect to be. You don't necessarily make the right choices, but it just happens, and leaves you with the fact that you have to deal with it somehow.
>
> We wanted the theme of frustration for all the characters; all of them are frustrated for different reasons, and we also wanted to make the story a bit absurd or funny, in a

way. So we tried to find a way to implement all those things, to create this absurd, kind of biblical but also contemporary revenge and sex-filled story. We wanted to create this idea that people are acting a bit like animals – and also that animals are acting like people – so they're intertwined, in a way. Not human beings, but animal-people.

Stumpf further explains,

The base idea of the film was trying to find the border where rational thinking ends and instinct starts. Every character in our film has this border, but in different ways. Every character can only take a certain amount of shit. That's the relationship between animals and human beings; human beings often don't think rationally, they think with emotions. And that is when things can fall apart, literally everything, as we show in the film.

The beginning of the end plays out in the final Chapter 4: *The End*, where, some time later, the caretaker is happily arranging a nursery for an expected child. We cut to a scene that could be initially construed as the caretaker giving his wife oral sex, but transpires to be him delivering their baby. Upon birth, he is shocked to find the infant, a product of his wife and the deer's tryst, has antlers (Figure 5.9). What ensues is one of the film's most visually untethered sequences as we see the caretaker's internal rage spiral. In an especially effective use of the digital risograph style, the ensuing montage sees him floating in a void populated by floating vaginas, into and out of which antlers fire and stab at him. The floating specters of his wife and her lover taunt him, followed by a succession of quickfire, hallucinogenic images that invite frame-by-frame scrubbing and callback to previous events in the film. For the directors, the unfettered nature of this sequence proved to be one of the more freeing aspects of the production.

Mihalyi:

With animation you have to plan, but for us it was also important to be spontaneous when putting it together. With the things that are in the montage we were just

Figure 5.9

Still from *SH_T HAPPENS* (Dir. Michaela Mihalyi, David Stumpf). ©2019 BFILM s.r.o. / Bagan Films / BFILM.cz s.r.o. / FAMU. Image courtesy of Michaela Mihalyi and David Stumpf

playing around with certain scenes that we have seen before and what kinds of symbols, colors and transitions we can put together, so we have these more visually loose parts (like him flying around between the vaginas) that we could mix it all together. The rest of the film was very tight and very scripted but this was fun and loose, playing around with our editor.

Adds Stumpf:

> The thing is, it happens at around ten minutes into the film, and it leads to an important plot point, so what we needed to do was break the former rules we'd established so the audience could focus again. We knew from the beginning that there would be a montage, but only knew approximately what would be in it, not specifically. So when the time came to animate it, we just went in and just broke all the rules we'd established. It was actually really fun to do, because the process was so different. Everything else in the film was really planned, the timing is super tight, the animation is pose-to-pose, while this is more free and fluid. So our approach needed to change, and after being in production for months it was refreshing to do something else for a while.

In despair, the caretaker removes the corks from the bottom floor, allowing the building to gradually flood as a storm rages. As the ark on which the apartment complex is built begins to sink, the man rows away in a lifeboat, leaving his life and the building's inhabitants behind. Hearing a rustling under a blanket covering supplies, he is nonplussed to discover the inebriated deer who cuckolded him is an unwitting stowaway on the same lifeboat. In another nod to the film's biblical origins, a bespectacled dove lands on the boat, proffering a literal olive branch. The caretaker joins his unlikely boat companion in getting drunk. Of the film's conclusion, Stumpf observes that

> Each of the three main characters at one point goes beyond what's reparable. We have all been each of them, and the more responsibility you have, the bigger the damage. So when Noah is destroying the arc, it's the biggest problem of all, because he's basically destroying the world. The audience are just observers, they're neutral – like we are, as the directors. We're not taking sides, we just observe things that lead to other things.

An enormous festival hit, receiving over 150 international Official Selections, the overall run of the film was somewhat fettered by the COVID-19 pandemic lockdown restrictions demanding online editions of many events (which failed to get in the way of it scooping up multiple grand prizes, audience awards and honorable mentions). The pair were fortunate enough, however, to attend several earlier screenings, including its premiere at the 2019 Venice International Film Festival and major industry festivals such as Sundance and Clermont-ferrand, where they were able to gauge the variety of audience responses firsthand. On the overall response to the film, Stumpf reflects:

> It really depends on the country. Some audiences are more conservative. You can tell, not only from when people are coming to you and talking to you about the film, but also when you are sitting in an audience, how they're reacting directly to the film. Even within European countries, there are differences between Belgium and Czechia. So it's fun to watch how the people are reacting, but in general I think the feedback is really good and we are super happy about it.

Adds Mihalyi: "In the US we were quite surprised that people really reacted to almost anything in the cinema, which we are more used to with European audiences. But in the US, if they laugh, they laugh really hard."

Figure 5.10

Still from *Lachsmänner* (Dir. Veronica L. Montaño, Manuela Leuenberger, Joel Hofmann). ©2020 YK Animation Studio GmbH

Another film that deals with sexual competition in a way that combines both human and animal instinct is *Lachsmänner (Salmon Men)* (2020) directed by Veronica L. Montaño, Manuela Leuenberger (two-thirds of the filmmaking trio responsible for *Ivan's Need*, explored in Chapter 2) and Joel Hofmann. The film follows a group of salmon/men hybrid creatures (Figure 5.10) clad in old-timey swimwear as they compete in a "testosterone-driven race" upstream toward a gathering of salmon women performing "a fertility dance," but a surprise awaits them at the spawning grounds.[12] As with many films, the original idea came from multiple points of reference. During the storyboarding stage of Hofmann and Montaño's 2018 film *Eisnasen*, while doodling, a drawing of a walking fish with legs and shoes materialized, providing the starting point for the film, as Hofmann explains:

> We just had some fun with this image – *What is this fish going to do?* Early on we came up with these muscular fishes that are competing upstream […]. Later on, we realized that the competition upstream alone wasn't enough.

In developing the film, Montaño references a conversation that influenced the next part of the story:

> A good friend of ours told me about a tribe of women who were able to fertilize themselves and they didn't need a man. I thought that was quite a fun thought that stuck in my head, because it was somehow funny. But as you start to process the thought in your head you think *When you don't* need *men to have babies, what happens?* That, combined with the fish-with-legs drawing, is how we started.

Within the animal kingdom, there are examples of animals who self-fertilize or, rather, can produce offspring without the need for fertilization, a process known as parthenogenesis[13]; however, such research was not part of the development process for this film. Hofmann asserts that

> We didn't do a lot of research from the biological side, because we thought it's such a comical and un-serious situation that we put these fish in, that we didn't want

to get stuck with these biological details. So in our opinion, it would have taken the fun out of the development of the story, if we had tried to get too accurate. Originally the log line was "How salmon reproduce; a sports documentary." So we tried not to take it too seriously.

This is a notion that codirector Montaño supports: "Animation has this great power to do everything. And I always think, if you get too accurate, if that's not the goal of your film, just kick it. So we can swim free and do what we want."

And swim free they do. The film itself is a colorful, rip-roaring, no-holds-barred erotic odyssey upstream that follows the competing swimmers as they race furiously toward their sexual counterparts. The designs of the male and female fish are somewhat reminiscent of the centaurettes section of Disney's *Fantasia*, with complementary color schemes and contrasting visual body types of the male and female fish, suggesting to the audience to consider which of the male piscine prospects might be successful in partnering with which of the females up ahead (Figure 5.11), a thought that is derailed to magnificent effect in the film's final section. As the men speed their way to the finish line, they explode from an opening at the top of the mount, hurling goblets of semen high into the sky as they do so, only to fall short of reaching the ethereal floating females, as they protect their collective ovum. The now disappointed salmon men wade among their defeated sperm looking skyward, when the females suddenly but gracefully dive in unison back into the pond and disappear. Momentary confusion quickly evaporates as the ovum begins to oscillate and wriggle, before releasing a flurry of adorably wide-eyed baby tadpoles. As they fall, they are caught by their new male caregivers in an inversion of the stereotypical gender roles often seen in our own species. The men fall instantly in love and seem overjoyed in their new roles as salmon fathers. The idea behind this twist ending draws upon, and adds to, the previously mentioned idea of self-fertilizing women, as Hofmann recalls:

One thought that we had was: *What does a fully emancipated world look like?* So we tried to invert the "classical roles," hopefully from earlier days, and include it

Figure 5.11

Still from *Lachsmänner* (Dir. Veronica L. Montaño, Manuela Leuenberger, Joel Hofmann). ©2020 YK Animation Studio GmbH

in the story; what if it was a fully emancipated world and women don't need men anymore to fertilize eggs? The children still need parents to take care of them – why can't men take this role?

Adds Montaño,

> When we had the idea about the kids, we thought that it was a really strong message, that the father can be a caring part of raising children. I think it's an area that still concentrates a lot on mothers, not on fathers. We recently had a big discussion in Switzerland about paternity leave and I think it's still a point that we have to discuss and give men this role of taking care of the kids.

The detail of the animation performance aids the comedy of the film, recurring use of extreme overlapping action and follow-through on the male genitalia, along with extreme camera angles often framing this motion also adds further to the feeling of speed and the need of each participant to beat their opponents as they swim, in thrusting action, to their supposed goal. Along the way, they also encounter obstacles, including a bear (which sets up a later background gag, being lured to distraction by one of the salmon men, the pair later seen engaging in analingus) and a large octopus who defends a vagina-like opening in the mountain, perhaps as a nod to the "tentacle erotica" subculture of hentai. The final shot of the film lingers, as we pull away from the sweet image of the new would-be fathers playing with their adoptive offspring, to the mountainscape itself, visually reminiscent of a woman's open legs and thighs. The previously spotted vaginal cave opening is combined with a phallic-like spout in which the salmon men and offspring play. This unified image, with its merging of nature and both sexual organs, perhaps suggests a coming together of the male and female salmon and the self-fertilization we have just witnessed.

The design work was largely created by codirector Montaño, who wanted to combine fish and humans, in an exploration of different body types. It was also important to find a style that would provide the energy needed for the film's more competitive and masculine elements as well as the more feminine energy of both the females and males, as they develop a softer and gentler side toward the end of the film. This need for vibrance and energy in the film was also partially inspired by children's drawings, as Montaño elucidates:

> I'm a really big fan of children's drawings. My friend has three kids, and we draw together a lot. I love their freedom when they draw. Also, when you do workshops with children, it's amazing how they just get into it and explore animation. So I really wanted to use this kind of energy in our film.

Although the design strategy came earlier in the process than the final scene, the style of coloring is given further credence when we see the children at the end and the different energy their presence brings to the film. While the filmmakers initially wanted to work with an analogue process, this proved untenable. Montaño explains,

> We were really stubborn in the beginning, in that we really wanted to have the texture of the pencils, as I thought we could express the energy really well with pencils and the direction of the line. If you draw with pencils you see the energy when you press the pencil harder or lighter. I wanted to include that in the outlines and in the coloring, but then I found a way to do it digitally. People asked if it was analogue, so I think it got the point across.

The trio were classmates at Lucerne University of Applied Sciences and Arts: Hochschule Luzern. It was there, during the post-production of their graduate film *Eisnasen*, that they decided to apply for funding for the film from the Albert Koechlin Foundation Young Talents Short Film Competition, which funded new talent working on their first or second film out of school. At the time it consisted of a two-step funding process that offered preproduction funding for four projects, from which one would go on to receive production funding as well. *Lachsmänner* received the preproduction support but did not receive the production funding, as both the funding and scheme timeline were not sufficient for the film. However, this situation suited the team well, as this allowed the trio to look for additional funding to support their vision for the film fully. They would later receive funding from the Federal Office of Culture, Pro Cinema Bern, Swiss-TV SRF – SRG SSR, Gemeinde Emmen, Burgergemeinde Bern and FUKA-Foundation Lucerne to make the film.

The trio would go on to set up the production studio Eisprung[14] (which means ovulation in English) in Bern, where Montaño and Hofmann have continued to work together on commissioned projects as well as their own ideas, Leuenberger leaving in 2020 to pursue her own projects. *Lachsmänner* enjoyed a strong festival run after great success at its premiere, winning Best Swiss Newcomer at the 2020 edition of the Locarno Film Festival in Switzerland. In flipping the narrative of sexual competition often found in nature to find a mate and maintain the species, the film also humanizes it. It achieves this with humor and re-introduces the idea of love, albeit in a different form than first expected.

The sometimes-futile nature of competition and matters of sexual conquest is also touched upon in Veljko Popović's *Cyclists*[15] (Figure 5.12), whose character design sensibilities were discussed previously in Chapter 3. Coming from a background in painting, Popović would study at The Academy of Fine Arts Zagreb and gravitate toward animation while working as an assistant to celebrated Croatian director Simon Bogojević Narath. Following the success of his first short film *Ona koja mjeri* (*She Who Measures*, 2008), Popović would be spurred on to form his own studio Lemonade3D, which would eventually rebrand in 2019 as Prime Render Studios,[16] continuing to direct short films that would amass over 70 awards between them. Following 2015's existential CG short *Planemo*,[17] in which the phenomenon of lone celestial objects that float through space without the need to orbit a star is analogized to the overwhelming sense of metaphysical dislocation a young man feels after he survives a car crash, both Popović and the studio were keen for their next film to be as different in tone and presentation as possible.

> There's two reasons for *Cyclists* – if you happen to stumble upon my films, you'll see that I go from doing a somber, serious film, exploring human nature and the nature of human society as a whole, then I try to pick a subject which is completely different. So after doing *Planemo*, which was a hard film to make and to watch, we in the studio really wanted to go into something that would cleanse our palate a bit.

As touched upon previously, the realization of *Cyclists* as a film would come from the studio's collaboration with the family of the late, much-celebrated Croatian artist Vasko Lipovac. Following several commissioned projects for his studio, Popović and team would be approached to come up with a short film based on Lipovac's works. Given the drastic shift in style from *Planemo* such an

Figure 5.12

Still from *Cyclists* (Dir. Veljko Popović). ©2018 Lemonade3D / Bagan Films. Images courtesy of Veljko Popović

endeavor would require (chiefly an excuse to work in 2D for the first time[18]), the studio enthusiastically took on the project.

> Vasko Lipovac is one of those artists who's really bridged that gap between fine art and popular culture. He created art, which was really fine art, but it was really accessible to the common people. I was really interested in getting access to his studio, going through his sketches and finding these little gems. He's loved by all walks of life in Split, including the conservative, "God fearing" folks, but he also had this series of works that he did late in his life which were these erotic, really bizarre drawings. There was a lot of kinky stuff there, a lot of sexual, really hardcore stuff. I think he kind of wanted to go, through these images, back to his teenage years. So my starting point was trying to create a film whose narrative structure would marry two themes – one is his *Cyclists*, which is a super popular series of works and sculptures – and these erotic themes.

These images would be interpreted as a story that takes place in an idyllic Mediterranean village; as it readies itself in preparation for a major bicycle race, we are introduced to the love interest of the film as a supine, voluptuous – and partially disrobed – woman luxuriating on her sofa in the Mediterranean heat, whose balcony overlooks the starting line. She flirtily wolf-whistles at the line of racers, two men interpreting it as motivation to win the race and, in turn, a romp with the woman herself. As with *Lachsmänner*, the representation of sexual competition through a literal race is at the forefront of the story, the two adversaries bolstered by fantasies of aggressive, impassioned sexual intercourse that dangle in their mind's eye like the proverbial carrot on a stick. The fantasy cutaways serve as a particularly strong comedic component of the film, marrying sensuality with an unabashed silliness that is well-served by the vocal performance of her boisterous sexual moans and grunts.

> I think the most difficult film to make is a humorous, funny film – at least for me. To get the audience to laugh is much harder than getting an audience to cry. So I really was interested in doing something different and experimenting, both in the narrative structure and in the visual approach and trying to create something different. If you try to create a humorous film and the jokes fall flat, it's kind of dead in its tracks, I think. So, in a sense, it was a bit of an experiment, and a leap of faith on our side, but I was confident in the material, I was confident in the satirical and comedic aspects of Vasko's work, that we could really pull it off and create a film which would amuse and have this satirical, humorous side to it.

As the riders push on, the world around them transforms from the established style of Lipovac's paintings into one more hand-drawn, monochrome and sketchy. Their fantasies fused with the route of the race itself, all other cyclists fade away as the two competitors ride through undulating land masses that take on the form of the woman they are fighting for. On top of giving their addled inner thoughts an extra dimension, this style shift also serves as a tribute to Lipovac's own approach to drawing.

> I had to find a way to try and get both styles and both approaches he had into the film. My original idea was to use the moment of the tunnel[19] to introduce this 2D hand drawn element. Then I started working with Sander Joon,[20] the Estonian animator (who also, incidentally, did a film about cyclists[21] back in 2015). I said "Why don't we try an experiment in expanding this 2D style outside the tunnel scene?" It broke up the tempo of the film and introduced a new style, so I kept it.

Unbeknownst to the cyclists, the woman who has so incentivized them appears far more interested in an approaching cruise liner than the race below. When one of the two frontrunners crosses the finish line, he sets out to enact his fantasy by visiting her apartment. Alas, she has already left to greet the boat's captain, a figure of far higher, authoritative standing in the local community; his status represented, in a faintly surreal way, by being nude from the waist down (a trait shared by the town's mayor).

> The mayor and the captain, they're the top Alpha dogs, and they're presenting their masculinity for everyone to see and they differentiate themselves in this way. So for me, it's a visual display of how sometimes someone's attitude is such that he presents himself as this very important man. For me, it has a slightly political connotation.

The ending of the film sees the townsfolk's attention diverted, the seemingly all-important race immediately forgotten and the victor's fantasy left unfulfilled, perhaps as a matter of karmic justice for his presumption of her interest to begin with. While it is a lighthearted comedy first and foremost, the ultimate message of *Cyclists* could perhaps be that, for all of their efforts, there will always be a greater competitor to contend with. As a political analogy, it also effectively communicates how power and dominance will often trump the hard slog of the common folk.

Figure 5.13

Still from *Dipendenza* (Dir. Panna Horvath-Molnar, Virág Zomborácz). ©2012 MOME Anim. Image courtesy of Panna Horvath-Molnar

A film that deals with both the idea of romantic competition and the nature of obsession (explored further in the next section) is *Dipendenza* (2013), a graduate project from MOME in Hungary by Panna Horvath-Molnar and Virág Zomborácz. The film follows the hulking but ostensibly lovable Bubu (Figure 5.13) and his attempts to retain the affection of his coworker and sexual partner, the selfish and easily distracted artist Angela. When the fish factory at which they both work hires a new male employee, his appealing physique and flirtatious nature turns everybody's heads, including, to Bubu's dismay, Angela's. As the new man quickly becomes her new muse, Bubu finds himself increasingly squeezed out of the love nest they once shared, eventually forced out of their bed and onto the floor.

Increasingly tortured by jealousy, Bubu tows the line until, while on a lunch break one day, he sees his love rival begin to choke. A helpful Bubu slaps him on the back, dislodging the choking hazard but, overcome by rage, the helpful gesture turns fatal as he continues to slap his adversary, repeatedly, to death. The conclusion of the film finds Bubu floating in a prison barge out at sea. When Angela visits, dressed in black, she releases her lover's ashes into the swell as Bubu watches on.

As well as the element of competition between Bubu and the new lover, *Dipendenza* acutely takes on the idea of toxicity in a relationship, or perhaps more precisely, the indifference of one partner to another. Throughout the first section of the film, we see how Bubu dotes on his lover – washing her hair, preparing her meals and, at one point, kissing her feet as she sits upon him like a chair and plays her harp – in the hope of a molecule of affection. While appearing to be at peace with the sexual component of their relationship as a reasonable trade-off, Bubu has made himself a doormat to a self-obsessed lover (Figure 5.14), whose lack of compassion or empathy drives him to despair.

The film's use of music and visual gags, among the pathos of the storyline, straddles the line between drama and comedy; although the film performed strongly at festivals, its dry wit led to some variation in programming, as Horvath-Molnar explains:

Figure 5.14

Still from *Dipendenza* (Dir. Panna Horvath-Molnar, Virág Zomborácz). ©2012 MOME Anim. Image courtesy of Panna Horvath-Molnar

> I was really happy to get into all the festivals, but it meant even more to be approached by various people personally and be told they liked my film. Those were definitely the best moments, although I had to learn that the predefined positioning of your film (which section, under what theme etc.) matters a lot. Having a long film like *Dipendenza*, with quite subtle gags did not always work within its section. There were festivals where a lot of people reacted and laughed, at other times complete silence followed.

Regardless, the story of the film itself has real intrigue and depth that, when paired with Horvath-Molnar's flair for design, creates an enigmatic, thoughtful piece that invites repeat viewing. It was Zomborácz, who primarily works as a live-action director and writer, who originally approached Horvath-Molnar to work on the film together. An affable collaboration soon developed between the filmmakers, as Horvath-Molnar recalls:

> [Virág] thought this could work as an animated film. I read it and immediately felt what she was talking about – the script had characteristics already which reminded me of my cherished Estonian animation. It was an easy decision. She gave me a free hand in basically everything related to animation, including the style. During the process, I showed her the partial results from time to time. She was a very good partner, we were on the same side and agreed on almost everything.

With Zomborácz's script giving off what Horvath-Molnar describes as "that Nordic/Estonian vibe," the design work for the film would draw upon multiple inspirations and references, including manga, European graphic novels, the short films of Priit Parn (in particular 2008's *Life Without Gabriella Ferri*) and Kaspar Jancis's *Crocodile*.

> It was easy to decide on which direction the film should take. We worked for almost a year on the storyboards and animatic. It was my first time making a film this long and a story this complicated and I really wanted to nail it as much as I could. I learned a lot from the process of how to change a live-action script into animation.

Figure 5.15

Still from *Dipendenza* (Dir. Panna Horvath-Molnar, Virág Zomborácz). ©2012 MOME Anim. Image courtesy of Panna Horvath-Molnar

> [*Life Without Gabriella Ferri*] was a really good example of how to make every single movement made by a character into a small gag.

The level of visual research created for the film is evident in the way the film maintains a balance throughout; there is a graphic feel to the film that draws as much from graphic novels as animated art, creating a monochromatic world in which we feel the central character's despair and his austere lover's need for excitement. While Angela comes off as unfeeling and stone-hearted, it is Bubu's lack of self-respect and misplaced assertiveness that proves to be his undoing (Figure 5.15). As suggested by the title (which essentially translates to "dependence" or "addiction"), *Dipendenza* shows how his inability to leave a toxic situation results in a love competition that may have been created unwittingly by Angela; whether she brings a third party into their relationship out of an agreed-upon understanding, or out of cruel indifference, it is a decision that ultimately leaves them both at a loss. The flirtatious interloper has lost his life at the hands of a jealous ex who has lost his freedom at the hands of his own temper. In the end, we are unsure if Angela's visitation denotes a continuation of their relationship or a dramatic display in reaction to the loss of two lovers, but Bubu's wary retreat into his prison cell suggests a potential loss of desire for her.

Obsession

Although a film that more explores hereditary mental illness, Signe Baumane's 2014 independent feature film *Rocks in My Pockets* touches upon the ways in which romantic delusions can manifest themselves as a form of mania and obsession in the story of her cousin Linda (Figure 5.16), one of five family members whose tragic struggles with mental health are explored as part of Baumane's own "crazy quest for sanity."[22] Remembering her as the prettiest and most academically gifted of all her cousins, at a young age, Baumane would attribute strength of character to Linda's sense of superiority and teenage moodiness. When the gifted cousin fails

Figure 5.16

Stills from *Rocks in My Pockets* (Dir. Signe Baumane). ©2014 Signe Baumane

a crucial exam at her desired university, a downward spiral begins. While initially seeming to be humbled and, as such, more approachable by the situation, Linda develops an obsession with the certainty that her life will be back on track the following year, with a husband to boot. Caught in the crosshairs of her increasing delusion is her tenant Ivars, who tolerates her one-sided infatuation for cheap rent.

Young Signe comes to learn of the situation when, while visiting Linda, Ivars hits on her, later confused when Linda announces a nonexistent wedding date. Things come to a head when Linda is eventually discovered by Ivars in the throes of a full breakdown, dancing in their garden wearing a wedding dress she has bought herself. In the fallout, Ivars is kicked out of the house, unable to convince the paramedics and her parents of the truth that there was never to be a wedding.

Although the root cause of Linda's mental health issues is never conclusively stated (and likely would not have been accurately determined at the time), it is heavily suggested that the weight of her studies might be an early contributor that snowballed. When she returns home from care, her academic future appears to have been put on indefinite hold, though she remains convinced that she will be married soon. A local man, either taking pity or being opportunistic, inserts himself into her life, leading to her falling pregnant, a situation she problematically considers to be "a great lever to force someone to marry you." The man turns out to be married with a family and will not be persuaded to leave them for Linda, triggering a repeat of the previous, wedding dress-clad breakdown.

While *Rocks in My Pockets* can be fairly described as a dark comedy, the story of Linda is one of its sequences where the darkness comes close to eclipsing any sense of levity. While we certainly are not encouraged to laugh at her for being so out of touch with reality, Baumane's signature approach to how her characters' internal processes are visualized, one that goes back to her early shorts, does help smooth out some of its harder edges. As with all of the film's stories, it is also told through Baumane's own written narration in a way that puts a certain amount of respectable distance between the audience and the family members being examined; the Linda of her story is depicted through the lens of the director's own memory, first and foremost. As we, the audience, do not become intimately familiar with her, nor see much of her version of events, there are certain gaps we are left to fill in ourselves. Linda could, on the one hand, be a pathological liar, carrying on a fiction that she knows very well is untrue in the vain hope that eventually its unwilling participants will start to go along with it. She could suffer from erotomania, a condition in which a person becomes unwaveringly convinced of another person's romantic interest in them, despite no such interest being exhibited. There could also be the cruel scenario in which both of her prospective husbands, sensing her emotional fragility, genuinely manipulated her and strung her along. In the context of the film and its overall premise, the second of these scenarios is perhaps the most likely.

Seeing the pregnancy through, Linda gives birth to a daughter and lives her life the best she can while medicating her delusional tendencies. While the reality of how her life turned out is always shadowed by the fantasy expectations of how things should have been, her story ends on one of the relatively happier notes in that it does not end in harm or tragedy.

The concept of obsession in a relationship can take many forms. In *Symbiosis* (2019) by Nadja Andrasev, we see how it can progress from curiosity to an all-encompassing fixation while also developing into something entirely different over time. After a brief stint in the animation industry working with famous Hungarian animation director Ferenc Rofusz, a subsequent drought of work in the industry pushed Adrasev into live-action. However, her desire to return to animation led her to apply to the Moholy-Nagy University of Art and Design (MOME) in Budapest, giving her more time to develop her craft. While studying she took part in the Animation Sans Frontières (ASF) program, a partnership between her host university and the Animations Institut at Filmakademie Baden-Württemberg in Ludwigsburg, Germany, The Animation Workshop, VIA University College in Viborg, Denmark (TAW) and GOBELINS in Paris, France. During this time, she worked on her idea for *Symbiosis*, pitching the film at the end of the program in Paris. This led her to join forces with French production company, MIYU, who coproduced the film with the Hungarian studio SALTO Films.

Symbiosis follows a wife who, upon uncovering her husband's various affairs, is at first jealous but slowly becomes curious – first about who these women are to her husband and then about the women themselves. The film spans a range of ideas and themes simultaneously, though, for Andrasev, the main theme is about

> how somebody can become so obsessed about something that they spiral into a state where they forget about their original motives and feelings, and they start to control the situation in a completely different way, through this obsession. For me, towards the end of the film, it's also about female solidarity.

As the protagonist's obsession increases, her need to keep track of and get close to these women grows too. In the beginning, she observes them from afar, stalking their online activity and collecting evidence of her husband's infidelities by keeping rogue hairs from his collar and collating texts from other women she finds on his phone. As time goes on, she begins to follow these women, taking pictures, stealing their trash from outside their homes and their underwear from laundromats.

On uncovering a matchbook in her partner's pocket, our protagonist finds her way to a sex club he attends. When she comes face to face with one of his mistresses, who is leading him blindfolded on a leash, her tethered, unknowing husband is offered back to her. The final scene sees the couple back at home on the couch. She leaves, ascending to the roof of their apartment building. Here we see snapshots of the lives of all the women her husband has been with, as well as many others, displayed in small sample boxes, a collection of women going about their days, just like her. The female characters in this film are complex and interesting. They all have different personalities, as shown in these closing moments, their motives shifting, their thought processes mysterious and undefined. For Andrasev, while the main character was loosely based on herself, other characters in the story took longer to decide upon as they were constructed from real-world strangers that Andrasev found in her daily life.

> It's a little bit autobiographical, but not exactly of course. I got answers in my own life that helped me shape the characters and some of the scenes. My phone was full of pictures of strangers. I started photographing women on the street and on the subway and on the buses. Some people – I hope they will never find out – I have maybe a hundred photographs of on my phone, because they were just so interesting and they all inspired me a lot.

This wealth of visual research allowed Andrasev to create a full cast of highly diverse characters, with the process of collecting people's identities and their assumed lives represented in the film's conclusion.

> The end of my film is about how, if you look closer or start observing better, you will see some nuances and that not everything is as clichéd as you imagine; everybody has their own problems and their own loneliness. I think it's interesting for the characters to change and imagine other people – and maybe guess wrong.

Throughout the film, animals are a recurring theme, sometimes in reference to its title, such as the mosquito that she lets drink from her in the film's opening sequence at a swimming pool as well as the Garra Rufa pedicure fish in the spa. Further readings explained by Andrasev include how, although our central character is in a relationship, she is also lonely, so finds a connection with the animals around her. Even if these connections are not immediately positive, they still draw her attention and she can identify with them. These layers of symbolism are deeper still, as Andrasev explains that she "also wanted the animals to be kind of feminine and be looking at the man as well. So they're partially her competition as well, and representative of other women." This idea can perhaps be seen mostly clearly through the captive tiger at the zoo, who makes consistent eye contact with the protagonist, a key moment that is mirrored in the final scene, as Andrasev explains how in the film there are

> moments when somebody sees her, finally, and one of these is the zoo scene with the felines, when they look at each other. At the end of the film it's very important

that she's looking at other women and they can see her as well. It's important that she's not unnoticeable.

The tiger, as a symbol of courage and strength, is also found in the tattoo the wife gets during the film from one of her husband's lovers, which could be read as symbolic of her letting go of the confines of her relationship and becoming more comfortable in her own skin.

Although the film deals with the obsessional nature of relationships concerning infidelity and self-pleasure, it is also a film that discusses the notion of loss of sexual arousal and interest, as seen when the main character attempts intimacy, both with herself and her husband.

I really wanted to emphasize that, even though this woman is in a relationship, some people who are in relationships have much less control of their sexual life, or their partner maybe doesn't even see them naked most of the time. They have this strange power play where it's always a compromise. I really wanted to show these awkward moments in a relationship.

Some people might feel lonely in having difficulties with these subjects in their own life. This is important to talk about, and it's important to show masturbation as well, I think. If you're in a heterosexual relationship, pleasure does not always come from your husband or your boyfriend, it can come from other places as well. I'm hoping to show that being single is not always so bad, because sometimes you can be much more liberated than when in a relationship. Of course, I'm not saying that relationships are terrible, I'm just saying that it's important to show what our needs and desires are, and to acknowledge them.

This idea of knowing oneself is a key factor in developing a healthy sex life, as putting all the onus on another person is not only unfair but unlikely to warrant full sexual gratification or add to a strong and healthy relationship with one's sensuality.

The film uses a combination of 2D animation created in TV Paint and collage that incorporates live-action footage, a combination that Andrasev explains as representative of the

collection of things in a woman's life. I figured it was the best time for me to experiment with mixed media, because while I was doing stop-motion films I was always hoping to get into 2D animation with painted backgrounds – that's why I made my graduation film, *The Noise of Licking*, in that style.

The Noise of Licking (2016), based on the short story *Megbocsátás* by Ádám Bodor, also includes themes of obsession between a woman, her plants and her neighbor's cat, with voyeuristic tendencies, who seem to derive pleasure or at least intense interest in watching the women undress and bathe among her growing collection of plants. Later, a man in a fur hat, who resembles the cat, invades the women's sanctum. The film's overt sexual overtones represent some degree of artistic license on Andrasev's part:

It was just my imagination running wild with the original story. It just involved a woman watering her plants and a man, a total stranger standing in her living room, just watching her doing it, and she heard the noises of the licking of the ice cream but she didn't turn around immediately. I thought that was really perverted and sexual in some way; even though the story itself is not sexual, for me it was. So I just went off of that completely.

During her time studying at MOME, Andrasev also wrote her thesis on animated sex scenes. From this and the two films discussed above, Andrasev has developed specific insights into the relationship between animation and sex.

> Animation is strange in this subject because there are so many different ways to show something, so it's always about your imagination. It's very free, and that's also sometimes the problem. Some people have different opinions, of course, but it's interesting to see how minimal you can be in showing sexuality and how symbolism can be really interesting as well. Sometimes rotoscope techniques or too much live-action puts people off, because animation is much freer, so why not use something more imaginative? So there are a lot of decisions, and that's always my question to myself, how directly I would like to show something.

The connection between animation and the themes explored in this book is echoed by many filmmakers working in this area. The process of animation itself can have an obsessiveness to it as well, one that creates synergy when exploring subjects such as those seen in *Symbiosis*. The obsession of the central character eventually leads to her finding a form of independence, the film's title itself a term that, more often than not, has positive associations; to live symbiotically is generally considered to refer to a mutually beneficial situation. In a healthy relationship, this may be a coupling that finds love, comfort, support and joy from one another while being able to maintain their own lives and sense of self. In Andrasev's film, there is a kind of symbiosis between the woman and the husband; however, this is not always positive. When an unhealthy form of symbiosis takes root in a relationship, through codependence or obsession, it can even become parasitic.[23] Obsessional love can be even more devastating if, as seen in *Dipendenza*, one or more of the partners is unfaithful or even cruel.

As explored so far, the subject of obsession has varying levels of extremity in as far as how it is handled from a story perspective, as well as the type of animation approach it is paired with. At its most excessive and comedically gratuitous, we find the work of UK animator and illustrator Ross Butter.[24] Known for his absurdist, graphically violent but hilarious short films, the energy with which Butter approaches animation is itself a form of mania, one that finds greater credence when paired with the subject of risky masturbation, as seen in *Base Wanking* (2012) or obsessional, overbearing love as in his short film *I Love You So Hard* (2013). Both films are the result of collaboration with Rathergood[25] founder Joel Veitch, having worked together previously since 2008. During his studies at university at Edinburgh College of Art (ECA), this working relationship helped bring about a longer-form project Butter could work on.

> [Joel] was making stuff for YouTube and his website. He wanted to have something that could get put out regularly. His email newsletter had this crazy sign-off, "I love you so hard," at the end of each one. He sent me a big Word document with dozens of different rants that could be turned into sketches. I picked out the four that I thought could be translated best into animation.

These visualized rants would be developed into four short videos that would eventually be edited together to become *I Love You So Hard* (Figure 5.17), a film that shares some of the DNA of the classic cartoon antics of the likes of Pepé Le

Figure 5.17

Still from *I Love You So Hard* (Dir. Ross Butter). ©2013 Ross Butter

Pew and Johnny Bravo, in which male characters aggressively pursue the object of their desire, despite visible disinterest or alarm. In Butter's case, this trope is taken to the extreme almost instantly, the film's male lead violently declaring his love by stating he will slice out his – and other people's – organs to show how much he loves the fearful woman he is chasing. Having locked herself in her house, his pursuit continues by shouting through her letter box and calling her on the phone, detailing increasingly surreal scenarios he would be willing to enact to gain her affection. Over the end credits, we see police taser and incarcerate him, as she weeps in the shower. This film, though primarily a comedy based on lunacy and an irreverent take on an obsessive kind of love, does speak to how real-life pathological infatuations may have more to do with ownership of the person at the focus of their mania and less to do with a genuine desire to be with them. In less-skilled hands, the film could tip over into being uncomfortable or unwatchable, but Butter's deft skill as an animator as well as his excellent comedic timing validate its extreme subject matter.

> A lot of my ideas are very lowbrow, [which] forces me to actually put the time into making sure that it's completely technically sound so that no one could question it. I think if I put no effort into it, I'd just look like an absolute lunatic!

The narration by Veitch was originally recorded on his phone with the intention of a professional re-record down the line, a route Butters insisted they not take for the sake of preserving the film's manic energy.

> There was something about the original performance that I think was just far better. I was sort of adamant that we stick with the scratch tracks and sacrifice the audio quality for the better performance.

The quality of the audio also takes on diegetic resonance during the final scene in which he continues his manic monologue via phone.

Butter cites pioneers such as Don Hertzfeldt and his analogue use of pencil on paper as an early inspiration, as well as early internet Flash cartoons, representative of a time in which animation was unrestricted by the meddling of larger organizations and producers.

> There were definitely edgier sensibilities back in the 2000s to the 2010s. There was a turning point where producers started to reflect on what may land them in trouble, but before then was a brief period where, in terms of the internet, it was very much the Wild West. Now you feel like you have to self-censor to make sure your social media page doesn't get shut down, because the main gathering places on sites [are] owned by companies with terms of service.

As an early beneficiary of this new form of animation distribution, Butter can see parallels between those early provocative works and the current trends on social media platforms.

> I'm not really up to date with Gen Z culture, but I know that they've created [specific terminologies for sensitive terms] so they don't get their videos demonetised. In the early days of YouTube, as the advertisers started to make it known that they didn't want their adverts appearing near questionable content, that definitely deincentivised people to make more edgy, adult content.

The provocative nature of Butter's work often means that, although selected at festivals, it is often part of out of competition, late night or fringe screenings. "I'm cool with that," states Butter, "If I wanted awards, I'd probably make something more serious, but I'd rather make people laugh than stroke their chins."

This sentiment is echoed in Butter's attitude to his online presence as well, which, in later years, would court mild controversy for his outlandish, hyper-violent, celebrity-lampooning skits *Eamonn Holmes Gives Birth to a Swan* (2020) and *Boris Johnson Eats A Pot Noodle in the Bath* (2021).

> There was a level of virality to both of them, but as soon as they started to get out of the sphere of people with similar sensibilities, there would be a point where someone would report them and get them marked as sensitive content. Then their reach would just completely flatline. That's the problem with having social media that's controlled by Terms of Service – there's a good reason for that, and I don't blame them. It's just very hard to get people off social media and watch it on a website. For the most part, a lot of my work lives on my website because I'm in control of that and no one can censor it.

Personal Growth

A filmmaking duo whose notable work covers many of the themes in this chapter are Chintis Lundgren and Draško Ivezić of the independent Croatian animation studio Adriatic Animation, who began writing films together with the 2015 short *Life with Herman H. Rott* (Figure 5.18), the first of what would make up something of an informal trilogy of shorts that share Lundgren's distinctive aesthetic style and a propensity toward examining relationships that are uniquely complicated. Coming from a background in painting, Lundgren's (who would animate and direct the film) early character development would come from a series of one-panel comics in which a "grumpy" rat would prove popular while

Figure 5.18

Still from *Life with Herman H. Rott* (Dir. Chintis Lundgren). ©2015 Chintis Lundgren

also drawing on a living situation she had found herself in with another couple, some years prior.

> We used to live together in a shared apartment as part of a little commune. They were such a strange couple, because the guy was a total punk, just playing video games, drinking, never cleaning anything, and then he started to date this girl who was the most *petite bourgeoisie* person I'd ever met. She had all these convictions about how things should work and was totally crazy about cleaning. The fact that these two would end up a couple was a big inspiration. But of course, I think all of our relationships have some clichés in them.

As a couple themselves in real life, Lundgren and Ivezić's working dynamic sits at some distance removed from the relationships they depict. Says Lundgren,

> I always thought that I would never work with anyone; I guess it's a kind of Estonian mentality; we don't trust anyone! But since we are a couple, I was always presenting [Draško] with what I was doing and he was giving me advice, which was very constructive. Slowly, it just happened that he was giving me more and more advice, and in the end we were just creating together. I think it worked out pretty well, because all my films before *Life with Herman H. Rott*, I actually never spent more than one day on the story, so they're funny, but they don't make a lot of sense. Draško questions things more – "*why* is he doing this?" – I think it works well together. With *Herman H. Rott*, I would always say at Q&As that I am the rat, and [Draško]'s the cat.*Rott*, I would always say at Q&As that I am the rat, and [Draško]'s the cat."

Adds Ivezić, "[The film] is not about our relationship, but we do talk about relationships a lot. Before we met, we were in a bad place, disappointed with other relationships."

Relationship disappointment is certainly a prevailing theme of the film. The character of Herman H. Rott is an archetypal bachelor rat prone to drinking, smoking and listening to death metal, a lifestyle that appeals to an observing cat (named Cat) who, watching him stumble home, sees him as a project. On this shaky foundation, Cat inflicts a relationship on Herman, arriving at his door with suitcases, a piano, domestic appliances and classical music records in tow. In spite of his resistance, she moves in and begins the process of civilizing him. Though initially resistant to Cat's efforts, he gradually begins to adapt to her ways. Doing their shambolic best to maintain some degree of domestic harmony, their pairing eventually implodes, ending in a fight wherein the pair begin destroying one another's possessions.

Herman packs and leaves, getting drunk at a bar where, in a moment of remorse, he buys a new vacuum cleaner with which to tidy their destroyed apartment. Cat returns, Herman seemingly a changed man, eager to help out around the house and dote on her; she swiftly loses her interest in him in favor of an attractive neighbor (an athletic wolf who, in later films, we come to know as Toomas). In a moment that marks the completion of his transformation into the man she had supposedly wanted him to be, Herman sits at the piano and plays elegantly; Cat leaves him for good, turned off by his new persona. Single again, he moodily lights up a cigarette. The scenario rings familiar to those who have experienced relationships, especially in youth, where a partner's wants and aims for a relationship prove fickle, or at odds with the reality of a supposedly ideal situation, especially once the initial honeymoon period has died down.

Says Lundgren,

> [Cat] is attracted to the kind of man that Herman *was*, and when he stopped being that, she was not attracted anymore. I think it's really a question for psychologists, in that we're often attracted to things we don't understand. We don't even know *why* we're attracted to them, we think we want it so much, but when we get it...

Adds Ivezić:

> ...It becomes boring and predictable [...]. We've noticed it's very often like this; someone gets what they "want," and then all of a sudden, it's actually not what they want. So she searches again, for another man who is like Herman. I guess we are trying to fix things that bother us about ourselves, so it's not a problem with another person, it's a problem with ourselves; our insecurity is at play.

Proving a multi-award-winning hit at festivals (a precedent that would be met by the films that followed), due in no small part to the relatability of the story paired with Lundgren's appealing analogue, hand-drawn, watercolor-textured approach to the visuals, *Life with Herman H. Rott* would pave the way for *Manivald* (2017), a prequel story of a gay fox in his early 30s who has developed an unhealthy codependency from living with his mother. The film marked a step forward in the pair's relationship as cowriters, now markedly more comfortable with the process having a first film under their belt. Ivezić recalls,

> We started to write *Life with Herman H. Rott* pretty soon after we met, so maybe we were still under the influence of exploring each other and trying to adapt to each other's way of life. For the second film *Manivald*, when we knew each other more properly, we were more comfortable to tackle intergenerational family affairs. This is more me, because I'm always surrounded by my family, but Chintis had the idea that Manivald should be gay, which came from a relative of hers she is very close to, they're almost like brother and sister. Also I had a relative who was an adult, nearing his thirties and still living with his parents. He's definitely not like Manivald,

Figure 5.19

Still from *Manivald* (Dir. Chintis Lundgren). ©2017 Chintis Lundgreni Animatsioonistuudio / Adriatic Animation / NFB. Image courtesy of Chintis Lundgren and Draško Ivezić

> but it made me wonder *How does this make him feel? Does he feel under accomplished?* Even though, economically, he could have afforded to move, it's more of a trend that kids are staying longer with their parents, and they don't want to take risks. So I guess this made me think about the idea of Manivald living with his mother, and the dramatic tension we could create from that.

When their washing machine breaks, the attractive wolf Toomas comes to repair it, stirring desire in Manivald who sees a potential relationship and opportunity to break free from his current routine and living situation. Inconveniently, his mother also has her sights on the buff repairman, kicking off an uncomfortable rivalry that Manivald initially appears to win (Figure 5.19). The pair sleep together, kicking off a joyfully ludicrous fantasy (set to a schmaltzy musical cue with vocals by fellow animation director Nina Gantz) in which they gambol among hillocks and horses, a sequence that proved important for keeping the tone of the film on track. As Lundgren explains:

> Because Manivald is such a shy and sweet character, we wanted to show that he really falls in love with this plumber. So we had to make it a bit "overly" romantic. In some first drafts of the film we had imagined that, instead of this love scene, that there would be some psychedelic scene where they're just going crazy and partying and strange things are happening, but it just didn't make sense.

Adds Ivezić,

> It was too awkward. There were some weird games they were playing in the room and we just realized that we were losing important focus. So we just deleted a whole chunk of the film and decided "Okay, let's start from scratch and have our focus be love." I think we managed that; everybody recognises when they see the film that this is about love, that it's not even about sex. So maybe that's what makes it more sweet than explicit sex.

Manivald is crushed when, the following morning, he finds that Toomas has bedded his mother also. Taking the incident as his cue to finally leave home, Manivald tracks Toomas down at his apartment to discover he has a wife and children. Both lonelier than they were before, Manivald leaves his mother behind for good to join a troupe of traveling musicians.

Says Ivezić,

> The band is an element which is present from the beginning [...]. The first time we hear the band, we hear it through the window. And it's almost like a call to him, "It's time to move out." We wanted to use this idea of freedom, the nomadic life of artists who are playing music as a symbol of finding your own voice. That he, at the end, sits with them, just fit very well.

On the heels of another bevvy of selections and awards for *Manivald*, the loose trilogy is rounded out by *Toomas Beneath the Valley of the Wild Wolves* (2019), again a prequel (the nonchronologically and interwoven story threads across the films partially inspired by Lundgren's enthusiasm for the writing style of French novelist Honoré de Balzac), which matches its predecessors distinct presentation style while paying specific homage to the cinema of sexploitation maestro Russ Meyer. Says Ivezić,

> We watched a documentary about Russ Meyer and started to realize that there is a power in camp filmmaking, where you can actually explore ideas that would maybe be a bit too bizarre in a different genre. This kind of film inspired us to explore this camp side of Toomas. So in a way it's almost the same world, but in my mind it is a completely different genre than *Manivald*, because one is a quiet dramedy and the other is playing on camp, cult classics.

"I also felt a little bit bored after *Manivald*," confesses Lundgren. "Which came out to be a very subtle and calm film. So I just wanted to do something crazy. This Russ Meyer connection seemed like the right thing to explore."

Taking place some time before the events of *Manivald*, we come to learn of the perpetually leered-at Toomas's "origin story" that sees him fired from his engineering job after rebuffing the sexual advances of his boss. Concerned for how he will provide for his two children and wife Viivi (Figure 5.20), pregnant with a third on the way, he keeps his situation secret and takes on odd handyman jobs, ultimately becoming a gigolo.

While certain story beats and characters would make direct nods to moments in Meyer's filmography, as with *Life with Herman H. Rott*, some aspects of the film would take their inspiration from Lundgren's own observations of people she knew in real life. With Toomas frequently away from home, Viivi becomes a devotee of female empowerment speaker (and dominatrix) Alexandra Horn-Eye, a character jointly inspired by Tom Cruise's role as a misogynistic seminar leader in *Magnolia* (Dir. Paul Thomas Anderson, 1999) and an acquaintance of Lundgren's.

> She figured out that there are men out there who will pay you to treat them not very nicely, and then you can order them to clean your room. I think a lot of people, even if you know that the other person wants it, would find it hard to do that, but she doesn't have any problems with it. So she just totally started to take advantage of that, and got a slave as a way of cleaning her apartment! She even orders groceries from him; if she says it, he has to do it – and at the same time he's paying her.

Figure 5.20

Still from *Toomas Beneath the Valley of the Wild Wolves* (Dir. Chintis Lundgren). ©2019 Chintis Lundgreni Animatsioonistuudio / Adriatic Animation / MIYU Productions. Image courtesy of Chintis Lundgren and Draško Ivezić

With Toomas increasingly in demand, his skill set lands him a role in a pornographic movie while Viivi begins to spend more time in the thrall of Alexandra, embracing her inner dominatrix and inadvertently stealing the devotion of one of her mentor's slaves in the process. In a similar respect to the contorted, in-universe logic of the bad behavior demonstrated in the characters of *SH_T HAPPENS*, the pair's infidelities and secrets come across as curiously innocent and well-intentioned. Toomas is not going down this path to hurt his family, but to keep it afloat (Figure 5.21), while Viivi is acting out of a dire need to reclaim

Figure 5.21

Still from *Toomas Beneath the Valley of the Wild Wolves* (Dir. Chintis Lundgren). ©2019 Chintis Lundgreni Animatsioonistuudio / Adriatic Animation / MIYU Productions. Image courtesy of Chintis Lundgren and Draško Ivezić

herself. While these are excuses that likely would not fly in a real-world scenario, in the universe that Lundgren and Ivezić have built it is somehow charmingly palatable. As Lundgren reflects:

> In some ways this all came naturally, because we started with Toomas and we already knew some things about him from *Manivald*. We knew that he fixes washing machines, he has no problem sleeping with people – but he has a family. So first we fleshed out that part, but then in the end, we were at risk of having a very weak female character in the wife, and we didn't want her to be weak. We had some early versions where she was having an affair, but it wasn't right.

Ivezić:

> It felt almost as though their power game was not really equal, because if she also had a lover then there would be no tension. In a way, Toomas's wife is not acting against him, she's acting against systemic gender expectations, or the patriarchy. So that gave her agency, on top of being pregnant and already having two kids. I think it's very clear what she represents – women who cannot use their own voice.

When Toomas rejects the drunken advances of the film's director, it sends the latter into a psychotic rage that tips the film into gleefully chaotic, *Beyond the Valley of the Dolls*[26]-esque farce. Fleeing for his life, Toomas arrives back home to find Viivi whipping her slave; before indignation can set in, a trailer for the porno he wrapped just moments previously appears on the television. All secrets exposed, the couple have their new child and move forward contentedly, Viivi embracing her own female empowerment career and Toomas throwing himself into life as an escort.

The juxtaposition of Lundgren's style, awash with saturated pink hues, pencil lines and playfully simplistic designs, against the fairly adult themes of toxic relationships and skewed sexual dynamics would, in other filmmakers' hands, run the risk of alienating audiences. The pair's shared clarity of vision and identifiable intent behind their work, however, make the films an altogether joyful experience. As Ivezić sees it, the degree to which the pair's work has been embraced is owed to an underlying humanity beneath the zanier exterior of the world they've created, and their shared desire to tell the kinds of relatable stories they themselves would like to see more of in the world.

> When you make comedy, people usually become an exaggeration; somebody who has desire becomes obsessive and ridiculous. The effect is that the audience will usually recognize themselves, because we are always, here and there, obsessed with something. I think this works, because then we start to laugh, and what we're laughing at is ourselves. I think with animation it is even more powerful, because our characters are animals, they're all kind of wearing masks, so you're not connected with a particular physiognomy, race or even gender. I think this also gives people "permission" to laugh, perhaps at very serious subjects, like problems in a relationship, or infidelity, or sex workers. One thing we are also trying to explore is "what is animation for adults?" In our animation festival bubble, we'll want to watch a new artistic film from somebody very famous in the animation world, but when we talk about entertainment for adults, animation is still not using its full potential, I think. I feel like I would like, as an audience, to watch more animated dramas for adults. It's not just entertainment, but I want to make people wonder about their life, about society, about rules.

Figure 5.22

Still from *Venus* (Dir. Tor Fruergaard). ©2010 Den Danske Filmskole. Image courtesy of Tor Fruergaard

As seen in the earlier case study *Drijf*, relationships are hard work, the challenges they throw up sometimes hard to recover from – but not necessarily impossible. The National Film School of Denmark graduation project *Venus*, directed by Tor Fruergaard and written by Sissel Dalsgaard Thomsen (whose later short film project *Growing Pains* was discussed previously in Chapter 2) is a sensitive, clay-animated stop-motion film that follows a young couple, Caroline and Rasmus, as they experience an unexpected lull in their sex lives (Figure 5.22). In a bid to relight their romantic fire, Rasmus suggests they visit a swingers club together. Caroline reluctantly agrees, setting the pair off on a voyage of sexual discovery that will ultimately leave them questioning their bond with one another and test the strength of their relationship. Having worked together previously during their studies, the director and writer were keen to pair up again to develop an earlier script of Thomsen's originally intended as a live-action film that never came to be. The story itself was inspired by a conversation with her husband at the time, regarding sex clubs and the misconception that men are the dominant force in these kinds of venues; due to the generally lower number of female participants, it is more often the women who call the shots. The intriguing perception of these clubs – and the flipped expectations and realities of the activities within – laid the foundation for what would become the eventual script for *Venus*.

Fruergaard did extensive research to have the look and tone of the sex club feel as genuine as possible. Initially, he and Thomsen attended an info night aimed at attracting new members. It was at this event that they were first shown the venue – it also, anecdotally, is where the line regarding the rules of the jacuzzi came from "If you use the jacuzzi, you swallow." Not satisfied with the lights-on, no-action version of the club, Fruergaard asked one of the owners if he could speak to any of the swingers; he was informed that this wasn't a good idea, due to their shy nature. He was instead invited to return for a free night, to experience the club in action for himself. With the go-ahead from his wife, he became a "fly on the wall in a swingers club," he watched when the lights were off, experiencing the sounds and the atmosphere of the night, something he made pains to replicate authentically within the film itself.

The result is an undeniable lived-in feel to the club – slightly romanticized, but with all the hallmarks of luxury on a budget, as the director explains: "In Denmark at least, all the swingers clubs are like this – red velvet on the walls, everything is painted gold, a cheap way of making it look very rich."

The film's characters are brought to life in a soft and almost naive stop-motion style. As Fruergaard recounts, this look was very much purposeful.

> I remember the guy who was doing the character designs, the first thing he came up with was this really dark, gritty animation style. Then I told him "No, it should be a lot more like *Postman Pat*, like 'Pat Goes to a Swingers Club'." It's also a little bit inspired by a Danish cartoonist called Claus Deleuran [...]. When I read the script, I knew that animation and these really explicit sex scenes would be a really fun thing to work with, because you get the idea of a sex scene but it's not pornography with live actors, which would be very intimidating, in a way. Here, it's more like a parody, or almost a metaphor for these explicit sex scenes.

"It also makes it a lot more accessible, in a way," says Thomsen, reinforcing Fruergaard's sentiment,

> Some people might have been a bit turned off if it had been a live-action film. It would have been much more provocative and much more of a niche film. Also, if the animation had been more realistic, or more dark and gritty, it may have also turned off some people – but I think it really opens up the film to a much larger audience; having this very innocent look to it makes it very accessible.

The look of the characters serves to effectively put the audience at ease, drawing them into the two lovers' fleshy world through the use of clay animation wherein the animators are able to create rippling flesh with a level of organic movement.[27] Being a student film, many of the animators were new to stop-motion, learning on the job. Toward the end, some scenes were changed and a professional stop-motion animator was hired to help out. However the possible tentativeness of the film's less-experienced crew members affords the animation a certain energy that complements the emotional journey of Coraline. She initially seems out of place and unsure of herself, before becoming confident in her sexuality and finding new heights of erotic pleasure with a temporary partner among the voyeuristic crowd. The starkness of the film's visuals is reminiscent of such films as Charlie Kaufman and Duke Johnson's *Anomalisa* in its naturalism and unflinching portrayals of "real" sex. It is at this point in the story that Rasmus comes into the room, having been unable to maintain an erection in his own attempts to participate in a group sex scenario elsewhere in the club. He joins the mounting crowd and is shocked by the image of his partner climaxing astride another man – as were some viewers, as Fruergaard recounts: "When *Venus* came out, there were a lot of men who reacted quite weirdly, in my opinion, asking 'How can he forgive her?'"

The reaction certainly seems incongruous given that the narrative makes it clear that the entire expedition was at Rasmus's own insistence, Coraline begrudgingly going along with it to appease him. "I think they forgot about all that and just saw that image of their own girlfriend having sex with another man. It's a strong image for some people," says Fruergaard.

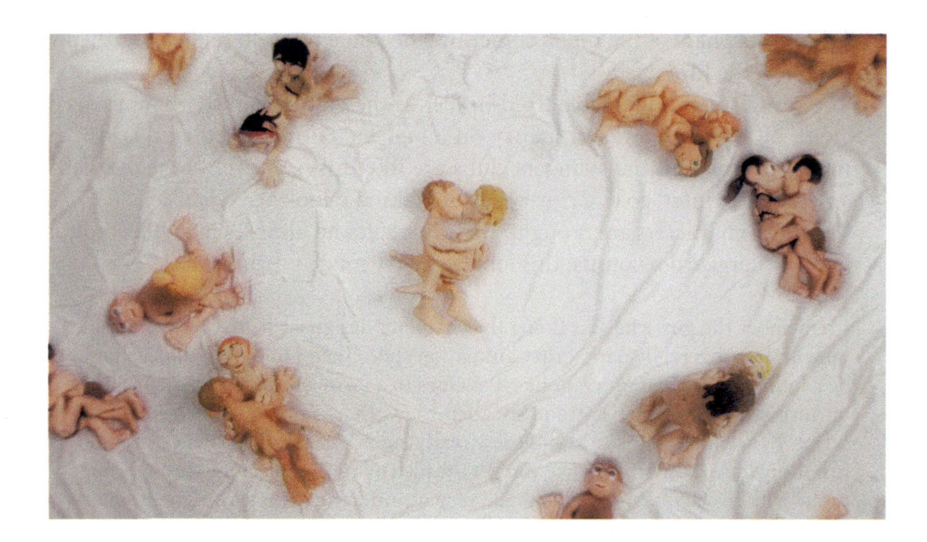

Figure 5.23

Still from *Venus* (Dir. Tor Fruergaard). ©2010 Den Danske Filmskole. Image courtesy of Tor Fruergaard

This double standard is also depicted within the film itself, when a distraught Rasmus flees and Caroline finds him re-dressing in the changing rooms. In the original script by Thomsen. Rasmus leaves Caroline at the club, ending the film on a sour note before Fruergaard suggested a cheerier conclusion to the film.

"The original script was a bit more cynical," explains Thomsen. "The ending was more like a revenge ending. Tor felt it would be really nice if they learned something and they actually ended up together."

The unexpected turn of events leads the couple into a new understanding and appreciation for one another moving forward, the closing scene of *Venus* sees Caroline and Rasmus sharing a nude embrace, floating ethereally on a bed of pleasure among other similarly entwined couples (Figure 5.23). As mentioned when discussing Fruergaard and Thomsen's later film *Growing Pains* in Chapter 2, sex and sexuality are recurring themes in much of the latter's work, themes that she uses to embody other aspects of the characters' emotional or psychological journey, suggesting that Caroline and Rasmus's re-engagement in monogamous sex in this scene could represent a newfound connection.

Venus enjoyed a successful festival run and to this day still receives requests for screenings. "It's amazing how it's still alive, in a way," Fruergaard contemplates of the film's reception and the interest it continues to generate. Over a decade since its release, it is a story that continues to tap into important aspects of long-term relationships, such as making time for one another, compassion, understanding and the importance of communication.

While compromise can be key to the longevity of a relationship, there are times when it runs the risk of morphing into rationalization for why we choose not to leave a toxic situation. The story of Signe Baumane's 2022 feature film *My Love Affair With Marriage* (Figure 5.24), whose impulse to incorporate informational segments into its narrative we discussed in Chapter 1, serves as a strong case study for the at-times irrational nature of love and attraction. Following the film's protagonist Zelma (Dagmara Dominczyk) from conception, through a humble 1970s upbringing on a farm on the Russian island Sakhalin, the seed of her lifelong quest

Figure 5.24

Stills from *My Love Affair With Marriage* (Dir. Signe Baumane). ©2022 The Marriage Project LLC / Studio Locomotive / Antevita Films. Image courtesy of Signe Baumane

for a soulmate is planted during childhood when she oversees a couple meeting, falling in love and getting married in quick succession. While steered by this quest, Baumane's film also largely explores the concept of womanhood itself, and the enormous pressures of conforming to the expectations of others.

> The film explores the question of how you become a woman. How much of that is biological? And how much of that is what society makes you? How does society form – or deform – you into a woman? Are you able to shake that off? The film also explores how the stereotype of "woman" can actually work against you, as a person. Those are the questions that the film raises, in a single story – with songs and with science!

As well as the previously mentioned Biology interjections, Zelma finds herself dogged throughout her young life by three Mythology Sirens (voiced by Iluta Alsberga, Ieva Katkovska and Kristīne Pastare, who make up the Latvian singing group Trio Limonāde) who passive-aggressively serenade her with musical numbers[28] about the importance of appropriate, womanly comportment in the eyes of society. As she matures, Zelma's individuality is frequently punished; fighting back when a male classmate picks on her earns the disapproval of her classmates, as does not exhibiting traditionally "feminine" behaviors. Navigating the usual pitfalls of early adolescence, such as bullies, rejection of friendships and unrequited infatuations, Zelma resolves to become more sexually desirable in the furtherance of her quest for a soulmate, ultimately losing her virginity at 17 to a concerningly older man she meets at an art gallery. As a post-coital impulse, the man proposes marriage, only to ghost her for months.

This scenario sets up a pattern of naive decision-making somewhat reminiscent of Pam's journey in Sara Gunnarsdóttir and Pamela Ribon's *My Year of Dicks*, in that it is predicated on Zelma thinking better of the men she finds herself drawn to than their own immaturities warrant. While Baumane's previous film *Rocks in My Pockets* explicitly served as a memoir of her own life and genealogy, *My Love Affair With Marriage* puts its protagonist Zelma at some distance removed from the director herself. As with Cynthia, the sexually adventurous lead of Baumane's episodic series *Teat Beat of Sex*, real-life experiences serve more as a springboard for the ideas and story of the film than a direct reference point.

> My life is a messy enterprise. So when you try to squeeze all this richness into what has to be around 80-90 pages of a script, you have to simplify, you have to generalize, and you also have to make it visual. So while the film was inspired by my real life events, when I strip them away from too much context, too much detail, they become more universal. I feel that these are not just my experiences, but experiences that a lot of women have gone through. I hope it is universal enough to reach other people, and that we can say that we experienced this thing together. As an artist, that's what I'm very much interested in.

In Zelma's first long-term relationship with Sergei (Cameron Monaghan), a young man she meets at university whose odor draws her in (desire activated by their histocompatibility, as the Biology character informs us), red flags such as constant comparisons to his mother, callow insensitivity toward the "banal" death of a friend and offering "forgiveness" for her having a prior sexual history are dismissed. Judgment clouded by a cocktail of norepinephrine, serotonin and dopamine rushing through her system, Zelma falls in love and accepts his marriage proposal. This marriage ends up going ahead, the wedding scene a darkly comic reprise of the friend's funeral (Figure 5.25) – their union presented as a

Figure 5.25

Still from *My Love Affair With Marriage* (Dir. Signe Baumane). ©2022 The Marriage Project LLC / Studio Locomotive / Antevita Films. Image courtesy of Signe Baumane

responsibility to the state. The analogous political throughline of the film, chiefly the lead-up to and knock-on effect caused by the collapse of the Soviet Union, is an aspect of it that carries particular weight, especially when considering the tumultuous and divisive climate during which much of its production took place.

> When I was younger, I ignored the larger world, the political world. I said, "It doesn't touch me, I'm not in charge of it, I don't fucking care." And then horrible things happen when you ignore the world, and you're not ready for them. It's like the pandemic, you're sitting here while this disease somewhere in China slowly comes to you, and suddenly your whole life is disrupted for two years. In 2015, I believed that we would have a woman president in the United States. It seemed obvious – then look what happened. Also, seeing what is happening in Ukraine, the attitude of these colonizing powers trying to take over, and the patriarchy – it's all connected, the way I see it. And I feel that Zelma is just trying to live her life and get on with it. She just wants love, and that's all she wants. Then the country she lives in collapses, which changes everything. I just find it interesting how we as individuals live our lives, and how the larger political forces influence our lives.

While national tensions simmer away, oxytocin deepens Zelma's love and bond toward Sergei. This comes at the cost of inhibiting the individuality that so defines her; while she is able to work, his own lack of confidence in himself manifests as controlling behaviors, alienating her from her friends, cultivating insecurities about her body and domestic abilities and excluding her from events. Conditioned to go along with the passive abuse due to fight or flight anxiety and a dwindling of oxytocin creating a fear of abandonment, she is easily manipulated into giving him a second chance when he inevitably cheats on her, only to be immediately let down. His second infidelity results in her reclaiming some autonomy, leaning into becoming an artist in her own right – but, thanks to oxytocin, still not completely resistant to his love-bombing and appeals for forgiveness.

It is testament to Baumane's abilities as a writer that Sergei's dialogue is so archetypically toxic; we see from glimpses into his childhood that he has his own traumas and complexities, the ultimate result being a skewed attitude toward women and the role they should have in a traditional relationship. In his attempts to contort Zelma's naturally free-spirited and artistically inclined persona into something he can control, he barrages her with a series of diluted monologues designed to make her pliant and supplicant. When she appears to find some success in her own professional life, his inability to fathom the situation while he himself is struggling manifests as spousal abuse. Zelma finally leaves Sergei for good, blaming her predicament on the concept of love itself, rather than his fundamental weaknesses of character.

Zelma's second marriage opens up even more fascinating psychological avenues of exploration (Figure 5.26). Maintaining her independence and strength, she resists Sergei's overtures to win her back (with the lure of a sudden uptick in his finances) and travels to Viborg for a gala, meeting Bo (Matthew Modine) while feeling particularly self-conscious about her appearance and mannerisms in a previously unexplored part of the world. Bo's contrast to Sergei, in and of itself refreshing, is boosted by easily romanticized qualities such as basic kindness, empathy and an ability to bring Zelma out of her shell, "magically" gifting her with an ability to speak English (a phenomenon credited to cortisol and a rewiring of her neural pathways unlocking knowledge that had lain dormant since childhood). These traits, coupled with an intense honeymoon phase and a

Figure 5.26

Signe Baumane animates Zelma and Bo in *My Love Affair With Marriage*. ©Image courtesy of Signe Baumane

unique sexual compatibility, are enough for Zelma to accept his marriage proposal, though she is partly relieved when national marriage laws determine it cannot happen immediately. His disappointment and sense of urgency for the marriage to happen swiftly raise mild alarm bells; unbeknownst to Zelma, Bo is wrestling with gender dysphoria and is likely over-reliant on the stability a traditional marriage might bring to his life.

Eventually moving to Toronto once wed, a troubling shift in their relationship occurs. Having previously determined that "Love means never be the cause of your lover's suffering," the stark decline in passion, coupled with frustrations toward the feminine characteristics Bo exhibits, results in Zelma's behavior becoming uncharacteristically judgmental and cruel, at times demanding he comport to certain standards of masculinity.

While Zelma's abuse toward Bo is not comparable to the worst she herself had received from Sergei, it remains a troubling and important narrative point when considering the ease with which she slips into her former spouse's role. Similarly, the behavior stems from a degree of personal disillusionment, the sense of self Zelma had built up during her time being single now eroding. The scenario hearkens the phrase "Hurt people hurt people," although it is not a complete inverse of her first marriage, Bo's struggles resulting in some toxicity on his part also. As an alternative to the dubious decision of bringing a child into the mix, Zelma suggests divorce as a better solution to a marriage plagued by such significant issues of communication. Their separation prompts Bo, with "nothing to lose," to come out as trans in an era and part of the world where "being gay or a pedophile or an exhibitionist was essentially the same thing."

This brings about a turning point in Zelma, as her hypothalamus links his struggles to conform to societal expectations of masculinity to her own schoolyard struggles with feminine comportment. Although it is her second consecutive marriage to end in failure, through this experience she finds peace and, confronting them one final time, gains control over the sirens who have been nagging her throughout her life.

> Change is more possible than ever. But I also feel that there are enough forces in society that don't want that change, so if you want to change, you have to press on. There was one thing that really struck me when I was working on the film, at the end where the gates open and she can finally see this new world. I had to write the end credits song, and thought *What is that thing that Zelma really needs and wants, that we* all *need and want? How can society be organized in a way where we, as individuals, would be happier and more equal, and would have true intimacy as well, without the need to lie and hide our true selves?* For three months, I couldn't come up with an image or idea of what it could be, and I realized that I had lived under these certain social structures for too long. I realized *Okay, maybe my generation shouldn't come up with these structures, maybe this new generation should understand what they want from the future society.* But I do think that the end credits song comes up with an answer, or at least a mood of hope and inspiration and desire for this equality, through intimacy and relationships.

Premiering at the Tribeca Film Festival and receiving the Jury Distinction for a Feature Film at Annecy mere days later, *My Love Affair With Marriage* would be selected for over one hundred events across 2022 and 2023, accruing multiple Best Film wins and culminating in a dedicated North American theatrical run from October 2023 in aid of Academy Award consideration. Many of these screenings would include filmmaker Q&As with Baumane and would actively engage local communities and interest groups, such as animation students, activists, feminist organizations and even domestic abuse survivors. While an Oscar nomination ultimately proved elusive, the film's journey is a laudable feat of indie perseverance, major cultural outlets praising it as "inspired,"[29] "remarkably beautiful"[30] and "visually stunning."[31] As with Baumane's previous work, perhaps the most valuable outcome is the direct engagement from her audiences that she was able to participate in.

> With *My Love Affair With Marriage*, some audiences are very quiet, they experience the film internally. And of course, it's a film that is not quiet. It's not a tragedy. It's a comedy. And I love to present it as a comedy. I have a special presentation to make people laugh before the film starts, and when they're given permission to laugh, they start laughing at the first scene and then they keep laughing. Of course, it can be a bitter laugh, or a laugh that has darkness in it, but when you're laughing together, something gets unleashed, some kind of shared experience. It's like hearing the story by campfire.

Heartbreak

As many of the prior-discussed case studies put forward, not all relationships are destined to withstand the rest of time – nor the difficulties created, forged or uncovered by those in them. UK animation director, artist, writer, producer and educator Joseph Wallace,[32] whose filmmaking process leans toward stop-motion and puppetry, has built a career on his innate ability to construct environments and characters with an especially appealing degree of texture and tactility.

Figure 5.27

Still from *Natural Disaster* (Dir. Joseph Wallace). ©2014 Joseph Wallace

With a body of work that includes music videos for Sparks, Parker Bossley and James, idents for the BBC and Adult Swim as well as animated segments for Edgar Wright's 2021 feature-length documentary *The Sparks Brothers*, Wallace is also known for several short films of his own, including the BAFTA Cymru-nominated Newport Film School graduation short *The Man Who Was Afraid of Falling* (2012) and the award-winning *Salvation Has No Name* (2022), a parable on xenophobia, ignorance and the societal othering of refugees.

Among the films made between those two projects was *Natural Disaster* (Figure 5.27), created during a time when Wallace lived in a shared house in France as part of the "sort of hippie" Caravel Collective, comprised of fellow animators met during the European training program Animation sans frontiers. Having collaborated on several short projects, Wallace drew inspiration from a difficult chapter in his life to create a slightly longer film on the destructive and derailing nature of heartbreak.

> It's probably the most real world, autobiographical, non-fantastical/fairytale film that I've made and it came from having been through a horrible, traumatic breakup, and using my art to explore the trauma of that. It was made for no money in a garage in the south of France, from French magazines that I collected and animated on a multiplane made from bricks and picture-frame glass.

The use of a multiplane (a method in which large glass panes are stacked on top of one another and photographed from above, each plane housing its own layer of animated or static elements to give a sense of depth) and cutout collage animation distinguishes *Natural Disaster* from much of Wallace's other, more puppet-oriented work. It tells the story of Mark, a man-made redundant from an unspecified job due to government funding cuts. He comes home to find his wife Rachel and her lover Paul (a man Mark appears to know), both partially undressed, having clearly been intimate. In the face of Mark's devastation, Paul meekly apologizes and leaves, while Rachel attempts to downplay the affair and unsuccessfully appeals to Mark that he stay and they work things through. The unenviable but somewhat common scenario pairs interestingly with the visuals; assembled from multiple magazine sources, each character presents as a chopped-up, fractured caricature of a person. While at first glance it is a look with almost comedic connotations (reminiscent in part of the collage aspects seen in Terry Gilliam's animated *Monty Python* skits, celebrity "cameos" in *South Park* and the short-lived UK sitcom *I Am Not an Animal*), the jarring nature of the approach feels appropriate given how disruptive and unreal the experience of a particularly harsh breakup can be.

> I think there's a sense of fragmented memories within the piece, using the cutout stuff. One of the things I love about animation is that the techniques we use – and the materiality, especially in stop-motion, of how we tell these stories – really add to how we interpret these films as viewers. So I think there's something for me about that sort of breakdown of reality when you're going through a breakup, heartbreak – everything's fragmenting and feels angular and sharp and unpleasant. There was something about creating this world from fragments of disparate imagery and putting that together to make some sort of whole.
>
> Looking back on it now, I wish I'd made it more fragmented. In my head at the beginning, I had this idea for it to be very Picasso-esque. There's one shot where the main character is watching television in the hotel, and there's a couple making out. That's much more of a Dada-esque sort of assemblage, very Picasso. In some ways I wish I'd made the whole thing more like that; maybe I got too neat with the imagery in the end (Figure 5.28).

Drifting off while at the hotel he has retreated to, Mark dreams of living in the clouds where an assortment of topless, buxom, fairy-sized angels beckon at him. He giggles with glee as a swarm of breasts encircle him, a reminder that, in spite of his emotional turmoil, he remains a common or garden variety red-blooded male whose desire for women and sex has not been completely obliterated.

> That was an interesting one, because I knew I wanted quite graphic, explicit imagery in there, so I went to a French supermarket in the town where I was living and

Figure 5.28

Still from *Natural Disaster* (Dir. Joseph Wallace). ©2014 Joseph Wallace

> bought a stack of these pornographic magazines in French. I had to have a slightly awkward conversation with the woman behind the till and explain in French that they were for a film. She was like "Yeah, sure!"

Mark's brief respite is disrupted as each angel's face is replaced with Rachel's, to his disgust and annoyance. Knives appear in his hands and, in a meta moment that partially acknowledges the paper-constructed world they inhabit, he slashes at the angels before waking up.

Although Wallace himself bears little by way of immediate resemblance to Mark, the degree to which the film appears to draw on lived experience comes through strongly in certain moments, the dream sequence, in particular, a palpable representation of how a person can be tortured by their own thoughts when muddling through heartbreak, whether cheated on, dumped or simply not having their love reciprocated. There is, however, something to be said for the therapeutic value of working through one's emotional ordeal through artistic expression.

> When the events in real life had happened, I sat and wrote three pages of angry heartbroken dialogue and ideas, and put them in a folder. So when I was thinking about ideas for a film that was gonna be around four or five minutes long, I came upon that again and thought Yeah, this has got a nice energy to it. It was exploring something that maybe I hadn't quite done before in other films, and it was interesting to do something that was a little bit more real life.
>
> There's always a sense of therapy in some ways with filmmaking, even when it's not such a personal story. I don't tend to do many autobiographical films, because I often just think my life is quite boring. But I like making films about things that scare me; I think I'm often drawn to themes that make me emote, that make me feel something deeply. And this is probably still, to date, one of the most personal films that I've done, emotionally and in terms of the story coming from my life, rather than coming from something that I've observed from somewhere else.

In achieving the overall look of *Natural Disaster*, Wallace drew inspiration from a number of sources, spanning the films of Yuri Norstein, a standout dream sequence in Henry Selick's 1996 adaptation of Roald Dahl's *James and the Giant Peach* and, outside of animation, collage artists including Hannah Höch and Jindřich Štyrský as well as the work of illustrator Ralph Steadman and experimental sculptor Geoffrey Farmer:

> He'd done an exhibition at the Barbican, of three dimensional sculptures made from paper and cardboard. They involved cut out magazine elements that you could look at from different angles, and they had different faces on each side. The representation of human form and that sort of angular collage look was really inspiring.

Toward the end of the film, we see Mark out shopping for groceries, where he runs into his wife's lover, Paul. In a moment of blind rage, Mark knocks Paul out with a hard baguette, an action beat that tows the line between tragedy and absurd comedy. The ramifications of the assault are left to the audience's imaginations, the film shifting into a more ruminant space as we see a montage of images of natural disasters, over which Mark contemplates the "miniature devastations" that occasionally hit us in life, concluding that "eventually, they subside."

> That hadn't been in the initial three pages of impassioned writing that I'd done at the time of the breakup. It came when I was making the film, and was more

> of a reflection on what had happened, and on these moments in our lives where big events take place and we feel as if the ground is falling out from under our feet, as if things will never be the same again. I suppose it was an analogy that came up partly from thinking about and exploring those emotions, but also from the images I was looking at. I had all these nature magazines, there were a lot of incredible landscapes and mountains, and I was thinking *I wonder if there's a way of bringing this in somehow?* It was a way of having an epilogue that took it into a slightly more philosophical space and was a reflection that stepped outside the grounded domestic reality that you've been immersed in for most of the film; a way of reflecting on things in a slightly more holistic manner.

In the wake of the film's completion, Wallace would employ variations of the collage animation approach for subsequent projects, including the Parker Bossley music video *Chemicals* and several striking sequences in *Salvation Has No Name*. Though arguably in the shadow of some of the director's other, more widely circulated projects, in relative terms it made a decent mark in the United Kingdom during its festival travels, with stops at Bristol's Encounters Festival, the much-missed Bradford Animation Festival and London Short Film Festival, earning itself a Critics Choice nomination at Canterbury Anifest and a glowing retrospective write-up on the respected film showcase platform Director's Notes.[33] Through these avenues, Wallace has been able to glean an audience response that speaks to its uniqueness as one of his more directly relatable film endeavors.

> [Mark] is probably quite an angry, toxic man – which I hope I'm not, but I think people responded to the emotion of it and the poignancy of it, which was nice, because it was a different type of storytelling exercise for me. And I think it's reached people in a different way than some of the other pieces I've made.

Following in a similarly self-reflective vain, we look to the work of Edinburgh-based Will Anderson,[34] whose involvement in Anna Ginsburg's 2016 animated documentary *Private Parts* (2016) we explored in Chapter 3, is not just a staple of the Scottish animation scene but well-known and admired among the international festival and short film landscape. Initially making a name for himself with his Edinburgh School of Art BA graduation film *The Making of Longbird*[35] (that enjoyed an extensive festival run picking up multiple awards including both a Scottish BAFTA for Animation and a BAFTA in 2012 for Best Animated Short Film), Will's subsequent work has spanned multiple short films, idents and micro-series for various channels, sites and media outlets, often with his long-term creative partner Ainslie Henderson.

Anderson's work often combines post-digital storytelling, meta concepts, naturalistic dialogue, intimate human connection and wit that reflects on both the conventions of filmmaking itself as well as the creative process in general. The self-reflective and jibing nature of his films are often paired with humorous stories boasting warmth and genuine connectivity. His 2017 film *Have Heart*,[36] which depicts the life cycle of a GIF-animated bird plunged into an existential crisis, is a prime example; a satirical and deeply moving film about the human condition and feeling trapped by the monotony of life.

> As freelance animators, we tend to make things that satisfy us and post them online, hoping for appraisal or that people see and like it. I was thinking about that when I was making this thing and how social media, in general, is this constant clamoring for attention, it's kind of an ugly thing but also what we have to do. It's

Figure 5.29

Still from *Betty* (Dir. Will Anderson). ©2019 Wanderson Studio. Image courtesy of Will Anderson

> sort of an unsettling feeling, so the GIF itself refers to that a little bit, the idea of trying and failing and trying and failing. Then having this thing that existed in the world on a timeline, I started to think about how I could develop it. I saw the rule – because I think it's important to have very strict rules to make work and tell stories – as "I'm going to just move chronologically from here and see where we end up." It was almost like an experiment to see how far I could take this little collection of shapes and where they would end up in the course of around a year.

With its minimal design approach, based largely on contrasting color, geometric shapes and effective incorporation of glitch art, the film laid the visual groundwork for his subsequent 2018 project *Where's the Butter, Betty?*[37] A micro-short coming in at under three minutes and somewhere between an absurdist skit and a style experiment, we meet Bobby, a bird-like character (birds being a recurring visual motif in Anderson's films) searching his kitchen for an elusive slab of butter, appealing to an unseen Betty as to its whereabouts (Figure 5.29). This piece would ultimately set up his lengthier film *Betty*,[38] a more elaborate and distinctly metaphysical musing on relationships, loss and self-reflection, drawing from Anderson's own processing of a recent breakup.

> [With *Betty*] I had just come out of a relationship and something didn't quite make sense about it all ending. I needed this project on the side so that I could make sense of it. I was feeling stuff that was evaporating into the atmosphere and not going anywhere. I wanted it to go somewhere useful instead of just disappearing, so in that way I wrote this fictional thing. That's what *Betty* was for. It's quite a pathetic thing, feeling heartbroken over someone. Everyone will have felt that in some way, but I needed to put it somewhere.

As the film begins, we hear Anderson describe its events over the top of the audio mix, initially akin to a director's commentary describing his process. The film begins by establishing how lovebirds Bobby (played by Anderson with a digitally pitched-up New York accent) and the mute Betty meet, hit it off and begin a relationship. As the story continues, the director's commentary concept begins to invade the film, to the point of continuous interjections and interruptions to the narrative flow, breaking down the character rigs, analyzing his workflow, pointing out mistakes and even halting the film completely to scrub through its timeline. While the intrusions seem to almost be an attempt to impede suspension of disbelief or emotional investment in the characters, certain qualities of production, such as Anderson's endearing voice performance as Bobby or the earnest musical score by Richard Luke, help to thwart his efforts.

With the overall look of the film and some of its themes building upon its predecessor *Have Heart* ("I like that there's clarity and simple bold shapes, geometry and minimal dialogue – the simpler it is, the more beautiful I find it"), this multilayered approach to the storytelling calls back to Anderson's first film *The Making of Longbird*, which similarly featured a metaphysical narrative regarding the production of the film itself, albeit one where the animated character berates the director. In *Betty*, overindulging these overlapping narratives run the risk of being too "film clever" (in Anderson's words) and alienating the viewer, yet they are interwoven well enough to instead elicit a dual investment; the brief, wholesome snippets we see of Betty and Bobby's relationship and their affection for one another are enough to cultivate an emotional connection as viewers of a piece of fiction, while Anderson's creative battles and personal inspirations for the events of the film prompt a sense of understanding and empathy.

When we cut to nine months later, we see the sheen has gone from their relationship, though only from Bobby's point of view (Betty remaining mute and offscreen) as he voices pet peeves such as leg hairs in the bathtub. The missing butter scene from *Where's the Butter, Betty?* is reused, though in the new context of this film, where their romance is waning, it feels less like a skit than something more forlorn and somber.

> It becomes representative of him trying to look for signs he can't quite grasp, which is a metaphor for his relationship. I suppose that there's some kind of method in telling the story, something that's really hard to talk about – "How do I get over someone? How do I find love?" But I think in the film, it makes sense, this symbol of him trying to hold on to something.

As it increasingly dawns on Bobby that he is alone (Figure 5.30), we see him embark on a pitiable, almost childlike search around his house and town in search of Betty, as though she's been misplaced. In what would ordinarily be considered the film's saddest moment, we find the defeated bird in an inverse of the earlier scene, appealing to his slab of butter "Where's the Betty, butter? Where's my Betty gone?" through plaintive sniffles. The emotional beat is laid on extra thick as we dwell on this scene being rewound and replayed multiple times. When Bobby's despair reaches a destructive crescendo, Anderson halts the action and wades in, snapping the viewer out of the moment and admonishing himself for the film's "pathetic, manipulative nonsense." Diminishing the endeavor as "a stupid little story to worm yourself out of a relationship that doesn't work" while belittling his design approach and attempts at symbolism, we come to understand that this is truly more about Anderson's struggle than Bobby's, if not as regards his real-life breakup than in catching himself (perhaps) disingenuously fishing for sympathy through his art.

> I don't really like showing weakness, I don't want to be like a victim or anything like that. With a thing like heartbreak, I wonder if it's really worth making a film

Figure 5.30

Still from *Betty* (Dir. Will Anderson). ©2019 Wanderson Studio. Image courtesy of Will Anderson

> about it. I don't know if I buy into it, but actually it's a pretty universal thing. Everyone's fallen in love, or most people have, or think they have.

This universality is another throughline in Anderson's filmography, in that much of his work touches upon experiences many of us go through, yet feel pointedly specific to us in the moment, such as the stuck-in-a-rut, existential crisis of *Have Heart* and the grappling with our own artistic worth as seen in *The Making of Longbird*. In *Betty*, Anderson ultimately acknowledges that the film is perhaps a product of something that was never truly real, but rather a way of making an intangible feeling he is struggling with somehow tangible. As the fourth wall breaks essentially derail the possibility of the story continuing as originally planned, he skips to the final scenes where we finally rejoin Betty, having been absent for much of the film.

> I thought [Betty] was a really important character in the beginning, when I was improvising. Then I realized that, in fact, it's really about her *not* being there. At the start of any film, there's this normality, then there's usually some kind of disruption and then you go on a journey to try and fix that thing that broke the normality. Then at the end you get to a place that hopefully shows a perspective you hadn't seen before that's perhaps better, or worse, or different from where we were. That's what that journey is for me. I don't know where it's going to end but it's going to end somewhere and I'm just yearning to find out what it will be.

The film's journey ends with Betty on her own at a party, observing a slab of butter on a food table suddenly disappear. It reappears back in Bobby's kitchen, where he sits alone. He returns it to the fridge, seemingly in acceptance of the relationship ending; as this moment is left to play out, uninterrupted by Anderson, it could be read that he too has reached a similar acceptance, not just for the relationship but the film itself.

> In the end, I genuinely felt that it helped. Although it is my job and I enjoy being creative, there's something about making animation where saying you're going to

tell a love story in this medium feels quite stiff and false. I would struggle to do it with a script and actors. If it was funded and there was a crew that were waiting for me to decide how I'm feeling that day, it wouldn't really work. It's like opening your sketchbook, I think – and it's terrifying opening your sketchbook and letting someone just peruse through and read it and make it public.

Although predicated on difficult periods of their directors' lives, these films strongly exemplify just how powerful and important the medium of animation – and any form of artistic expression – is in conveying the intangible and inarticulable. Animated filmmaking can act as a form of therapy in solidifying our thoughts and feelings, in healing and in finding new ways to be. As seen elsewhere in this book, it can also be used to celebrate, elevate, uncover and discover those aspects of our emotional lives that benefit from being shared with audiences, whether or not they can relate directly.

Through the case studies discussed in this book and the insights so graciously offered by the artists behind them, it is clear that this is an important era for compassionate, thoughtful, diverse filmmaking, whether to entertain, educate or simply let those who might be watching know that they are not alone in dealing with the complexities of love, relationships and intimacy. The spirit of this book, much like the films it explores, has been to open up conversations, provide insights and champion the impact these bold, uncompromising and progressive works can have on the world. We hope that our musings on these subjects prove useful, or at least interesting, and encourage you to further explore the world of intimate animation, either as a viewer or in your own work. We implore you to move forward, make love and make animation!

Notes

1 www.bitterfilms.com.
2 Highlights of which include the feature film *It's Such A Beautiful Day* (2010) and a plethora of adored shorts such as *Rejected* (2000), the three-part *World of Tomorrow* series (2015-2020) and the musical odyssey *Me* (2024).
3 www.juliapott.com.
4 www.davidoreilly.com.
5 www.kirstenlepore.com.
6 www.efabmanimation.com.
7 Best Undergraduate Animation, 2019.
8 A film that, alongside subsequent co-directed (with Sophie Marsh) projects *Blooming* (2022) and *The Gardener*, Blosse-Mason considers part of a trilogy, "because they're all about nature, sex, death, queerness and women."
9 www.windingsnake.com.
10 In an amusingly coincidental instance of parallel thinking, upon finally reaching dry land after their respective ordeals, both Celyn and Heledd of *Cwch Deilen* and Aurora and Jeremy of *Drijf* look out at the now-calm waters from which they have emerged, to be greeted by the sight of frolicking dolphins.
11 A notable offshoot of this collaboration is the changing of the film's title for French-speaking territories from *SH_T HAPPENS* to *Le Gardien, sa Femme et le Cerf*, a nod to Peter Greenaway's *The Cook, the Thief, His Wife & Her Lover.*
12 YK animation (2022) *Lachsmänner (Salmon Men).* 25 August. Available at: https://vimeo.com/742967491.

13 As mentioned in the discussion of TED-Ed in Chapter 1.
14 www.eisprung-studio.ch/.
15 www.bonobostudio.hr/en/distribution/cyclists.
16 www.primerenderstudios.com.
17 www.bonobostudio.hr/en/distribution/planemo.
18 Although Popović himself had previously dabbled in 2D for his 2010 short film *My Way*.
19 A scene that initially proved contentious, as mentioned in Chapter 3.
20 https://sanderjoon.cargo.site/.
21 https://sanderjoon.cargo.site/velodrool.
22 *Rocks In My Pockets* film logline Baumane, S. (2015) *Rocks In My Pockets*. Available at: https://www.rocksinmypocketsmovie.com/.
23 BBC (2024) *Bitesize Symbiosis*. Available at: https://www.bbc.co.uk/bitesize/guides/zp9887h/revision/1.
24 www.rossbutter.com.
25 www.rathergood.com.
26 Russ Meyer, 1970.
27 Clay as a representation of flesh can also be seen in another film *Sexy Laundry* (2015) by Izabela Plucinska, which is also thematically linked, in which a mature couple attempts to rekindle their relationship through sexual play and new experiences. Although set in a bougie hotel the space holds a lot of the same hallmarks of the sex club in *Venus*, with its dark light, plush red drapery and faux opulence.
28 Composed by Kristian Sensini, who had previously worked with Baumane on *Rocks In My Pockets*.
29 Linden, S. (2023) *"My Love Affair With Marriage" Review: An Animator's Tough and Zingy Musical Exploration of Womanhood*. Available at: https://www.hollywoodreporter.com/movies/movie-reviews/my-love-affair-with-marriage-review-dagmara-dominczyk-1235609149/.
30 Winkelman, N. (2023) *"My Love Affair With Marriage" Review: A Tale of Love and Loss*. Available at: https://www.nytimes.com/2023/10/05/movies/my-love-affair-with-marriage-review.html.
31 Sobczynski, P. (2022) *A Look Back at Tribeca 2022: The Narrative Features*. Available at: https://www.rogerebert.com/festivals/a-look-at-tribeca-2022-the-narrative-features.
32 www.josephwallace.co.uk.
33 Munday, R. (no date) Making an Audience Care about Cut-Out Characters in Joseph Wallace's Animated Short "Natural Disaster." Available at: https://directorsnotes.com/2017/06/13/natural-disaster-joseph-wallace/.
34 www.wanderson.xyz.
35 www.wanderson.xyz/portfolio/the-making-of-longbird.
36 www.wanderson.xyz/portfolio/haveheart.
37 www.wanderson.xyz/portfolio/butter.
38 www.wanderson.xyz/portfolio/betty.

Appendix A: Intimate Animation Podcast Episode List (2016–2022)

The *Intimate Animation* podcast series, on which this book is based, can be found at **https://www.skwigly.co.uk/podcast_type/intimate-animation/** or as part of Skwigly's **Animation Podcasts**, available on Apple Podcasts, Podcasts on YouTube, Spotify, TuneIn and SoundCloud.

Season 1 (2016)

- Episode 1: Michaela Pavlátová (*Tram*)
  Release date: August 31, 2016
- Episode 2: Anna Ginsburg (*Private Parts*)
  Release date: September 14, 2016
- Episode 3: Veronica L. Montaño and Manuela Leuenberger (*Ivan's Need*)
  Release date: September 29, 2016
- Episode 4: Lori Malépart-Traversy (*Le Clitoris*)
  Release date: October 20, 2016
- Episode 5: Réka Bucsi (*Love*)
  Release date: November 3, 2016
- Episode 6: Andreas Hykade (*Ring of Fire*)
  Release date: November 24, 2016

Season 2 (2017–2018)

- Episode 1: Signe Baumane (*My Love Affair With Marriage*)
  Release date: February 9, 2017
- Episode 2: Kim Noce (*Love in Idleness*)
  Release date: March 27, 2017
- Episode 3: Diane Obomsawin (*J'aime les filles*)
  Release date: May 31, 2017
- Episode 4: Chintis Lundgren and Draško Ivezić (*Manivald*)
  Release date: July 11, 2017
- Episode 5: Dario van Vree (*Tabook*)
  Release date: October 13, 2017

- Episode 6: Veljko Popović (*Cyclists*)
  Release date: September 19, 2018

Season 3 (2019–2020)

- Episode 1: Caitlin McCarthy (*Coldsore*)
  Release date: August 19, 2019
- Episode 2: Floor Adams (*Mind My Mind*)
  Release date: September 24, 2019
- Episode 3: Elizabeth Hobbs (*I'm OK*)
  Release date: February 6, 2020
- Episode 4: Natasza Cetner (*Nigel*)
  Release date: March 13, 2020
- Episode 5: Michaela Mihályi and David Štumpf (*SH_T HAPPENS*)
  Release date: June 12, 2020
- Episode 6: Nadja Andrasev (*Symbiosis*)
  Release date: October 7, 2020

Season 4 (2021–2022)

- Episode 1: Shoko Hara (*Just a Guy*)
  Release date: April 2, 2021
- Episode 2: Will Anderson (*Betty*)
  Release date: August 18, 2021
- Episode 3: Renee Zhan (*Soft Animals*)
  Release date: September 27, 2021
- Episode 4: Alberto Mielgo (*The Windshield Wiper*)
  Release date: March 18, 2022
- Episode 5: Lori Malépart-Traversy (*Caresses magiques*)
  Release date: June 7, 2022
- Episode 6: Phil Wall, Chloe Beale (*Woodland*), Julia Wiza (*Bogdanka*)
  Recorded live at the Manchester Animation Festival November 16, 2022
  Release date: December 13, 2022

Appendix B: Suggested Further Viewing and Resources

Scan the above QR code or visit **https://www.skwigly.co.uk/intimate-animation/** to access a comprehensive list of animated projects that deal with themes of love, relationships and sexuality, as well as additional resources and exclusive Skwigly Online Animation Magazine site content.

Appendix C: Suggested Further Reading

Forbidden Animation: Censored Cartoons and Blacklisted Animators in America
Author: Karl F. Cohen
McFarland, 1997
ISBN: 9780786420322

Women and Animation: A Compendium
Editor: Jayne Pilling
BFI Publishing, 1992
ISBN: 9780851703770

Animating the Unconscious: Desire, Sexuality, and Animation
Editor: Jayne Pilling
Wallflower Press, 2012
ISBN: 9780231161992

Women and Film Animation: A Feminist Corpus at the National Film Board of Canada 1939-1989
Author: Marie-Josée Saint-Pierre
CRC Press, 2024
ISBN: 9781032685366

On Loving Women
Author: Diane Obomsawin (Translated by Helge Dascher)
Drawn & Quarterly, 2014
ISBN: 9781770461406

Notes to Boys (And Other Things I Shouldn't Share in Public)
Author: Pamela Ribon
Rare Bird Books, 2014
ISBN: 9781942600879

Caresses magiques (French language)
Caresses magiques II (French language)
Authors: Sophie Bédard, Sara Hebert, Sarah Gagnon-Piché
Independently published, 2015, 2016

Independently Animated: The Life and Art of the King of Indie Animation
Authors: Bill Plympton, David B. Levy
Universe Publishing, 2011
ISBN: 9780789322098

Unfiltered: The Complete Ralph Bakshi
Authors: Jon M. Gibson, Chris McDonnell
Universe Publishing, 2008
ISBN: 9780789316844

Index

E

F

G

H

O

P

Q

R

Z

9781032541501